The
Black Book

The
Black Book

**WHAT IF GERMANY HAD WON WORLD WAR II -
A CHILLING GLIMPSE INTO THE NAZI PLANS
FOR GREAT BRITAIN**

M J TROW

JOHN BLAKE

Published by John Blake Publishing Ltd,
3 Bramber Court, 2 Bramber Road,
London W14 9PB, England

www.johnblakebooks.com

www.facebook.com/johnblakebooks
twitter.com/jblakebooks

This edition published in 2017

ISBN: 978 1 78606 515 5

British Library Cataloguing-in-Publication Data:

A catalogue record for this book is available from the British Library.

Design by www.envydesign.co.uk

Printed and bound in Great Britain by Clays Ltd, St Ives plc

1 3 5 7 9 10 8 6 4 2

© Text copyright M J Trow 2017

The right of M J Trow to be identified as the author of this work has
been asserted by him in accordance with the Copyright, Designs and
[...]

Paper [...] natural, recyclable products
ma[...] from wood grown in sustainable forests. The manufacturing
proce[...] conform to the environmental regulations of the country of
[...]

Every [...] copyright-holders,
but s[...] appropriate
[...] people [...]

John Blake Publishing is [...]ing
[...]

CONTENTS

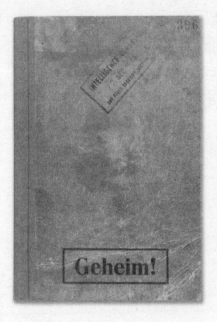

The front cover and a sample page of the *Sonderfahndungsliste GB* (the Special Search List Great Britain).

Reproduced with kind permission of the Imperial War Museum, © Crown Copyright, IWM.

SEARCHING THE LIST

In July 1940, as the seemingly invincible Wehrmacht stood poised across the Channel to invade Britain, Walter Schellenberg, SS *Brigadeführer*, leader of Amt IV EII of the Reich Central Security Office (RSHA), was ordered to compile a list. It would contain the names of individuals, British and foreign, who could be seen as the spearhead of anti-Reich elements in the United Kingdom. A similar list had already been drawn up for Poland and the result was that most of the 61,000 names on *that* list had been imprisoned or murdered by the end of 1939.

Officially called the *Sonderfahndungsliste GB* (the Special Search List Great Britain), it came to be known as the Black Book. It was almost certainly typed on upright Mercedes typewriters with their QWERZ keyboards in the bowels of RSHA headquarters in *Sicherheitsdienst* (SD) Office III near the Hohenzollern Strasse buildings occupied by SS *Obergruppenführer* Reinhard Heydrich. Did Adolf Hitler, the ultimate originator of the List, actually see it? We do not know. He never set foot in a concentration camp either but we know that he created the mindset that gave rise to them. There were originally 20,000 copies run off but today only two originals survive. The rest were either burned in the Nazi rush to destroy evidence at the end of the war or were buried in the falling masonry of intensive Allied bombing raids.

When the two copies fell into British hands, by September 1945, the *Manchester Guardian* carried an article naming a handful of famous Listees. The reaction from some is very telling. Noel Coward (C96 on the List) wrote later:

> 'If anyone had told me at that time that I was high up on the Nazi black list, I should have laughed and told him not to talk nonsense. In this, however, I should have been wrong, for, as it ultimately transpired, I was.'[1]

Sefton Delmer, the *Daily Express*'s Berlin and Paris correspondent, who was about to join the Special Operations Executive (SOE) as the List was compiled, said:

> 'This list...was among many secret documents captured by the Allies in Germany in 1945. Number 33 on the list was a certain Sefton Delmer . . . He was to be handed over, said the list, to Dept. IVB4 of the Central Reich Security Office . . . I like to think it was my maiden broadcast that put me there.'[2]

Victor Gollancz, founder of the Left Book Club, said:

> 'I was very high on Hitler's list of people to be dealt with in England. I think, as a matter of fact I was number seven out of about 2,000.'[3]

SEARCHING THE LIST

Walter Shirer, the influential American journalist who covered many of the big stories of the Second World War, referred to it as 'among the more amusing "invasion documents"'.[4] There speaks a man whose own country had never been bombed and was not staring invasion in the face. There is nothing remotely amusing about a list of people ear-marked for death – ask the 61,000 Polish dead and their families.

Shirer was the first to refer to the List in his now iconic *The Rise and Fall of the Third Reich* in 1961. The complete list was not available to the public in Britain until 1969 and the first historian to discuss it was David Lampe in *The Last Ditch* (Cassell & Co. 1969). His Appendix E reprinted the List for the first time without any detailed evaluation of its contents. Lampe was more concerned with the proposed invasion itself and how the British, especially the Auxiliary units, would have responded. Over thirty years later, Norman Longmate used the List for his counter-factual work *If Britain Had Fallen* (Greenhill Books, 2004) but again, it only forms a fraction of his central thesis. The full List appeared again as an adjunct to Walter Schellenberg's *Gestapo Handbook*, published in English translation in 2004.

I am not surprised that so little has been written on the Black Book. The original typing is not that clear and there are innumerable 'typos' – the List was compiled in a hurry, clearly by different hands – and the photocopying necessary for research purposes has blurred the font still further. We should not imagine that either the collation of evidence or the typing itself was done by fanatical, diehard Nazis. Most office work in the Reich, as elsewhere in Europe, was carried out by women and most office workers had pressures put on them which had nothing to do with ideology. Marie 'Missie' Vassiltchikov was certainly not a Nazi. She was a Russian who found herself, by a variety of circumstances, working in Berlin in 1940. She did not work on the List, or for the RSHA, but her *Berlin Diaries* contain a wealth of information on the humdrum, everyday experiences of office life – jamming typewriters, breaking tapes, lousy coffee and the office octopus! We should bear all this in mind when we find numerous clerical errors in the List.

The original copies had ruled lines for the insertion of other names which would have been added by the Gestapo or *Einsatzgruppen* as they rounded people up. There were also photographs of twenty-nine Listees (there may once have been more), which now are of too poor a quality to reproduce but which would have aided identification at the time. The twenty-eight photographs (two are of the same individual, Captain Albert Brandon, also known as Albert Burrell) are across the spectrum. G. Anderson-Foster (A48) was a British agent. A82, Werner Aue, was a vice consul in Antwerp. Josef Forst (F80) was a Czech officer, attached to the headquarters of the exiled government under Edouard Benes (B98). H50, Hans Hartmann, was a brewer. Richard Israel Merton (M120) was a businessman. Wilburn Smith (S112) was a major in the US army. V49, Adrianus Vrinten, with several aliases, was a Dutch spy.

Contrary to Gollancz's arrogant assertion, the List is strictly alphabetical, so rather than seventh of Britain's 'most wanted', he is actually number 939 – even, alphabetically, his wife Ruth came before him! Figures on the List vary with each account, ranging from less than 2,000 to more than 3,000. Many of the names are duplicates, if only because the compilers were unsure of real names (as opposed to aliases) and because the Germans seem to have had particular difficulty with double-barrelled names. So U10, 'Ustinov, Journalist, London', has the *Deckname* (alias) Middleton-Peddleton. But he also has the alias of Peddleton-Middleton, so the same man, in fact, appears three times. He was the father of actor Peter Ustinov, rejoicing in the nickname *Klop* (bed-bug) and, as the List knew, was 'brit N-Agent'; a spy. One account says that Peddleton and Middleton were on a bus route that passed his home and gave Ustinov the idea to confuse the enemy as far as possible.

Alongside each name is a date of birth, if known, and a place of residence. An occupation is there although, of course, this is misleading. Paul Robeson (R80) features as *'negersänger'* but it was the man's outspoken Communism that offended the Reich. His colour and his music, though both objectionable to the Nazis, were secondary. There were locksmiths, nursery-school teachers, racing drivers, even a private detective, but this has little to do with their inclusion on the List.

Where possible, the current whereabouts of a Listee is included, vital for the marauding *Einsatzgruppen* execution squads to do their job. Taken at random, Dr Artur Tester (T15) could be found at 14, James Place, London SW. Eberhard Heinrich (H90) was a draft-dodger, hiding at 63, Grafton Way, W1. The Jew David Curitz (C112) lived at 'Four Winds', Prescelly Rd, Cardiff, and so on. In some cases, we even have telephone numbers. Rupert Vansittart (V6), for example, the Permanent Under-Secretary of State for Foreign Affairs until 1938 and chief diplomatic adviser to the Foreign Office, could be contacted on MAYfair 1144.

Alongside each name, too, is the Office (Amt) of the RSHA which wanted to talk to the individual. 'Talking' would have meant interrogation, with or without the use of torture, depending on circumstances. The RSHA itself was very new in 1940 and the Amter were still being modified and reorganised. Their particular specialisations are outlined in this book, giving us a clue, where nothing else exists, of exactly why these people are on the List at all. In some cases, *täterkreis* are added. This is a difficult word to translate but it loosely means 'circle' or 'ring' and is a reminder that many of these people were linked, by political inclination, religion, business pursuits or cause. Know one, know them all and, under interrogation, those ominous black lines in the original List could have been filled in.

I have no great faith in quantitative history but the List does throw up some interesting statistics. By my reckoning, allowing for duplications, there are 2,694 people on Schellenberg's books. 231 of them were women, which immediately confirms the sexism of the time. There were no women in Churchill's cabinet, none in the higher echelons of business and none in the church. Had this been a list of Nazis, the number would have been far lower because of the Reich's concept of womanhood. With a few now infamous exceptions, breeding and housewifery were about as exciting as it got! The women who *are* on the List were either writers or politicians in the broad sense. Virginia Woolf (L116) is there. So are Viscountess Rhondda (R51) and Eleanor Rathbone (R12). They were remarkable people in a time dominated by men and the war itself was about to change all that. Many of them were mothers, wives, sisters and sweethearts of men who had died in the trenches of the First World War and they are on the List because they opposed war in a dozen different national and international committees.

Many of the 2,463 men on the List felt the same way. Most of them were Victorians, born in the *fin de siècle* atmosphere of the last decade of the nineteenth century. Then, a European war was unthinkable. Britain was not only (just!) the 'workshop of the world' but stood at the head of the greatest empire in history. Those attitudes stayed with them, reflected in the diaries of men like Harold Nicolson (the List's N31) and Alfred Duff-Cooper (D114), both of them working for the Ministry of Information, which was a peculiarly un-British institution set up in response to the war.

The bulk of the List (1,840 names) is made up of 'foreigners'. In managing the numbers for the purposes of this book, I have broken the chapters down into various headings – political, academic, literary and so on. This is artificial, because there is a high degree of overlap. Harold Nicolson, for instance, is described as '*Schriftsteller*' (writer) but also as '*Politiker*' (politician). In the rough count of heads, I have made assumptions based on a person's name and place of pre-war residence, which may not be strictly accurate. Some Jews, for instance, were among those academics forced out of Nazi Germany after 1933 by the increasing stringency of the Reich's anti-Semitic laws. Others, like Viscount Samuel and the Rothschilds were 'home-grown', their families just as British as the Aryans the Nazis favoured.

Alphabetically, the largest number can be found in the 'S' category on the List, itself divided under that letter into four sections, each starting again from number one. Unsurprisingly, there are no 'Q's or 'X's and only five 'Y's. 'K' and 'Z', equally unsurprisingly, contain a high concentration of European names.

Many of those listed will probably always remain enigmatic. Their names must have been collected from a huge range of sources and no doubt folders of varying thickness would once have been held on them in the filing system of the Reich Security Office. They went up in the flames of Berlin as the Allies advanced in the twilight of the Nazi state.

Various commentators have suggested that the List was

little more than a paper exercise, compiled by men who were obsessed with such things, the meticulous attention to detail for which the Reich was famous. I do not believe this to be true – the Polish example is proof of that. The Special Search List GB represented a core of leadership in all walks of life that had to be eliminated so that a British Reich could rise.

When she read the *Manchester Guardian*'s résumé of the List in September 1945, the novelist Rebecca West (W63) sent a more accurate telegram than she knew when she wrote to Noel Coward, 'My dear – the people we should have been seen dead with.'

CHAPTER ONE

THE WAR THAT WAS – SEPTEMBER 1939-JULY 1940

It was Friday, 1 September 1939 and little Sam Pivnik was out with his friends, playing football. It was a day he would always remember well because it was his birthday. He was thirteen. He could not quite remember, years later, who was with him – Jurek was there, the Gutsek boys; probably Yitshak Wesleman, lads he had known all his life.

What he does remember clearly about this particular birthday, though, was the burst of activity. The normally quiet town of Bedzin, Poland, was full of people, grim-faced and muttering on street corners. Bedzin was a garrison town and, shortly before lunch, the local regiment, the 23rd Light Artillery, rattled out of their barracks, with creaking wheels, snorting horses and the clash of hoofs on the cobbles. All very exciting to a boy just turning thirteen but nothing holds a kid's attention for long and Sam and his friends were soon kicking the ball around again.

That was when they heard it. The drone of aircraft coming from the west. It took a while for them to stop their game and focus in the bright glare of the sun. They were fighter bombers, pale blue on their under-wings with tell-tale black crosses. Sam had no idea that these planes had already hit Wielun, 100 kilometres away, leaving a blazing ruin and 1,200 bodies in the rubble. The first bomb on Bedzin smashed through the roof of the railway station. 'It's funny,' Sam remembered long years later, 'you don't just hear a bomb going off, you feel it. The shock was like being hit in the pit of the stomach.'⁵

This was *Fall Weiss*, the German code name for the invasion of Poland, engineered by a cynical lie. It was necessary if Hitler was to add East Prussia to his Third Reich, to give his people the *lebensraum* (living space) he claimed they needed. The victors of Versailles – Britain, France and the United States – had created the artificial Polish 'corridor' that gave the Poles their only access to the sea, with Danzig (today's Gdansk) as a free port for use by all. That corridor lay between Hitler and his next objective and it had to be closed.

Accordingly, on the last day of August, Operation Himmler was launched. At 8pm, six SS men in Polish army uniforms crashed into the German radio station at Gleiwitz near the Polish border. There was a roar of gunfire, bullets biting into the plaster walls and the bewildered staff were pistol-whipped. One of the raiders grabbed a microphone and announced in immaculate Polish:

'People of Poland! The time has come for war between Poland and Germany. Unite and smash down any German, all Germans who oppose your way. Trample all resistance! The time has come!'

They killed no one at the station but the body of a concentration camp inmate, also dressed as a Pole and referred to in the codes of the time as 'canned goods', was left on the floor.

The next day, Hitler announced to the German people that 'the attack by regular Polish troops on the Gleiwitz transmitter' was the direct cause of the war that was about to begin. Even before his broadcast, Army Group South, commanded by Field Marshal Gerd von Rundstedt, had crossed the Polish border with fifty-three divisions, six of them armoured. One eye witness who was not supposed to be there was 27-year-old Clare Hollingworth, who died in January 2017 aged 105. She was a correspondent for the *Daily Telegraph* who grabbed a diplomat's car and drove to the frontier. She hung out of an upstairs window with a telephone receiver held out so that her editor, on the other end of the line, could hear the snarl and roar of the tanks. Sixteen hundred aircraft accompanied the advance, the terrifying Stuka dive-bombers snaking over the countryside as the bringers of blitzkrieg, lightning war. Against them, the Poles had twenty-three divisions of infantry, one armoured division, insufficient artillery and an impressive, but obsolete, cavalry force. This was 1939 and blitzkrieg was a new, mechanised and faster-moving kind of war than anything the world had seen. Rumour rode with General Heinz Guderian's *panzers* and, for years afterwards, people believed the myth that Polish lancers had charged the German tanks with the inevitable slaughter that would result. It never happened.

Throughout September, the Wehrmacht pushed the Poles back, confident that, because of the treaty that Hitler had signed with Stalin weeks earlier (the Molotov-Ribbentrop Pact), there would be no opposition from the USSR's Red Army. Poland was to be dismembered, split down the centre by the vastly more powerful states on its flanks. Germany would have the lion's share of the country and Russia would control the rest as well as Lithuania, Latvia, Finland and Estonia. Despite the uneasiness with which the ideologies of Fascism and Communism worked together, the geographical elements were a marriage made in heaven. In fact, a British cartoon appeared soon after this time showing a smiling groom, Joe Stalin, arm in arm with Adolf Hitler as his blushing bride.

By the day after the invasion, Runstedt had crossed the Warta river. In the south, the Lodz army collapsed and this led to a bizarre scene in Sam Pivnik's home town. Bedzin, on Monday, 4 September, was full of excitement. The rumours rode again – this time, it was the British and French who were riding to the rescue. People lined the streets to welcome them, the girls and women holding flowers to give to their saviours. But it was not the British and French. It was the dark motorcycles and side-cars of the Wehrmacht's motorised units: 'Hard men,' Pivnik remembered, 'and hard faces. Behind them came grey-painted trucks, all crashing gears and rattling tailgates...between [them] came armoured cars, with cannon and machine-guns – the face of total war.'[6] The cheering stopped. The smiles vanished. The flowers were thrown to the cobbles.

And four days later, hell came to Bedzin. The *Einsatzgruppen* arrived, Hitler's execution squads. Shots echoed in the streets and the smell of the burning synagogue filled the air. When the Pivniks came out of their self-imposed home prison after three days, Sam saw his first corpse. In fact, dozens of them; old Jews with Orthodox ringlets, beards and black clothes lay in the gutters, smashed by rifle butts, slashed with bayonets. Others hung from lamp-posts in the town square, swaying with the wind. The names of some of these men were on the Polish Special Search List. This was the reality of which the people of

Britain, as yet, knew nothing. And many refused to believe it when they did.

The September War, as the Poles called it, was in many ways a foregone conclusion. Warsaw, the capital, was pounded by the full might of Goering's Luftwaffe in a foretaste of what all major cities would experience in the coming months. A Polish government in exile was set up in London with Wladyslaw Raczkiewicz as the new president and the unpopular Wladyslaw Sikorski as commander-in-chief of the armed forces, some of whom had got away in the four destroyers the Polish navy had been able to extricate from the *Kriegsmarine*. On 3 October, the remnants of the Polish army that stayed surrendered near the town of Luck. The Germans took 700,000 prisoners, the Russians 200,000. *Fall Weiss* had been a total success and Poland had ceased to exist.

* * *

Neville Chamberlain's plummy, out-of-touch tones crackled over the radio waves on Sunday, 3 September 1939, reaching a numbed British population who would spend the next six years glued to their wireless sets. Some of the men who heard Chamberlain remembered all too well the last time they had clashed with Germany, only twenty-five years before. It had been the Kaiser's Germany then, a new nation flexing its military muscles on the world stage. It was Hitler's Germany now and the men and women who listened to Chamberlain that Sunday had watched in growing disbelief as Germany had risen from the ashes of defeat in just six years. Most Englishmen found the Führer funny; he had awful hair and a silly moustache. His high-stepping minions in the black-shirted SS were something of a joke. But some of those listeners were impressed by the economic miracle that Hitler had brought about in a nation all but destroyed by defeat and the Wall Street crash. Some of them believed that the Allies had been too harsh in punishing Germany at Versailles in 1919 and that Hitler's rise was wholly explicable. Still others rather admired the stand he took against the Bolshevism that had made a monster out of Russia. And a few, although they would spend the rest of their lives denying it, thought that he had a point in his detestation of the Jews.

From that Sunday, Britain was at war with Nazi Germany. So, with immediate effect, were Australia and New Zealand, whose men had bled in the trenches of Gallipoli in the First World War. Chamberlain – the arch-appeaser who had stood by and watched as Hitler annexed the Saarland, sent troops to the demilitarised Rhine, forged an alliance with Austria and snatched first the Sudetenland, then all of Czechoslovakia – called a meeting of his cabinet. Alongside the time-servers and paper-shufflers who did not believe this moment would ever come were two who knew that it would: Anthony Eden, Secretary for the Dominions, the old empire which, fifty years earlier, had been the largest in the world; and Winston Churchill, the maverick anti-Nazi of the Thirties, now First Lord of the Admiralty.

Minutes after the Prime Minister's announcement and before the cabinet assembled, the tell-tale whine of an air-raid siren wailed over London. It was a noise that would strike terror to millions over the next six years. Churchill and his wife Clementine went up to the roof of their town house. They saw, in the hazy midday sun, thirty or forty barrage balloons, floating like huge beached whales in the sky. Then, with the *sang froid* that he would show for the next six years, Churchill made for the nearest air-raid shelter 'armed with a bottle of brandy and other appropriate medical comforts.'[7]

The raid was a false alarm. Churchill's shelter was the basement of a house with no sandbags and the all-clear sounded after fifteen minutes, followed by someone walking along the street calling out the same. No doubt the famous British sense of humour kicked in – 'Is that all they've got?' 'Typical – late for their own war.' Many people would learn to laugh at death in the coming months.

At 5pm on that Sunday, France, whose own ultimatum to Hitler over Poland had not yet expired, followed Chamberlain's lead and declared war on the old enemy. And then …nothing.

The strange lull before the storm that the West experienced has been called 'the bore war' because it was so dull. The French knew it as *drôle de guerre* (the funny war). The Germans, who were, in fact, busy in the East, called it *sitzkrieg* (the armchair war). The British coined the expression of an American journalist based in London and the 'phoney war' was born. Even that first weekend, there was a peculiar sense of time standing still. Most football matches on the previous day had been cancelled because of a shortage of players. By the time of Chamberlain's broadcast, many of the West Ham team were already wearing their itchy new battledress khaki, scanning the empty skies with the Essex regiment's searchlight section.

Behind the scenes and unbeknownst to the British public, the government had set up Code Yellow and Code Black, mass movement unprecedented in history. People were on the move to safety. The BBC closed down its infant television station at Alexandra Palace, right in the middle of a Mickey Mouse cartoon (unlike Nazi Germany, which continued to broadcast throughout the war). Realising the vital need to keep radio going and to provide news, the rest of 'Auntie's' operatives moved to Bristol and Evesham. The Bank of

England abandoned Threadneedle Street and became the Little Old Lady of Overton, Hampshire. The National Gallery began the huge task of moving its art exhibits, of the sort that Hermann Goering was fond of collecting, to caves in a slate quarry in Wales.

But the biggest movement of all was of children. The horrific experiences of the town of Guernica in the Spanish Civil War two years earlier had brought a new word and a new concept to warfare – blitzkrieg.[8] A reporter who was there told a disbelieving world:

'I saw a priest in one group . . . His face was blackened, his clothes in tatters. He couldn't talk. He just pointed to the flames, still about four miles away, then whispered, *'Aviones . . . bombas . . . mucho, mucho.'* In the city, soldiers were collecting charred bodies. They were sobbing like children. There were flames and smoke and grit and the smell of burning human flesh was nauseating.'[9]

The *'aviones'* were the Heinkel IIIs, the Dornier 17s and the Junkers 52s of Germany's Condor Legion, the pride of Goering's Luftwaffe, and Guernica was their dummy run for the war that was to come.

To avoid this unimaginable horror, on the last day of August, vast numbers of London schoolchildren had been marshalled by adults as bewildered as they were. They carried toothbrushes, sandwiches and one favourite toy, taken to their schools by tearful mothers and then by bus or Underground to the nearest mainline station. Their faces all stare out of grainy black and white snapshots today, clutching all that was left of their world. Journeys by train took hours and there were often no corridors. Toilets overflowed. Children were sick, with excitement and fear. They missed their families already and they had no idea where they were going. The whole thing was chaos. Large hotels in the country waiting to receive their cohort got no one. Tiny village cottages were swamped with siblings who refused to be separated. Many of them were crawling with lice and fleas. They had rarely seen soap and did not own a comb. To many of these townies, seasons and cows were just words that their teachers sometimes used.

★ ★ ★

The land war may have been 'phoney' but the story at sea was different. The *Kriegsmarine* had fifty-eight submarines (U-boats), thirty-nine of which were at sea by early September. Although not a new weapon, the U-boat was regarded with apprehension by everyone. Until sonar (underwater radar) was perfected, a submarine was a silent killer, able to strike anywhere and disappear in minutes. Surface shipping, including that of the Merchant Navy and civilians, was at serious risk. Fifty-three such ships had been sunk by 3 September and it was not until four days later that the first British Atlantic convoys set out with destroyer escorts. On paper, the Royal Navy had the edge over the *Kriegsmarine*, although the Anglo-German naval agreement of 1935 had allowed Hitler to build warships openly and four years of hectic arms manufacture had produced impressive results. The aircraft carrier *Courageous* was sunk on 17 September in a routine submarine patrol and, after that, the carriers were withdrawn. They were too important and too expensive to be squandered.

Most notorious of the *Kriegsmarine*'s fleet was the pocket battleship *Graf Spee*, which sank nine ships between September and December. By the end of October, 196,000 tons of Allied shipping had been lost, at the expense of five

U-boats. The biggest blow, however, fell on 14 October, when U-boat commander Gunther Prien took his U-47 into the naval base of Scapa Flow and sank the *Royal George*. Goebbels and his Ministry of Propaganda and Enlightenment had a field day. The next month, on 23 November, the merchant cruiser *Rawalpindi* was blown out of the water by the *Scharnhorst*. What no one realised at the time was that the *Kriegsmarine* were able to intercept British codes and plan their strategy accordingly.

What was the mood in Britain? The people only knew what they were told by the media, and both the BBC and the mainstream newspapers were soon tightly controlled by the government's Ministry of Information. The paranoia of the period believed that there was a Fifth Column operating across the country, in constant touch with Nazi Germany and prepared to undermine morale in a thousand ingenious ways. Given this situation, the Ministry behaved not unlike Goebbels' Ministry of Propaganda and Enlightenment, exhorting people to 'Be like Dad – keep Mum', 'Tittle-Tattle Lost the Battle' and 'Careless Talk Costs Lives'. The public could only see things through official channels and those channels, naturally, tried to put a brave face on things. Spreading alarm and despondency was the last thing anyone wanted to do. Today, a number of historians believe that, in general, the media told the public the truth. I dispute that. On 10 May 1941, in the heaviest – and last – of the Luftwaffe's Blitz on London, the Air Ministry claimed to have shot down twenty-eight German aircraft. In fact, the figure was seven and that was scant recompense for the terrible punishment that London had taken. The BBC reported it nonetheless.

Harold Nicolson provides a fascinating candid snapshot of reaction to the news. He was a National Labour MP for

West Leicester when war broke out and would serve as a Parliamentary Secretary to the Ministry of Information from May 1940 to July 1941. Despite his 'establishment' status, his diary was written strictly for private purposes, not publication and the highs and lows of international developments give him a rather schizophrenic aura – suicidal in the morning, gung-ho in the afternoon (or vice versa), depending on the situation.

He had grasped the situation clearly by 6 September: 'If we insist upon the continuance of battle, we may condemn many young men to death. If we urge acceptance, we are ending the British Empire.'[10]

In those early days of the war, Anthony Eden was seen as the hawk of the Commons, broadcasting to the nation. Nicolson's schizophrenia is shown by his diary entry for 11 September: 'If Anthony had said "We will consider peace" I should have been wretchedly relieved. As he said "We shall fight to the end" I am stimulated and happy.'

On 20 September, Chamberlain, Nicolson observed, was tired and depressed. At least ten MPs nodded off during his speech to the House. It says a great deal about the difference between illusion and reality in the opening weeks of the war that one of the people Nicolson dined with that night was the double agent Guy Burgess, the BBC journalist who worked for Section Nine of SIS, the Secret Service and who would spectacularly defect to the Soviet Union in 1951. Nicolson noted the appearance of Winston Churchill 'like the Chinese god of plenty suffering from acute indigestion. He just sits there, lowering, hunched and circular' but when he got up all the benches cheered him wildly.

It would not have surprised men like Nicolson to know that Hitler was already planning to strike west and he told his chiefs of staff precisely that on the 27th. He may have expected wholehearted support – after all, the Polish campaign was all but over; in fact, the reception was not only lukewarm, it was downright hostile. Harold Nicolson believed the Germans were naturally a diffident people and Hitler's high command seemed to bear this out. Blitzkrieg had not yet made its true impact. The tank had been underused in Poland, with conventional infantry tactics being preferred by the more staid of the Wehrmacht generals, almost all of whom were veterans of the First World War.

The French army, its mobilisation surprisingly slow, had marched into the Reich at Saarbrucken and patrolled until 17 September, when news of the imminent collapse of Poland made Eduoard Daladier's War Cabinet call them back.

By the middle of October, four British divisions had crossed to France. It spent time improving the defences of the Maginot Line while the Germans improved theirs – the *Westwall*, which the British called the Siegfried Line. Despite this flurry of activity, involving miles of barbed wire and hundreds of Royal Engineers, not a shot was fired.

One of the many myths to emerge from this period is that Britain had so slavishly followed the government's line of appeasement to Hitler that she was totally unprepared for war. This is patently untrue. Thanks to the pioneering genius of men like R. J. Mitchell, Britain had the Spitfire, the best fighter plane of the war. We had a small but professional and well-equipped army that would be augmented by conscription even before war was declared. And, of course, the navy, despite its losses, had a reputation second to none. We also had an experienced and large workforce and had made enough adaptations to changing technology to stand against any country in the world in terms of arms production. These were the positives but would they be enough?

On 6 October, Hitler kept the world guessing and held out an olive branch to the West. In a speech to the Reichstag, he said that all Germany had done to date was to correct the vicious unfairness of Versailles. He believed that a Munich-style conference of European leaders could produce results – as long as warmongers like Churchill were not present. Harold Nicolson told R. A. Butler, Under-Secretary at the Foreign Office, that Chamberlain should consider this, with various guarantees. In the event, the Prime Minister rejected the idea out of hand, as did Daladier in France. It is unlikely that Chamberlain shared the same happy-go-lucky *sang froid* of songwriters Jimmy Kennedy and Michael Carr, who were 'gonna hang out the washing on the Siegfried Line', but the man had been permanently scarred by the Munich Conference in 1938; he wasn't about to make the same mistake again.

Three days later, in Directive No. 6, the Führer made his aims clear: 'Should it become evident in the near future that England, and, under her influence, France also, are not disposed to bring the war to an end, I have decided, without further loss of time, to go over to the offensive.'

On 5 November, the Wehrmacht's commander-in-chief, Field Marshal Walther von Brauchitsch, was summoned to the Reichs Chancellery to talk strategy. He told Hitler that the army was not ready for the planned strike west scheduled for a week's time. Hitler went into one of his carefully planned but increasingly frequent rages and shouted the man down. But the weather, at least, was on Brauchitsch's side. Between 7 November and 16 January 1940, the strike west was postponed an astonishing fourteen times!

As the year closed, the Winter War, fought in the snow of the frozen north between Finland and the USSR, continued, the vastly superior Red Army getting a bloody nose for its pains against a tiny but committed and professional force. The *Graf Spee*, driven for shelter into the River Plate in Argentina, scuttled herself rather than face the Royal Navy in open waters.

The new year brought economic sanctions on all sides in the war. In Germany, Hermann Goering was put in charge of war industry. The former air ace and larger-than-life Nazi was the most preposterous of the *goldfasanen*, the golden pheasants, who strutted around in glitzy uniforms. Four years earlier, in his famous 'butter or guns' speech, he had spelled out the determination he expected from the German people. Germany, he told his listeners, 'must have a place in the sun... What's the good of being in the concert of nations, if we are only allowed to play a comb?'[11]

In Britain, bacon, butter and sugar were added to the growing list of rationed goods, increasing the power of the Ministry of Food and extending the remit of the black market. France, too, was suffering. On 11 January, the government announced that Friday would be a meatless day (many French Catholics thought it already was) and that no mutton, beef or veal would be sold on Mondays and Tuesdays either. Grim though the economic figures were, it was still possible to afford pre-war luxuries if you knew the right place or person. Keith Simpson, the Home Office pathologist, continued to enjoy slap-up meals at L'Etoile in Soho's Charlotte Street for the rest of the war and, on the day of the French pronouncement, Marie Vassiltchikov in Berlin drank champagne at Ciro's nightclub in the city.

Militarily, it became a race for Norway. The country produced heavy water and could supply safe, deep-water harbours for U-boats in its fjords, thus avoiding the Allied naval blockade that had crippled the Axis powers in the First

World War. In the event, the Germans struck first and it was not until early April that the British navy moved on Norway. The Germans were already there, forcing Copenhagen to capitulate after a single day. In the brief fighting that took place, of the 16,000-strong Danish army, there were only 13 deaths. Churchill was off form in the House, shuffling his papers, mistaking Sweden for Denmark and generally giving the air of a man who had been outthought and outfought by the speed and efficiency of the Reich. MPs muttered among themselves that, if Norway fell, Scotland might be next. There were successes at sea, with seven German destroyers sunk, but the army fared less well and there was talk of evacuation. Churchill was a victim of his own (dubious) reputation. He had made serious mistakes at the Admiralty over the Gallipoli campaign in the First World War, to the extent that he had been forced to resign. Many were surprised to see him back in post twenty-four years later. 'Today,' wrote Harold Nicolson, 'he cannot dare to do the things he could have dared in 1915.'

In Berlin, Marie Vassiltchikov, a Russian émigré, with her perfect English, listened illegally to the BBC – 'People here are rather staggered by this precipitous pull-out [from Norway]. Many Germans still have a lurking admiration for the British.'[12]

At the end of the month, King Hakkon and his government left collapsing Norway with the country's gold reserves on board the cruiser *Glasgow* to become yet another government-in-exile in London. British and French forces evacuated soon after, leaving valuable equipment behind. All in all, it did not bode well for the future.

Harold Nicolson wrote one of his longest diary entries for 8 May. There was a debate in the House over the Norwegian situation and it turned into a vote of no confidence in

Chamberlain. The first stab was inflicted by Herbert Morrison, MP for Hackney South, and the Prime Minister took the attack personally. Ashen-faced, he rounded on Morrison – 'I have friends in this House.' It all sounded rather spiteful and like school-playground antics. In the frantic behind-the-scenes lobbies in the mother of parliaments, grown men bitched and plotted. Chamberlain was prepared to jettison Samuel Hoare and John Simon, his cabinet cronies. Duff Cooper of the Ministry of Information and David Lloyd George, the Welsh wizard who had led Britain in the First World War, savaged Churchill in the chamber. Forty-four, including Nicolson, voted against the government. Thirty abstained. MP John Wedgwood (the List's W38), carried away with the emotion of it all, sang 'Rule Britannia' and, all around the chamber, shouts of 'Go, go, go, go!' filled the Prime Minister's ears as he left.

The next few days were turmoil in the corridors of power. 'Germany,' wrote Marie Vassiltchikov, 'has marched into Belgium and Holland.' Harold Nicolson saw the same newsstands as he caught the London train from Brighton. The rumour machine followed him, with stories of the bombing of Lyons and an imminent invasion of Switzerland. On his arrival in the capital, he was immediately in the thick of politics. In the light of the news, some people contended that Chamberlain must stay. Samuel Hoare refused point blank to leave the Air Ministry. What about, some wondered, a triumvirate of Chamberlain, Churchill and Lord Halifax, the tall, stately Foreign Secretary? News from the Continent, arriving by the hour, was grim and there was panic in Whitehall. What made it all worse, Nicolson remembered, was the gorgeous spring day, with bluebells and primroses everywhere. He was back home in Sissinghurst by nine o'clock that night, in time to hear Chamberlain's tones, still plummy, still out of touch, but now desperately tired, offering his resignation. There was to be no triumvirate. There was to be no Halifax at Number Ten.

Marie Vassiltchikov wrote, 'It comes as a shock as this means the end of the "Phoney War"...Paris is being evacuated, Chamberlain has resigned and Churchill is now Prime Minister. This, probably, kills any hope for peace with the Allies now.'

When Churchill appeared in the House for the first time after he had kissed rings at the Palace, he got a rousing cheer from almost everyone *except* his own party. He would have to use his prodigious energy to win friends, and quickly – the same negative advice was being drip fed into his ears, as it had been into Chamberlain's. Basil Liddell-Hart, arguably the most influential independent military adviser in the country, had said in March that the only solution was to 'come to the best possible terms as soon as possible ...we have no chance of avoiding defeat.'[13] Lord Beaverbrook used his Express Newspapers fortune to create a realistic team of peace candidates in the House. Halifax, who had actually turned down the premiership because, sitting in the Lords, he felt out of touch, also thought that coming to terms with Hitler was the only way forward.

The Dominions were not happy either. At the start of the war, Canada had waited a week before declaring war on Germany. In South Africa, it had taken a change of government in Johannesburg for that to happen. Now, Robert Menzies, the Australian Prime Minister, told his High Commissioner in London that Churchill was a publicity-seeker and that the real enemy was not Nazi Germany but Bolshevik Russia.

And it was to get worse. On 10 May, *Fall Gelb* was launched, a simultaneous attack on the Netherlands, Belgium and France. In the north, Field Marshal Bock's twenty-nine

divisions of Army Group B moved against a pitifully weak
Dutch defence. The flat nature of the Netherlands offered very
little in the way of natural barriers to slow the Wehrmacht
down. In the centre, Army Group A, under von Rundstedt,
marched confidently into Belgium from the *West Wall*. This
was the major thrust of the campaign, forty-five divisions,
crashing through the forest of the Ardennes with a speed that
bewildered everyone except Heinz Guderian, whose *panzers*
now came into their own. Against them, the Belgian army
was feeble. The Dutch and Belgian reserves were based in
the west, nearest to the coast. The Germans had forty-two
divisions in their reserve, stationed in the north but ready to
reinforce the line wherever needed.

In the south, Wilhelm Leeb's Army Group C stretching
from the Swiss border near Basel to Luxembourg, faced the
French Maginot Line. Much has been written about these
fortifications and the 'defence mentality' that they bred. The
French Army Groups 2 and 3 manned it, under Generals André-
Gaston Prételat and Antoine-Marie-Benoit Besson. Further
north, along the French border, the 1st Army Group under
General Gaston Billotte had twenty-two divisions. Further
north still, along the Somme of bitter First World War memory,
Field Marshal John Gort's British Expeditionary Force had
nine divisions and at the coast near Dunkirk, General Henri
Giraud's seven divisions included two motorised and one light
mechanised.

On paper, the sides seemed evenly matched but the reality
was very different. While Leeb feinted in the south, Runstedt
simply bypassed the Maginot Line and pressed forward between
Luxembourg and Aachen. The advantage that the Germans
had was that the three army groups were co-ordinated by
von Brauchitsch at OKH, the Army High Command. Against

that, there was less co-operation than there should have been, certainly in the planning stage, between the Dutch, the Belgians, the French and the tiny British force involved. They had all had eight months since the outbreak of war to prepare for this moment but the possibility of establishing peace with Hitler, arrogance and inertia had combined with fatal results.

The French command was especially weak. General Maurice Gamelin, the commander-in-chief, did not have the confidence of the government or many of the officers under him. He was too old to appreciate the situation facing him. Even by the end of the first day's fighting, everything had gone to the Wehrmacht's plan and the Dutch and Belgians were struggling to hold out. In the air, the Luftwaffe's superiority was clear – 3,000 combat aircraft to 2,000 of the Allies. It prompted the question from many disgruntled British squaddies in the days ahead, 'Where the bloody hell was the RAF?'

Two days later, the Wehrmacht marched into Sedan unopposed. The French army retreated, determined to hold the Meuse with their heavy artillery. As Queen Wilhelmina and her advisers left for England to become *another* government in exile, Giraud's Seventh Army was in full retreat, pushed back by Guderian and, another rising star in the Wehrmacht galaxy, Erwin Rommel.

That was the day that Churchill made one of his most famous speeches in the House. 'I have nothing to offer you,' he said, 'but blood, toil, tears and sweat.'

Rotterdam was flattened by aerial bombing on 14 May and the Dutch were staring surrender in the face. In Britain, the Local Defence Volunteers were formed. Subsequently mocked as 'Dad's Army' it was a last-ditch defence organisation composed of old men, teenagers and those with various disabilities. Without uniforms, guns or, at first, a structured command, they seemed as desperate as the times. The Dutch surrendered on the next day and the French First Army pulled back. The German commanders were at the front with their men, spearheading attacks as the Germans had for centuries.

In Britain, Air Marshal Hugh Dowding persuaded Churchill's War Cabinet not to send any more fighters to France. They would simply be swallowed up in the German advance and Britain had neither the planes nor the pilots to spare. Instead, Bomber Command was given the green light to target the Ruhr, Germany's industrial heartland, to damage war production. This may seem an obvious decision but it was directly at odds with the opening weeks of the war. Then, only leaflets were dropped because, after all, the factories in the Ruhr were private property!

Churchill flew to Paris on the 16th. He learned that the French Reserve had virtually ceased to exist. Minions in government offices were already burning top-secret papers and a radical shake-up in that government effectively removed Gamelin two days later. Marshal Phillipe Pétain, the hero of the First World War at Verdun, became deputy prime minister under Paul Reynaud, and General Maxime Weygand took over the supreme command. With hindsight, the aged Pétain was a poor choice; he had little faith in his own army and was overawed by the speed of the blitzkrieg that they faced.

In the case of the British Expeditionary Forces (BEF), Gort was increasingly uneasy about the situation. He had the right to refuse French orders if he felt his own units were compromised but exactly when to pull out was difficult. At home, Harold Nicolson had been asked by Churchill to step up to the plate. In the Prime Minister's own words, 'Harold, I think it would be very nice if you joined the government and helped Duff [Cooper] at the Ministry of Information.' Nicolson was like a schoolboy in his 'sunny little room' in a building belonging to London University, with pins and coloured wool showing troop positions across the Channel. By that day, Guderian's *panzers* had carved a twenty-mile corridor from the Ardennes to the French coast. As he played with his pins, it may have dawned on Nicolson that the Third Reich was just over one hundred miles from him and getting closer every day.

On 21 May, a unit of British Matilda tanks hit back at Arras, where their fathers had fought in the First World War, but they were too few to do much damage and the French general Billotte was killed in a car crash. Walter Monckton, Director-General of the Press Bureau of the Ministry of Information, heard a loud laugh at the Foreign office that morning – 'a sound which I have not heard for a week'. It was probably hysteria. Hitler held a high-level conference in Berlin that same day. This was the moment when Admiral Erich Raeder suggested to his Führer that it may be necessary to invade Britain.

In the House, the Emergency Powers Act was passed, giving sweeping new authority to the magistracy, the police and the emergency services, which would have been unthinkable in peace time, and a new army of 'little Hitlers' threw their weight about in a society ever more afraid for its own safety.

Harold Nicolson was expecting the worst. He advised his wife, the novelist Vita Sackville-West, to fill the tank of her Buick with petrol, grab her jewels and a twenty-four-hour food supply. 'I should imagine that the best thing you can do is to make for Devonshire.' He was not talking about invasion yet, but the need for the government to get out of London. If the Luftwaffe's bombers were to be based on the French coast, then the British capital was well within their range.

The Royal Navy was now in action in the Channel, firing in support of Allied troops pinned in at Calais and Boulogne.

Under Defence Regulation 18B, Oswald Mosely, the British Fascist Leader and Captain Archibald Ramsay, chairman of the Right Club, were interned along with many others. In the rising tide of panic, anyone with obvious German or Austrian connections was rounded up and placed under lock and key, including, ironically, several who would appear on Walter Schellenberg's List in a few weeks' time.

On 24 May, in a move that surprised everyone at the time and has been debated ever since, Hitler ordered a halt to the attack. Goering was demanding a more central role for his Luftwaffe and the Wehrmacht's tank crews certainly needed rest. Whether he deliberately soft-pedalled in his advance against the British in an effort to bring about peace talks is still argued today; but if he did, he reckoned without Winston Churchill.

Beaverbrook's *Daily Express* could scream in its banner headlines on 11 May, Now we're at their throats! but the reality was that we were David throwing pointless rocks at Goliath and the story was not turning out as it did in the Old Testament. On 4 June, Churchill made what is probably his best-known speech in the Commons:

'We shall not flag or fail. We shall go on to the end. We shall fight in France, we shall fight on the seas and the oceans, we shall fight with growing strength in the air. We shall defend our island, whatever the cost may be. We shall fight on the beaches, we shall fight on the landing grounds, we shall fight in the fields and in the streets, we shall fight in the hills. We shall never surrender.'[14]

By the time he made this speech, Churchill knew that fighting in France was no longer an option. There had been upbeat moments of good news – 'Our army has fought the most magnificent battle in Flanders,' Nicolson wrote on 31 May; two days earlier, he had talked of erecting a Corunna Line[15] around Dunkirk and 'hope to evacuate a few of our troops.'[16]

Operation Dynamo was the name given to the evacuation from Dunkirk that began on 26 May. Thanks to Churchill's genius as a rhetorician, the phrase 'Dunkirk Spirit' entered the English language and a victory was born. In fact, as most people realised at the time, Dunkirk was a defeat and an embarrassing one at that. First Norway, now France; the much-vaunted British army had been well and truly beaten twice. Photographs of the Tommies returning home to Dover give a false impression. Their grins are those of relief, not pride. Some of these men were jeered in the streets. A few were spat at.

'Our great-grandchildren,' said the writer J. B. Priestley in a broadcast on 5 June, 'when they learn how we began this war by snatching glory out of defeat…. may also learn how the little holiday steamers made an excursion to hell and came back glorious.'[17]

The 'little ships of England', privately owned motor boats, made the dangerous Channel crossing more than once. They could carry few men, however, and virtually no equipment. These were transferred to Royal Navy transports and warships at a suitable distance from the coast. The rows of dispirited men, in battle bowlers and greatcoats, sleeping exposed on the Dunkirk beaches, were sitting ducks for the fighters and dive bombers of the Luftwaffe. On 31 May, they had thirty-eight planes shot down by the RAF, who themselves lost twenty-eight. It was all too little, too late. By the next day, 64,429 men had crossed the Channel but four British destroyers were sunk and five others seriously damaged. On 2 June, the last British units left, a little before midnight.

The evacuees included 112,000 Frenchmen, who would form the Free French army in exile under General Charles de Gaulle in London, itching for a chance to renew the conflict on their own soil. Eighty ships had been lost and the navy's resources were now seriously depleted. Of the 180 destroyers in the navy list at the start of the war, only 74 were still fully operational. Eighty of Dowding's RAF pilots had been killed – altogether a more expensive commodity than Gort's BEF ground troops and more difficult to replace. As if to add insult to injury, five days later, the *Scharnhorst* and the *Gneisnau*, marauding along the coast of Norway now that the British and the Norwegian royal family had abandoned it, came across the aircraft carrier HMS *Glorious* with two destroyers as escort. All three British ships were sunk.

'And now comes Italy,' moaned Harold Nicolson. 'What a mean, skulking thing to do...They are like the people who rob corpses on the battlefield .... The Greeks had a word for it.'

In fact, it would be another six days before Benito Mussolini officially declared war on Britain and France, and both he and his country's military effort were to become, in the months ahead, an acute embarrassment to Hitler. At the time, of course, this was not the point. Mussolini, who became the Fascist dictator – Il Duce – of Italy in 1922, was very much the senior partner in the totalitarian stakes. Germany and Austria were Fascist, so was Italy. So, too, was Spain, although, exhausted by her civil war, she took no active part in the Second World War. It made sense for Italy to throw in her lot with Germany, and the Pact of Steel now created sent a shudder through the corridors of Whitehall. The Italian army was not first rate and the economy would find it difficult to sustain a prolonged war. The navy, however, was formidable, with state-of-the-art battleships nearing completion and the largest U-boat force in the world, 116 strong. The British possessions of Gibraltar in the west of the Mediterranean, Malta in the centre and Cyprus in the east, could all come under serious threat of invasion.

Immediately, in Britain, people with Italian surnames or connections were rounded up under Regulation 18B. Ice-cream parlours vanished overnight. And, with the signposts taken down from roads and barbed-wire entanglements embedded into the beaches, it was not going to be a wonderful summer! 'What makes me gnash my teeth,' Nicolson wrote to his wife on 12 June, 'is that Hitler said he would be in Paris by 15th June and I think he will meet that date, thereby increasing his mystic legend.'

Nicolson was anaesthetised by the situation. Convinced that Britain would be bombed and invaded in three weeks, he and Vita had taken steps to commit suicide with cyanide capsules – the 'bare bodkin', as he calls them – 'I am quite lucidly aware that in three weeks from now Sissinghurst may be a waste[land] and Vita and I both dead.'

The very last of British and Canadian troops were evacuated from France by 18 June. Churchill hit exactly the right note again in the Commons, broadcast to the nation later:

'What General Weygand called the Battle of France is over. I expect that the Battle of Britain is about to begin ...The whole fury and might of the enemy must very soon be turned on us. Hitler knows that he will have to break us up in this island or lose the war... Let us therefore brace ourselves to our duty and so bear ourselves that, if the British Commonwealth and its Empire last for a thousand years, men will still say "This was their finest hour".'[18]

Weygand had also said (although Churchill did not make this public for well over a year) that he expected, within three weeks, for Britain to have her neck wrung like a chicken. William Shirer, reporting for the Columbia Broadcasting System, was in the forest of Compiegne on Saturday, 22 June to witness France's total humiliation. Hitler had insisted that the very railway carriage in which the Kaiser's army had surrendered to Field Marshal Ferdinand Foch in November 1918 be used again; this time with the Führer in Foch's seat, literally as well as figuratively. The sun shone through the elms and cedars that afternoon as Shirer watched history reverse itself. The whole thing, with formal salutes and grim faces, lasted for fifteen minutes. Then the German band struck up *'Deutschland Uber Alles'* and the *'Horst Wessel'* song, which was virtually a Nazi theme tune. Shirer noted the inscription, as did Hitler and his cronies, that the French had erected there in 1918 –'Here on the eleventh of November 1918, succumbed the criminal pride of the German Empire, vanquished by the free peoples which it tried to enslave.' Twenty-two years later, the free peoples were vanquished after all.

★ ★ ★

Britain now stood alone, separated from Hitler's Reich by twenty-one miles of water. As if to signal the next move, on 30 June, the Wehrmacht occupied the Channel Islands, technically setting foot on British soil for the first time. The following month came to be known to the *Kriegsmarine* as *die gluckhche zeit* (the happy time) because of the high hit rate on Allied shipping in the Atlantic.

And on the second day of the new month, the OKW, the German High Command, issued a new order called The War Against England – 'The Führer and Supreme Commander has decided that a landing in England is possible.' Luftwaffe attacks on Allied ships intensified. The next day, Churchill made one of the most difficult and fateful decisions of the war. Concerned that the French navy would fall into German hands, he ordered the Royal Navy to open fire on the French and destroy as many ships as they could. Those in British harbours were seized quietly and with minimum bloodshed. At Mers-el-Kebir, however, demobilisation talks broke down and Admiral James Somerville opened his broadsides on Admiral Marcel-Bruno Gensoul's ships, sinking the *Bretagne* and damaging two other battleships.

Probing Britain's south coast and anxious to show what his airmen could do, Goering unleashed a Stuka squadron on a convoy off Portland Bill. Five of the nine ships were sunk. As an obvious prelude to a seaborne invasion, it was vital that the Germans should knock out the RAF first. Poland's excellent air force had been caught off guard by the suddenness of the invasion but Goering could hardly count on the element of surprise now. Throughout June and July, there was frantic work in the RAF and its support industries to build planes and train pilots. Churchill later wrote:

'This was a time when all Britain worked . . . to the utmost limit and was united as never before. Men and women toiled at the lathes and machines till they fell exhausted... and had to be ordered home... Nothing moves an Englishman so much as the threat of invasion, the reality unknown for a thousand years. Vast numbers of people were resolved to conquer or die.'[19]

The British reckoned 10 July to be the opening of the Battle of Britain. There were dog-fights over the Channel,

Messerschmitts and Hurricanes snarling through the summer skies to try to down each other. The gloomy thinking throughout the Thirties was that 'the bomber will always get through' and a squadron did that day, hitting the docks in Cardiff and Port Talbot in South Wales. Most of the Luftwaffe's attacks were on shipping in the Channel and they sustained the heavier losses. In terms of fighters, however, the tally was about equal and the Luftwaffe easily outnumbered the RAF in that respect.

The French had lost heart. Their army beaten, their air force shattered, their fleet non-existent, they rolled over to German occupation, giving the British a foretaste of what might come for them. President Lebrun resigned and was replaced by Petain, the war hero-turned-collaborator. All over the country, his grim countrymen formed Resistance movements, just to show how far they were removed from him.

Two days later, Hitler issued Directive 15. The full blast of the Luftwaffe's strength was to be unleashed on 5 August. The summer of 1940, now invested with a nostalgic glow as the 'Spitfire summer', was unusually hot and dry – excellent flying weather. Goering fell at the first. Having promised Hitler that the RAF stood no chance, he now had to report that his cohorts would not be up to strength by the 5th and precious days were lost.

The next day, Directive 16 was issued in Berlin. 'I have decided,' said the Führer with all the confidence that a dictator of a police state can afford, 'to begin to prepare for, and if necessary, carry out, an invasion of England.'

It had taken Hitler weeks to come to this decision and the rather curious wording implies, perhaps, a lack of conviction. Why prepare for invasion and not carry it out? With hindsight, we know that many of the German High Command were sceptical; that they fully appreciated the difficulties of invasion. But, if they dithered, all Hitler had to do was to point to Poland, the Netherlands, Belgium and France. Blitzkrieg was unstoppable. Some of today's historians have taken this apparent indecision to extremes; that Hitler never had any serious intention of invasion and that he would much have preferred to make peace.

On 19 July, the Führer made 'a final appeal to common sense' in the Reichstag, the last olive branch of peace that he would offer to Britain. The reaction in Whitehall was fascinating. Harold Nicolson was convinced that the Germans would invade in 'the next few days', even though Hitler had now fixed the airborne attack, *Agler Tag* (Eagle Day), for 13 August. Lord Lothian, the Right-wing peer who had been shunted to the role of British ambassador in Washington, essentially to keep him out of the way, rang Halifax on the 22nd begging him not to respond to Hitler's offer in a way that might close the door on peace. In the event, Halifax did just that. To paraphrase – and invert – Churchill's epithet, it was to be 'war, war, not jaw, jaw.'

Harold Nicolson – and, indeed, many of Churchill's War Cabinet – seem to have had only the vaguest notion of what actual invasion would bring, even though Nicolson's Ministry of Information had already issued pamphlets on the subject! 'It may be that Hitler will bomb us first with gas. At the same time, Italy and Japan will hit us as hard as they can.' In fact, Hitler had already turned down Il Duce's offer of military help and Japan was almost six thousand miles away. There was one thing, however, that Nicolson got right – 'It will be a dreadful month.'

The gas rumour emerged in Germany too. Marie Vassiltchikov wrote on 25 July that 'some gas bombs were

found in the wreckage of a recently shot down British plane.'
There were even more bizarre stories. 'Today, at the office, I
received, by mistake, a sheet with a yellow strip across – it
was an alleged rumour about a riot in London, with the King
hanged at the gates of Buckingham Palace.'

* * *

Eagle Day was imminent. Tanks, mechanised transport, men
and machines were massing at Boulogne and other bases along
the newly-captured French coast. Another campaign. Another
dazzling victory for the glorious Aryan armies of the invincible
Third Reich.

And, as part of that preparation, Walter Schellenberg,
deputy leader of Amt IV of the Reich Central Security Office
and personal aide to Heinrich Himmler, *Reichsführer* SS, was
ordered to compile a list. It was the *Sonderfahndunglist* G.B,
Special Search List Great Britain and it contained the names
of 2,694 individuals who, once the eagle landed, would find
themselves dead.

CHAPTER TWO

THE WAR THAT WAS TO BE –
AUGUST 1940

When Winston Churchill talked of the experience of invasion that the British people had not known for a thousand years, he was talking about 1066, still regarded by many as the best-known date in British history. There have only been three identifiable foreign invasions in recorded history, not including drifts of demography by the Celts, Saxons and Vikings.

The first was the arrival of Julius Caesar – twice! – in 55 and 54BC. This was more of a fact-finding mission than an attempt at conquest and was part of Caesar's far more ambitious campaign in Gaul. The second was the appearance of Aulus Plautius and his four legions in 43 AD. Although it is not possible to be accurate in terms of numbers, Plautius's full strength would have given him about 20,000 men; perhaps double that if we factor in the auxiliary units that the Romans habitually used.

William of Normandy's invasion of 1066 was a much less

impressive venture. Rome was a super-power, dominating the Europe of the ancient world; Normandy, by comparison, was a small, obscure duchy with little to recommend it. Again, numbers are hazy but it is likely that the Normans had no more than twelve thousand men, some estimates going as low as eight thousand.

The Roman invasion worked, not only because of the superb qualities of the Roman fighting machine, but because Britain, at the time, was a rag-bag of independent tribes; the Romans picked them off, one by one. In 1066, the English king, Harold Godwinson, had to fend off an invasion in the north before turning south with an exhausted army to face William at Senlac (Hastings). It would all be very different in 1940.

In pondering the task before the Germans in the Spitfire summer, Joachim von Ribbentrop, former ambassador to London, believed it would be a walk in the park. 'English territorial defence is non-existent. A single German division will suffice to bring about a complete collapse,' he told Mussolini in Rome. But then, the ex-champagne salesman was not a military man and his gaffes, in public and private, were legendary. At a royal reception in 1937, he had greeted George VI with a Hitler salute instead of the bow and handshake he ought to have given. He reported to Hitler that the British were lethargic and paralysed and would never go to war over Poland. Most of his peers had nothing but contempt for him. The far more able Josef Goebbels, for instance, wrote, 'Von Ribbentrop bought his name, he married money and he swindled his way into office.'[20] William Keitel, by contrast, was far more realistic. Recently promoted to Field Marshal, the man was old-school Prussia – tall, erect, with a monocle flashing over his left eye. As the war went on, the independence he still showed in the summer of 1940 disappeared. He became known, behind his back, as 'Lakaitel' (flunkey) and 'the nodding ass'. On trial for his life at Nuremberg after the war, he said, 'I was never permitted to make decisions, the Führer reserved that right to himself... '[21]

Keitel may have been aware that two other planned invasions of Britain had come to grief, in both cases because of command of the seas or, rather, lack of it. In the summer of 1588, irritated by English privateers raiding his silver convoys and giving aid to Dutch protestant rebels, Philip II of Spain unleashed his Armada against England. One hundred and thirty ships carrying 18,000 soldiers and manned by 8,000 sailors sailed up the Channel to link up with the Duke of Parma's force in the Spanish Netherlands – another 30,000 men. By sixteenth century standards, this would have been a formidable force and England had no standing army to stop them. In the event, naval clashes off the south coast were inconclusive and it was the weather that destroyed the Armada, the ships battered on the British coast and scattered as far west as Ireland.

The threat of 1804 was, in many ways, greater. At Boulogne, that summer, was camped *L'Armée d'Angleterre* – the army of England – 200,000 regulars commanded by the 'god of war' who crowned himself emperor in that year. This time, England did have a regular army but it was scattered far and wide in defence of its colonies and the recently raised militia and yeomanry forces were untried and badly trained. Against them would have come Napoleon's *'grognards'* (grumblers), who had achieved phenomenal success against all the powers of the *ancien regime*. Once again, it was the weather that came to the rescue. The French could not get their huge army across the Channel, either in conventional transports or on the vast rafts built for the purpose – Nelson's navy was there to stop them. And stop them it did, off Cape Trafalgar on 21 October 1805. Even before that, Admiral St Vincent, First Lord of the Admiralty, understood the situation perfectly – 'I do not say they [the French] cannot come. I only say they cannot come by sea.'[22]

But if Philip II and Napoleon Bonaparte could not do it, perhaps Adolf Hitler could. The men responsible for planning the invasion of 1940 were the staff officers of OKW (*Oberkommando der Wehrmacht*) in collaboration with OKH (*Oberkommando des Heeres*). The genesis of both, overlapping, organisations, was the Prussian General Staff, which morphed into the Great General Staff (*Grosser Generalstab*) under the Kaiser. In Napoleon's day, military success rested above all with the ability of army commanders. The Prussian Frederick the Great had been brilliant. So was Napoleon. Other rulers of states, less so, but they were still expected to command armies in the field and make military decisions they were rarely qualified to do. After Napoleon's defeat of the Prussians at Jena in 1806, the Germans set up the *Kriegsakademie* (War Academy) under Carl von Clausewitz, one of the foremost military authorities in Europe. Under the hugely impressive Helmut von Moltke in the middle of the nineteenth century, the General Staff prepared for war with any European country, collecting data of all kinds, drawing maps and investing in technology. By the time a united Germany came into being in 1871, the General Staff was the most efficient and organised in the world. The French, by comparison, rested on their laurels as the country that had bred Napoleon (he was, actually, of course, a Corsican) and paid the price of that arrogance at Sedan when they were smashed by Otto Bismarck's Prussians. As if to point up the disparity between the combatants, the Germans took their troops to the front along twenty-six railway lines; the French had one!

Under the terms of the treaty of Versailles, the General Staff was banned but, even under the liberal Weimar government in the 1920s, it re-emerged under the euphemism *Truppenamt* (Troop office), run by the military reformer Hans von Seeckt. In 1935, with the Nazis in power, the old *Kriegsakademie* re-emerged. Despite its defeat in 1918, the German army was a formidable organisation – Hitler's introduction of conscription and the oath of allegiance to him personally in 1934 also meant that it was growing enormously. Its officers were still largely conservative and traditionalist and, in 1940, not many of them were committed Nazis. They disliked the 'little corporal' who now ran Germany and were disquieted by the street gangsters of the SA (*Sturmabteiling*), which, at one point in the Thirties, outnumbered the Wehrmacht. By the outbreak of the war, the army had less influence than it had enjoyed in 1914, partly because of the rise of the Luftwaffe as a strike force and because there was no crony in the army as close to the Führer as was Goering for the air force.

Since before 1914, the major strategic problem for Germany had been the war on two fronts. If Russia were to join forces with Britain and France (as happened at the outbreak of the First World War) then Germany had to split her forces. The answer in 1914 was the Schlieffen Plan, which was to knock France out quickly while the ponderous Russians, with their nine million man army, were still mobilizing. In 1939, the same realpolitik no longer existed because, until Operation Barbarossa in June 1941, there was no threat to Germany from the east. The Axis powers could concentrate all their resources on Britain.

On *Agler Tag*, the OKW issued its invasion plans. They were divided, in terms of information gathering, into three sections. Part 1 dealt with an introduction to a country that relatively few Germans would ever have visited, including weather and climate, the industrial infrastructure, transport and, most tellingly for this book's purposes, population and social conditions. Part 2 broke down individual geographical areas in terms of strategic and military importance. Part 3 went further with this and included the sort of information found today in tourist guide books. Model questions included, 'Which is the shortest way to…?' and 'What is the name of this town?' One of the most bizarre was, 'Where is the next tank?' Bearing in mind that citizens had already been told to say nothing in response to questions from the invader, it is debatable how useful this section was!

Portfolio A, the country's general description, contained photographs and maps. The latter were widely available from HMSO bookshops and were standard Ordnance Survey. The concentration of Britain's industrial areas was more diverse than Germany's Ruhr. Coal and steel were centred in Tyneside, Lancashire, Yorkshire and South Wales. The aviation industry was clearly labelled, as was shipbuilding and 'explosive products'. Individual cities, marked with road and rail linkages and key installations, included London, Liverpool, Birmingham, Manchester, Leeds, Cardiff, Coventry and Bristol. All of these would be targeted in the Blitz which began in September, but other areas were included in the Invasion Plan. South Shields was there, as were Sunderland and Bradford. Derby featured too and, most bizarrely, Oxford. The city was the home of the Morris-Cowley car industry, now converted to war production, but it was also the home of the country's oldest university and Hitler, thinking in terms of invasion, did not intend to damage that or Cambridge. They would become the great Anglo-German centres of Reich learning in the future.

Portfolio B focused on London. As the capital, the cities of London and Westminster held a special place in the country's history. They were symbols of power and national resistance since the time of the Roman invasion. The government was based here, from the royal family at Buckingham Palace to the mother of parliaments at Westminster and a labyrinth of executive offices along Whitehall. In the East End, the largest docks in the country were a tempting target for Goering's Luftwaffe. The maps here were overlaid with an artillery grid.

Portfolio C was devoted to potential landing places along the south-east coast. The planners of 1940 ignored the fact that the only two successful invasions had hit single, narrow areas and had fought their way inland. Aulus Plautius and his legions landed at Rutupiae (Richborough) and marched on London. William of Normandy's ships ground into the shingle near Pevensey and he faced Harold Godwinson's English a little to the north of that before, again, making for London by a circuitous route. In 1940, an attack in Kent was ruled out. The whole nature of warfare was different now and the Medway was a barrier which the defenders could hold for a prolonged period. The original idea was to land on a broad front from the Isle of Wight in the west (with a reserve at Bridport) to Ramsgate in the east. These units would have converged and could cut London off from the rest of the country. The south-east was agriculturally rich and could provide easy billeting of troops once the Wehrmacht was on dry land.

The invasion of Britain was given the codename Lion (*Löwe*), later changed to Sealion (*Seelöwe*), perhaps by

Hitler himself. The initial plans had been worked on by the *Kriegsmarine* soon after the outbreak of war, if only because it would be their responsibility to get the Wehrmacht ashore. The initiative came, as we have seen, from Admiral Erich Raeder, who raised it with the Führer at various meetings in June and July. This does not mean that he was a gung-ho commander anxious to sail into glory – in fact, as time went on, he realised how suicidal the whole venture was. It was merely that he was a supreme professional and needed as much time as possible to get his battleship ducks in a row. It has to be said too that the German navy was playing third fiddle in 1940 to the air force and the army. The Wehrmacht had just won spectacular victories east and west, astonishing everybody by the speed of their advance. The Luftwaffe, too, had swept aside the opposition of the Polish and French air forces and Goering had come to believe his own advertising about the almost magical brilliance of his fighters and bombers. The navy had been useful off Norway but the *Graf Spee* had gone and the *Bismarck* had yet to be commissioned (24 August 1940), although she had been launched in February 1939. Raeder had to get it right.

The plan was for the *Kriegsmarine* to create a narrow 'corridor' across the Channel, supported by long-range artillery firing from Cap Gris-Nez, flanked by minefields to keep the Royal Navy away and to prowl the area with U-boats. Through the corridor, the army would be landed in two waves – the first of 100,000, the second of 160,000 men – under the overall command of von Runstedt. He would eventually set foot on British soil, in Bridgend, South Wales, as a prisoner of war in 1945. Halder, as Chief of Staff, demanded forty divisions to take the various bridgeheads of the south coast. Four of these had to hit Brighton and there needed to be a significant presence in the Deal-Ramsgate area. Raeder alone seems to have understood the impracticalities of this. His European harbours would be too cluttered with shipping to accommodate all the men involved and no one seemed to grasp the need for speed to avoid the bad weather of late September and the fogs of October. No one not wearing the uniform of the *Kriegsmarine* had any grasp of tides at all. For all the German war machine was supremely mechanised by 1940, it still relied on the arbitrariness of the weather, and the Wehrmacht planned to bring several thousand horses with it, to haul artillery and equipment.

Doubts and arguments raged in the weeks and then months after Dunkirk. The number of troops was reduced; forty divisions became thirteen. An essential prerequisite was the knocking out of the RAF's Fighter Command, whose Group 11 in the south-east was on constant readiness in what would come to be known as the Battle of Britain. Goering promised Hitler he would do that in four days; the entire RAF in four weeks. Until that was achieved, no army crossing could be made at all.

Once air supremacy was achieved, the rest would be relatively plain sailing. The Sixteenth Army, moving out of ports from Rotterdam to Boulogne in huge, difficult-to-manoeuvre barges (mostly commandeered from Europe's canals), would wade ashore at Hythe, Rye, Hastings and Eastbourne. The Ninth Army, out of all ports between Boulogne and Le Havre, would attack between Brighton and Worthing. The beaches taken, using amphibious craft that could run up the shingle and the sand, bridgeheads would be established, the Luftwaffe's Stukas hurtling down on enemy troops being rushed from further north to hold the coast. The two armies would then merge and sweep in a huge arc over the South Downs and make, as all would-be conquerors had, for London. Within an estimated seven days, the Wehrmacht would have established a line from Gravesend to Portsmouth. The Sixth Army, in reserve, would land in a third wave at Weymouth, to reinforce the rest.

Because none of this worked and Sealion was effectively abandoned by the end of September, it has assumed a fairy-tale quality, an exercise in futility and yet another example of the wishful-thinking ramblings of a maniac. All military historians today see the huge flaws in the plans of the General Staff, the shortcomings of all three services involved and the lack of clear-sighted preparation, all of which contributed to the venture being shelved. But it was not like that in the summer of 1940. Bizarrely, an increasing number of people were putting their faith in Churchill. They believed wholeheartedly his bulldog public appearances and were impressed by his speeches. But this was a man who suffered badly from depression – his 'black dog' as he called it – and, only three months earlier, his own party had cold-shouldered him in the Commons over the ousting of Chamberlain. He was no more infallible than anyone else, believing that there was a secret, if undirected, army of 20,000 Fifth Columnists walking Britain's streets. And he had, after all, been at least partly responsible for the Norwegian debacle which had swept him to power.

The British army, frantically pushing untrained men into uniform, was woefully ill-equipped and understrength. On paper, they had twenty-nine divisions but they were scattered all over the country (including Northern Ireland) and were still shell-shocked from Dunkirk. Much of their equipment had been left behind there. The Local Defence Volunteers, who officially became the Home Guard in August, were a keen bunch but they were civilian amateurs and the Second World War was no country for old men. There were nearly 40,000 service personnel in Britain from other armies – Poles, Czechs, Free Frenchmen, Dutchmen, Belgians – but how useful they would be in an alien country with an alien language was debatable.

An American opinion poll was printed in *The Times* on 12 September. At the outbreak of war, 82 per cent of Americans expected Britain to win. By the time of the fall of France, that had dropped to 32 per cent. Joseph Kennedy, the ambassador to the Court of St James, who had Nazi leanings and was never impressed by Britain, used phrases like '*when* the Germans occupied London', not *if*. A week before the poll was published, the American politician Cordell Hull reported to the United States cabinet, 'England is undergoing a terrific attack. As a matter of fact, it has been getting worse and worse over there... '[23]

The stationers might sell placards to stick up in the windows of front rooms which read, 'We are not interested in the possibilities of defeat. They do not exist,' but, of course, they did. And the British high command knew it. Their infantry divisions were barely at half strength (11,000 all ranks). Of the sixteen in question, nine had reached a 'fair' standard of training, five had done very little and two none at all. The equipment available to them was almost laughable and, although the munitions factories were working around the clock to rectify this, it would hardly dent the first wave of the Wehrmacht. There were 54 anti-tank guns, which had already proved useless in France, 42 field guns, and 163 medium and heavy guns (with limited ammunition and some seriously old). There were less than 500 tanks and nearly half the available armoured cars were in Northern Ireland, making sure that the spectre of an Irish rising along 1798 lines never happened.[24]

It was estimated that there were 70,000 rifles in Britain in the summer of 1940. Thousands more were handed in by civilians to police stations but some of these were obsolete smoothbores with no suitable ammunition. Axes, golf clubs, assegais and packets of pepper to be thrown in Aryan faces were all on standby, just in case. The novelist Margery Allingham wrote, 'All this looks childish written down, but it was a direct, childish time, quite different from . . . any other piece of life which I, at least, have experienced.'[25]

Churchill consistently, at least in public, played down the reality of invasion, even when he talked of fighting on the beaches. He also believed an invasion of the south coast was impractical, which is odd in a man who saw himself as an historian. In 1688, William of Orange had landed successfully at Lyme Regis; two hundred years earlier, Henry Tudor had come ashore at Milford Haven in Pembrokeshire. William of Normandy's ships made for Pevensey and Julius Caesar's not far away. In fact, the only invaders who had *not* done this were Harald Hardrada's Vikings in 1066, destroyed by the English at Stamford Bridge.

German radio propaganda was doing its bit to rattle the island defenders. William Joyce had been on the air since the war began but the plummy, over-the-top accent of 'Lord Haw-Haw' was more a source of hilarity than the drip-drip of fear. The New British Broadcasting Station, beginning its broadcasts with 'Loch Lomond' and ending with the National Anthem, was altogether cleverer. It gave the impression of the enemy within, that perhaps there *was* a Fifth Column after all and that Churchill and his gang were increasingly clutching at straws. *Workers' Challenge*, broadcast on 8 July, tried the hypocritical approach of a people's revolution. Trade Unions had been banned in Nazi Germany, the Fascist Labour Front of Dr Robert Ley operating instead. That did not stop the broadcasters, in pseudo-Scots accents, urging the workers to overthrow their public-school-educated government. The 'Christian Peace Movement' had a go too, with equal hypocrisy, since the Nazis were interested in neither Christianity nor peace. The propaganda they all spouted was largely nonsense – but such is the way with propaganda. The Jews were giving the War Cabinet bungs to keep the war going. Foot and mouth disease was decimating the countryside. The banknotes in listeners' wallets were forgeries. The tins of meat they opened were poisoned by agents working in Argentina. When the first German parachutists arrived, they could stay in the air for up to ten hours, choosing their landing grounds with precision – oh, *and* they took 'fog pills' which made them invisible. The only answer was to horsewhip Churchill and burn the property of the warmongering elite.

Unwittingly, the Invasion Warning Sub-Committee of the Combined Intelligence Committee was helping to create the sense of panic. It first met at the Admiralty on 31 May and its early meetings were dominated by the likelihood of Irish attacks backed by the IRA. On the other hand, seeing bogeys in bushes where there were none, was perhaps preferable to ignoring those that were obvious. When the RAF reconnaissance aircraft brought back clear photographs of a shipping build up at Kiel, the Committee believed that they probably had something to do with 'mining or other temporary restrictions'. When the RAF snapped the transport barges massing at Ostend at the end of August, they were probably there to fetch iron, steel and textiles. When it became known that all Wehrmacht leave had been cancelled for 5 September, the Committee calmly reflected, 'Any leave is stopped from time to time without special incident.' Had the public known about these misconceptions and blatant ostrich behaviour, they may have asked whose side the Invasion Warning Sub-Committee was actually on!

Years later, Peter Fleming wrote of these bizarre months:

'Would tanks, one day, come nosing through the allotments? Would tracer bullets flick across the recreation ground? Would field-grey figures carrying stick grenades and flame-throwers work their way along the hedges towards the flimsy pill-boxes opposite the Nag's Head?'[26]

Had he remembered it, Fleming would already have had his answer. On 4 September, Hitler spoke to ranked thousands of his adoring subjects in the *Sportpalast* in Berlin, the scene of so many oratorical triumphs. 'When people are very curious in Great Britain,' he said, 'and ask, "Yes, but why doesn't he come?" We reply, "Calm yourselves! Calm yourselves!"' And, as always, his voice rose to a massive crescendo, '"He is coming! He is coming!"'

CHAPTER THREE

WHEN THE INVADER COMES

London thought that Hitler was coming at 5.30 pip emma on Saturday, 7 September. 300 bombers, with a 600-strong fighter escort, roared over the Kent and Essex coast, making for the capital. This was part of Field Marshal Albert Kesselring's 2nd *Aeroflotte* from Denmark and Norway and was designed to force Fighter Command to commit its carefully protected Reserve so that it could be destroyed. No one in the RAF was ready for this change of tactic and the results told their own story. The Luftwaffe, still with a huge numbers advantage lost forty-one aircraft; the RAF twenty-eight, with considerable damage to more. As darkness fell, Field Marshal Hugo Sperrle, commanding another Air Fleet, unleashed 250 bombers to hit London by night. In this situation, the RAF could play no part;[27] dog fights in darkness were pointless suicide missions. Only the searchlight batteries and the ack-ack guns on the ground could hope to stem the tide.

The assumption was made that the invasion would be

preceded by a massive aerial bombardment, rather as formal battles in the past had been opened up by cannon fire before the infantry advanced to grapple with each other. The Deputy Chief of Staff at GHQ Home Forces sent out the codeword *Cromwell* soon after eight o'clock, as Sperrle's leading bombers were circling to go home. It was sent initially to Eastern and Southern Command, IV and VII Corps (the Reserve) and HQ London District.

The very word *Cromwell* caused all kinds of confusion. The original code, *Caesar* (which made some sense historically in terms of invasion), had been changed on 5 June to that of the Lord Protector, who had only ever invaded Ireland by sea. Many of the night-duty officers, juniors with limited experience, had no idea what *Cromwell* meant. Some units jumped to it with the speed expected. The Home Guard in particular ('cometh the hour, cometh the man') rang church bells furiously. Since the outbreak of war, these had been silent, much to the annoyance of campanologists and the sound of them now, in villages and towns all over the south-east, caused a frisson of confusion and panic. Telephone operators refused to handle non-military calls. Road blocks of carts, furniture and lumps of concrete were dragged across roads from which signposts had long since disappeared. With his typical British *sang froid*, Harold Nicolson wrote calmly:

'At Sissinghurst, we have tea and watch the Germans coming over in wave after wave. There is some fighting above our heads and we hear one or two aeroplanes zoom downwards. They flash like silver gnats above us in the air.'

Denis Richards, the RAF's official historian, writing years later, summed up the situation perfectly, 'the brute fact that the world's largest air force was now within an hour's flight of the world's largest target.'[28] To those caught on the ground, it mattered little that the Luftwaffe had only about twenty-eight minutes' time over London before they had to turn tail to refuel. The damage was done in seconds. Angus Calder, in *The People's War*, makes the point:

> '... the bombs poured chiefly on Stepney... where nearly two hundred thousand people lived... on the tailors of Whitechapel; the factories, warehouses and gasworks of Poplar; the woodworking firms of Shoreditch; the docks of West Ham and Bermondsey...'[29]

And that, of course, was just the start.

In the night attack, only one bomber had been shot down and a shell-shocked London emerged, blinking into the sunshine of Sunday, 8 September. T. H. O'Brien, writing in 1955 when there was no longer any need to minimise the grimness of the situation, wrote that the docks had been very badly hit. Woolwich Arsenal, so crucial to the war effort, was a smoking ruin. So were Beckton Gas Works, West Ham Power Station and street after street of the City and the West End. In one photograph taken that morning, a double-decker bus is lying on its end, the driver's cab pointing to the sky. The front bumpers are resting on the shell of an imposing Victorian house. On the ground, bewildered men in tin hats and shirtsleeves are doing what they can to clear the debris. The entire population of Silvertown had to be evacuated by river. There were nine 'conflagrations' (the vortex created by fires merging into one that would destroy Dresden three years later), fifty-nine large fires and over one thousand smaller ones. It was vital to put these out quickly, not just to reduce further damage but to deny the next night's raid an illuminated pathway to follow. On the second night, 412 people were killed and 747 badly hurt. Every railway line to and from the south was out of action.

As it turned out, this was the start of the Blitz, an attempt, futile as it turned out, to so terrify and demoralize civilians that all systems would collapse and the government would be forced to sue for peace. The change of tactic gave Fighter Command – Churchill's 'Few' – a chance to regroup and rest their shattered nerves. It also gave time to build more aircraft and train more men.

On Monday morning, as if to illustrate the fact that 'London could take it' and it was 'business as usual', *The Times* reported that a great crested grebe had been found in an air-raid shelter in Euston! Despite the veneer of calm, however, the prospect of invasion was still starkly, terrifyingly real and the government acted accordingly, the Ministry of Information going into overdrive to exude calm mixed with defiance. Harold Nicolson was largely responsible for the most famous sheet, issued in June. It was called *If the Invader Comes* and by 8 September that could easily have read *When*. The first sentence was bold and confident: 'The Germans threaten to invade …. If they do so they will be driven out by our Navy, our Army and our Air Force.'[30]

This ignores the fact that the air force could be presumed to have been destroyed by the time the Wehrmacht came ashore, that the army only had twenty-nine weak Divisions and that the navy's use, once invasion was a reality, would be very limited. The pamphlet made the fair point that the civilians of the western-European countries overrun by the Germans had been caught napping; that could not happen to the British and everyone must be ready.

There must be no panic – no clogging of roads and public transport in a frantic effort to get away: 'You must remain where you are. The order is "Stay Put". If not, you are bound to be machine-gunned from the air.'

The naiveté of this is extraordinary. Machine-gunned on the blocked roads or buried under the debris of your house did not, to most people, make much difference. Point 2 talked about the Fifth Column – the sneakiness of the Germans in spreading confusion and panic. Most people knew their local bobby and ARP warden: 'You can also tell whether a military officer is really British or only pretending to be so. [?] Use your common sense.'

When the house you live in or the school your children go to is being flattened by bombs, when Guderian's tanks are crashing through your back garden, taking with them the walls and the washing, how much 'common sense', people must have wondered, was it possible to muster?

If anyone saw anything suspicious, they were to report it at once to someone in authority. Astonishingly, even the Home Guard had this instruction. They were not to tackle a potential spy themselves (there were a few isolated and unfortunate shootings in this respect as tensions rose that summer) but to find a policeman. The fact that the police, especially in the Metropolitan area, were stretched to breaking point seems to have passed the Ministry of Information by.

Next in the MOI's leaflet came the terror of the skies, the parachutist. With more hope than experience, the government told its readers that such men would not be 'feeling at all brave'. They would not know where they were or where their companions were and they would have no food. The experience of airborne troops who preceded D-Day, the Allied invasion of Europe in June 1944, was exactly the opposite. Units were indeed scattered by the wind and navigational errors in the drop zones, but the parachutists came down in clusters and easily linked up with each other. They had rations for three days. How brave they felt depended very much on the individual but the *esprit de corps* of the Wehrmacht and committed Nazis easily matched Europe's liberators of four years later.

'Do not give the German anything,' the MOI insisted. People were expected to hide their food, their maps and their bikes. If they had a car, the rotor arm must be removed to make it useless. The fact that the Wehrmacht could simply help themselves to most of those commodities, with or without the owners' permission, was another little irrelevance in Whitehall's corridors of power.

Today, owners of companies are buried in a welter of regulations about employment, health and safety, insurance and so on. In 1940, they were expected by the government to defend their premises. Everyone in such companies must know who is in charge and how orders are to be transmitted. Ex-officers and NCOs were naturally the best people to turn to in this situation.

The leaflet ended, 'Remember always that the best defence of Great Britain is the courage of her men and women. Here is your seventh rule – Think before you act. But think always of your country before you think of yourself.'

Peter Fleming paints an amusing picture of the model citizen that summer. He always carried his regulation gas mask (which, of course, was never needed and had an asbestos lining to the filter). He carried his National Registration Identity Card (which, if he lost it, could lead to a fine or imprisonment). He carried a ration-book with coupons that allowed him so much food and comestibles per week (not fully abandoned until eight years after the war ended!). If he worked for a company, large or small, he had to have a security pass to get him in. If he owned a car (unlikely in 1940 – car numbers have been estimated at well below ten per cent of the adult population), it could not have a wireless set and its headlights had to be dimmed by a grille. The house he left to go to work every morning (and, astonishingly, bearing in mind the need to work for the war effort, there were still nearly a million unemployed that summer) had sticky tape over the windows to minimise the risk of flying glass. There were sand and water buckets in all major rooms to put out the fires of air raids. He could not hoard food (a punishable offence) but he had to make sure that his household was provided for. He would already have handed in his shotgun and his binoculars. His wife had long ago dispensed with half her pots and pans because that nice Lord Beaverbrook needed them to make Spitfires and Wellingtons, Blenheims and Hurricanes. His children, after 6 July, could not fly kites or balloons, presumably in case they had any connection with signalling to the enemy. He must never shoot carrier pigeons – how could he, since the local constabulary had his gun? He must replace his begonias with carrots and turnips, ignore malicious rumours and never doubt for a moment that Mr Churchill had everything in hand.

'The reader,' wrote Fleming, his tongue well and truly in his cheek, 'will scarcely need to be told that this paragon did not, in his totality, exist.'[31]

Some people got out, their nerves shredded by it all. The official line from the United States government was that its citizens should leave. Hundreds did. One group that did not formed the American Squadron of the Home Guard in London, with a red eagle flash on their shoulders once they actually had uniforms to sew them onto. There was another move to evacuate children from the cities but it was much more half-hearted than at the outbreak of war. The vast majority of those children had drifted back and little boys in particular watched the dog-fights of the Battle of Britain, hoping to find bits of crashed aircraft or even, in their wildest dreams, being able to capture a German airman! Those who left were reduced to a trickle after 17 September, when the *City of Benares*, carrying ninety such children, was sunk by a U-boat. Only eleven survived.

There were demands for peacetime pastimes to stop. Horse-racing, dog-racing and cricket matches were among those frowned on and even the serious business of Bridge was being disrupted by air raids as the Bridge Correspondent of *The Times* told a disbelieving world on 3 September. There was a mild panic in London when the Zoo was hit. Poisonous snakes and scorpions had been destroyed when the war began but other animals flourished, watched over by a tiny cadre of snipers in case a dangerous one got out. A few of the birds did but the only quadruped escapee was a zebra, recaptured in the Zoo's grounds later.

The show, despite tension, had to go on. The Windmill Theatre, with its chorus girls and risqué reputation, never closed, despite an official order that it must, and other theatres followed suit by the end of September. Concerts were held at noon in the National Gallery. Ballet dancers strutted their stuff in the Arts Theatre Club and Donald Wolfit, then arguably the nation's leading 'luvvie', wowed his office-worker audience with soliloquies from *Hamlet* and *Macbeth*.

Rumours, despite the MOI's order that they should not be spread, flew. In August, the Channel was said to be 'white with bodies' of a failed German invasion. Even Churchill believed this one because it had good propaganda value; if the British public believed that an invasion had been beaten back, that could only work wonders for morale. The government, in turn, formed the 'Silent Column' in June, pledging to shutting down rumour by prosecution. Since Duff Cooper of the MOI was its figurehead, they came to be known as Cooper's Snoopers. Defeatism was a crime; so was being foreign. In that same month, a Dane and a Swede were arrested in Liverpool for 'their foreign appearance' and fined £15 each. And, according to the *Daily Mail* of 9 June, Dr J. J. Paterson, Medical Officer of Health for Maidenhead, had his house turned over by the police because, before the war, he had travelled widely in Germany. Everywhere, Mr Knowall, Miss Leaky Mouth, Mr Pride in Prophecy, Miss Teacup Whisperer and Mr Glumpot were all being listened to, plotted against, fined and imprisoned. It was a miserable time. And it was exactly the kind of discord that Adolf Hitler, still planning his invasion, was hoping for.

★ ★ ★

On 20 June, the day before Hitler crowed over the French surrender at Compiegne, the thriller writer Dennis Wheatley had lunch at London's Dorchester Hotel with Sir Louis Greig, an RAF Wing Commander, Lawrence Darvall (same rank) and J. S. L. Renny, a Czech arms manufacturer. They met to discuss a paper that Wheatley had written which was of interest to the chiefs of staff – and would have been of more interest, almost certainly, to the OKW.

Wheatley was the son of a Mayfair wine merchant and had been expelled from the exclusive Dulwich College for allegedly forming a secret society. Since, after the war, Wheatley became Britain's best-known occult novelist, this is not perhaps surprising. In 1940, he had a few highly successful thrillers under his belt and had offered his services as a writer to the MOI. He was mortified not even to get a reply but, since his wife worked as a driver for MI5, his potential reached the secret service. Out of this almost chance contact emerged Wheatley's first paper on the prospects of beating an invasion. The fact that he had no military experience was precisely the point. A sharp mind not hidebound by the services nor wedged into a cupboard somewhere along Whitehall was needed. It was a maverick time – Churchill's idea of the creation of the Special Operations Executive on 22 July to 'set all Europe ablaze' was yet another manifestation of it.

Wheatley worked like a demon, smoking over 200 cigarettes and downing three magnums of champagne over a 48-hour period. His resistance to invasion is fascinating, involving fishing nets, fire-ships, broken glass, flaming oil, 'tiger pits', tank traps, camouflage, armoured trains and gliders. It was *Boys Own* stuff but it was exactly the sort of thing that Churchill's commandoes of the SOE would use in the months ahead, taking the war into the Reich. It was also the sort of tactic planned by the Auxiliary Units who were currently under training as 'Churchill's Secret Army'. Most fascinatingly, Wheatley had the idea of undermining enemy morale by dropping leaflets over Germany. They would read:

'Come to England this summer for your holiday and sample the fun we have prepared for you. Try bathing in our barbed-wire bathing enclosures. Try rowing in our boats which will blow up as you touch the tiller. Try running up our beaches covered in broken glass. Try picnicking in our lovely woods along the coast and get a two-inch nail through your foot. Try jumping into our ditches and get burnt alive. Come by air and meet our new death ray (this sort of lie is good tactics at a time like this). Every Nazi visitor guaranteed death or an ugly wound. England or Hell – it's going to be just the same for you in either.'[32]

The meeting at the Dorchester went further. Wing Commander Darvall asked Wheatley to prepare a plan for the invasion of England as though he were a member of the Nazi High Command. It ran to 15,000 words and was delivered to 'Mr Rance's room at the Office of Works' (actually the Joint Planning Staff's HQ at the War Department).

With a novelist's verve, Wheatley put himself in the position of every villain he had created or was to create. 'It is British hypocrisy, duplicity and greed,' he wrote as devil's advocate, 'which has consistently barred the path of German advancement... There is no room in the world for a great and prosperous Germany and a still powerful Britain.' He was wrong there. Repeatedly during these months and even as late as the flight of Rudolf Hess to Scotland in May 1941, the *modus vivendi* which Hitler described was that Britain should be left alone to run her overseas empire, giving Germany a free hand in Europe. The British government never seriously considered that and neither, for his 1940 black propaganda purposes, did Wheatley. The novelist, posing as an OKW adviser, advocated the use of bacterial warfare and poison gas. He pushed the idea of landing in Ireland with its huge anti-British sentiment. He demanded the first wave of troops ashore be 600,000 strong with a further million in the second wave. Nothing was too costly to achieve the German objective, so the loss of thousands of men, most of the air force and a considerable number of ships was a small price worth paying.

Infiltration should already have happened. Apart from

those interned under Defence Regulation 18B (who would of course be released once the Wehrmacht rescued them), there were thousands of refugees in Britain who may already be secret Nazis or could be easily 'turned' in that direction. New signposts would be erected quickly by these Fifth Columnists, who would poison water supplies, dig tunnels, provide lights for landing strips, break out prisoners and those in asylums, cut through telegraph wires and spread as much doom, gloom and panic as possible. Fake orders would be issued by men in fake uniforms. Trains would be sabotaged. Gas mains would be blown up by men in overalls. Drugged cigarettes would be given out and women would be placed in front of advancing troops as human shields. Assassination, though difficult, must be attempted. Government ministers, senior soldiers and airmen, must be targeted in their homes. Open grounds like golf courses, cricket pitches and race tracks must be commandeered to allow parachutists to land. Booby bombs with delayed detonators would be essential.[33]

Wheatley's 15,000 words detail the progress that must be made by the Wehrmacht on successive days, together with the objectives of the Northern, Midland and Southern Forces.

Taking off his OKW braided hat with its eagle insignia at the end of this section in his paper, Wheatley turns on the stuffed shirts whose job it is to prevent the invasion he has just described:

'These men have proved themselves lacking in vision, tortoise-like in adjusting... to new conditions, incompetent and gutless. [They are] unworthy to serve under our lion-hearted Prime Minister... The public is asking that a full inquiry should be instituted into the men responsible for this cowardly policy which has cost the nation so dear at such a vital time and that those who have shown themselves incapable of leadership should forthwith be relieved of their responsibilities.'

Rather cutely, he added later in an editorial note, 'Dear, dear; I had got myself into a tizzie, hadn't I?'

* * *

In one chilling respect, Dennis Wheatley had got inside the heads, not only of the OKW, but the SS too. In the section marked 'Assassination', he says that the 'directing brains of British defence' should be put out of action quickly 'and this policy will be pursued after the conquest to prevent any leaders of public thought forming an unauthorised government or even leading local riots.'[34] He advocates the shooting of every officer above captain in the army, lieutenant in the navy and flight-lieutenant in the air force. That would include all politicians, past and present of the Commons and Lords, all industrialists, editors and journalists, leading barristers, prominent churchmen, magistrates and well-known sportsmen.

Nearly seven hundred miles away, in Berlin, *Reichssicherheirshaupstant* Walter Schellenberg had creepily similar ideas. And he was preparing such a list of personalities. Unlike the amateur Dennis Wheatley, Schellenberg was a professional. And he intended to put his theories into practice.

CHAPTER FOUR

THE LIST MAKERS

On the afternoon of Thursday, 9 November 1939, a young man was sitting in Café Bacchus in the little Dutch town of Venlo, half a mile from the German border. Hauptmann Schaemmel of the Transport Department of the OKW had been waiting for a while, downing cups of indifferent coffee and nibbling *peperkoek*. He was a good-looking man, clean cut with neat, brushed-back hair and a tweed jacket. He was twenty-nine years old and had a smattering of Dutch, although he spoke German, French and English fluently. He wore a monocle on his right eye and that, as well as the duelling scars on his cheeks, gave him an aristocratic, Prussian look.

In fact, Hauptmann Schaemmel was not quite what he seemed. And as he waited, the hectic events of the last twenty-four hours must have been whirling in his head. He knew that Adolf Hitler, Germany's Führer, had gone to a Munich hospital the previous afternoon to cheer up a friend of his. She was the

Honourable Unity Valkyrie Mitford, the strangest of the misfit children of the English aristocrat Lord Redesdale. Obsessed by the man who ran Germany, and an ardent Fascist, she had met the Führer 'accidentally' in Munich and rumours flew that they were lovers. Since the outbreak of war two months earlier, Unity had become increasingly depressed and had shot herself in the head in a suicide bid – hence the stay in hospital as she had bungled it.

Later the previous day, Hitler had undertaken one of the key visits of the Reich calendar. It had been sixteen years to the day since he and his 'old fighters' had marched towards the Felderrnhalle into the bullets of a police barricade. This was the Beer Hall Putsch, Hitler's failed attempt to wrest Munich from the Communists in the chaotic early years of the Weimar Republic. It produced sixteen martyrs, an opportunity to publicize the infant Nazi Party and a mythology of its own. Posters produced at the time boasted, 'The regime of the November criminals[35] is today declared deposed.' That proved a little premature, but sixteen years on it had certainly been borne out. The peace-makers of 1918 were either dead, in exile or languishing in the camps that the Reich was starting to build in increasing numbers. The rebels of 1923 had set out from the Burgerbraukeller and it was at this virtual shrine that Hitler had spoken on the evening of 8 November 1939.

By Hitler's standards, the speech was short – disappointingly so to his fanatical audience. He began speaking at 8.10pm and finished at 8.45. Not only that but he and the *Stellvertreter*, Rudolf Hess, left the beer hall and the city, bound for Berlin in the Führer's private train. Twenty minutes later, the Burgerbraukeller blew up, shattering glass and crumbling masonry. There were deaths and serious injuries and Munich was placed immediately under martial law.

Hauptmann Schaemmel was almost certainly among those who heard the official radio broadcast from Berlin early the next morning. There was 'profound gratitude [among] the German people to the Almighty for watching over the Führer's safety.' While neutralising the churches throughout the Reich and replacing God with his own image, it was extraordinary how often the Führer would invoke the Almighty!

The radio went on:

> 'The instigators, the financial backers, the people who are capable of so infamous, so execrable an idea, are the same ones who have always employed assassination in politics! They are the agents of the [British] Secret Service! And behind them stand the British war agitators and their criminal satellites, the Jews.'[36]

There were no surprises here. The Jews were behind everything – they were already being made to pay inside Germany and those in Poland were following suit already. The 'war agitators' were, of course, Churchill and Eden, the hawks in Neville Chamberlain's cabinet. The involvement of the British Secret Service *may* have surprised some listeners but not Hauptmann Schaemmel. That was because he was actually Walter Schellenberg, Party Number 3504508, SS Number 124817 and he had received a phone call the previous night from his ultimate boss, Heinrich Himmler, Reichsführer of the SS. A sting in which Schellenberg was already involved must be brought forward.

'"There's no doubt the British Secret Service is behind it all. [The Führer] now says – and this is an order – when you meet the British agents for your conference tomorrow, you

are to arrest them immediately and bring them to Germany,"
Himmler had said.'[37]

★ ★ ★

The Netherlands were, of course, still neutral in November
1939 and any neutral country during the Second World War
was fertile ground for espionage, each side trying to discover
the other's secrets. The British had two agents in The Hague
– Major Richard Stevens and his number two, Captain
Sigismund Payne Best. Stevens was officially a passport
control officer (the passport offices were generally a cover for
Intelligence work) and Payne worked for the maverick Claude
Dansey of MI5, who had set up his Z System, planting spies
abroad under legitimate business cover. The future historian
Hugh Trevor Roper described Dansey as 'an utter shit, corrupt,
incompetent but with a certain low cunning'. The Germans
had a high regard for British Intelligence but it was actually
creaking badly by the outbreak of war – Stevens and Payne
Best are evidence of that. They did not get on – Payne Best was
far more experienced than his superior officer – and their task
was a daunting one.

Today, largely because of the huge charisma of Winston
Churchill, his speeches and his wartime leadership, most
people regard Neville Chamberlain as a dud; yet another in
the long line of statesmen duped by Hitler. In fact, behind
the scenes in the opening months of war, Chamberlain,
through his Intelligence network, was trying to link up with
disaffected groups in the German military machine who
detested Hitler and despised Nazism. A man with Hitler's
ardour won adoring millions of fans but he made enemies too.
Chamberlain's private secretary, Jock Colville, wrote, 'What
is needed is a moderate conservative reaction in Germany;

the overthrow of the present regime by the army chiefs.'[38] We know today that there *were* army chiefs who were unhappy with Hitler and his megalomania. They tried to kill him in the failed bomb plot of July 1944. It was exactly what Hitler was hoping for in Britain after May 1940 when Churchill went to Number Ten. Accordingly, Stevens and Payne Best, working under the auspices of Stuart Menzies, poised to become the new 'C', director of the Secret Intelligence Service in Whitehall, made contact with potential allies inside the Reich. The disgruntled German who took the bait was a Dr Fischer, who had once spied for Dansey in the Twenties, and he claimed to speak for General Gustav von Wietershein, commander of the 14th Panzer Corps, currently creating havoc in Poland. Wietershein was old-school Prussian, just the sort to loathe the 'Bohemian corporal' *and* a man with clout in the German High Command.

In fact, Fischer was a double agent and had long been in bed with the German secret service, the SD (*Sicherheitsdienst*). Since 21 October, there had been a flurry of casual, secret meetings at various places just inside Dutch territory, within reach of the German border. Working out of a safe house in Dusseldorf, stashed with telegraphic and telephonic communications, Schellenberg liaised with a German agent in Holland only referred to as F479. This was almost certainly Dr Franz, a German émigré. Schellenberg had never met him and the man proved to be less than reliable, leaving the SD man to his own devices.

The first meeting took place at Zutphen in the pouring rain. Captain Payne Best's German was excellent and he and 'Schaemmel' shared a love of classical music. Lieutenant Coppens and Major Stevens met them at Arnhem and Schellenberg went into his anti-Hitler pitch with apparent sincerity.

Coppens was actually Dirk Klop, a Dutch agent and Schellenberg fed them false names of men active in a German underground resistance movement. These were Captain Seydlitz and Lieutenant Grosch, a man with the unlikely name of Colonel Martini and the handsome Hauptmann Schaemmel, who, as things turned out, had been the brains behind all this flurry of underground activity.

On that final day, 9 November, the Englishmen were late. It was an hour and a half after the agreed time that they and Klop turned up in Stevens' Buick. As Schellenberg walked out to greet them, a car with SS markings came out of nowhere, crashing through the barriers at the end of the street that marked the Dutch-German border. Klop fired at Schellenberg. The man was unarmed and he dived for cover, not before being fired on too by the trigger-happy SS *Sonderkommando* who mistook him for Payne Best![39] It was probably the monocle that caused the problem. Payne Best was taller than Schellenberg but a new man, brought into the SS detail at the last minute, could not tell them apart and thrust his pistol in the SD man's face. Quick thinking by the SS commander saved Schellenberg's life. The confusion of those moments has produced, unsurprisingly, confused accounts but the upshot was that Stevens and Payne Best were bundled over the border at the end of the street to be whisked away to Gestapo headquarters, first in Düsseldorf and then in Berlin. And, for nearly five years, that was where they stayed, in isolation at Sachsenhausen, the 'camp for the capital'.

The Venlo incident was a major coup for the SD and Germany generally. A delighted Hitler congratulated all concerned personally, handing out iron crosses, first and second class, to the Kommandos. More recent writers have tried to play down the fact that MI6 was in tatters as a result of what the prisoners told their captors. The whole SIS network in the Netherlands was compromised, as was Dutch neutrality. It gave Hitler a justifiable excuse, if he needed one, to invade the Low Countries on 10 May 1940.

Two weeks later, a triumphant Himmler announced that the bomb-maker of the Burgerbraukeller had been found. He was carpenter Georg Elser and he had confessed to planting the bomb under orders from Dansey's Z Office in Switzerland (another neutral country that was chancing its arm).

What is important about Venlo from the point of view of this book is that it gave Walter Schellenberg a great deal of raw material from which he compiled the Special Search List in the summer of 1940. All that Stevens and Payne Best were obliged to do – in fact, all they were ordered to do by SIS – was to give their names, addresses and cover information. Stevens, in particular, sang like a canary. Spies, in reality and fiction, risk sticky ends if they are captured. Two women, one innocent, the other less so, had been shot by firing squad in the First World War – Edith Cavell and Gertrude Zelle, better known as Mata Hari. Between 1940 and 1942, fourteen hapless agents faced the hangmen Albert Pierrepoint and Stanley Cross at various prisons around Britain. José Waldeburg, Carl Meier and Charles Van Dem Kieboorn were caught disguised as refugees in the same month that Stevens and Payne Best were kidnapped. Karl Drucke and Werner Walti came ashore via a dinghy in Scotland. What gave Walti away was the length of *knockwurst* in his kitbag! That little slip did for Josef Jakobs too in August 1941. Because he was an ex-NCO in the Wehrmacht, he was shot, rather than hanged. Karel Richter only survived for fifteen minutes after burying his parachute before a local constable found him. José Kay and Alphonse Timmerman were hanged on the same day, 7 July

1942, their downfall the large quantity of cash and invisible ink in their holdalls. The list goes on.

Yet Stevens and Payne Best, important professionals with a lot to hide, survived the war, one actually going on to write his memoirs. It was, after all, in the interests of Schellenberg and the SD to keep them alive – they were a mine of information. At the time of Venlo, there was panic in Whitehall, the SIS issuing a D notice to the Press, which meant that no information on the 'Dutch brawl' was allowed to be published. Payne Best blabbed. His contacts were all written down in a notebook in his pocket, so perhaps 'professional' is not quite the right word to use about him. SIS was badly mauled – and rattled. No more 'peace feelers' were so much as looked at in Whitehall and the entire service was highly wary of the SD in general and, once his involvement was known, Walter Schellenberg in particular. On several pages in his Special Search List, he refers to his source as being the '*täterkreis* [spy ring] Stevens/Best'. The information they gave him would have, had things gone differently in the summer of 1940, led to the deaths of hundreds.

* * *

Walter Schellenberg was born, the seventh child of a piano manufacturer, in Saarbrucken on 16 January 1910. The family moved to Luxembourg when the French army occupied the Saar basin soon after Versailles, believing that German industrial workers were deliberately sabotaging their own work to avoid paying the crippling reparations that the victors of the Treaty had imposed on them. The financial collapse of 1924, with chaotic hyperinflation destroying the German economy, hit the Schellenbergs hard; who buys pianos at a time like that?

Having left the *Reform-Realgymnasium*, Schellenberg attended the university of Marburg in Hesse, a sixteenth century institution with a strong Protestant bias. He himself had been brought up a Catholic by a very devout mother. Not surprisingly, his name does not appear among any alumni today but those who do prove the university's cosmopolitan reputation. The brothers Grimm, folklorists of the nineteenth century, the poets Ortega y Gasset and T. S. Eliot and the writer Boris Pasternak all passed through the college's Gothic portals. Tiring of medical studies, Schellenberg transferred to Bonn in 1929, his tuition fees paid by his fiancée, Käthe Kartikamp, a seamstress three years' his senior.

Bonn was undergoing radical change during Schellenberg's time there. Strapped for cash in the drying-up of state funding (Weimar Germany was once again shattered financially by the Wall Street crash), there was a frantic search for sponsors and the students themselves became decision-makers under a new constitution. Schellenberg was now reading Law but maintained his language studies too. With his father's permission, he joined a student *Schlager* corps, which gave him his sabre scars, proved his honour and meant that he could both take and give punishment. His leaving the university coincided with the rise of Hitler to Chancellor in that year. While both Schellenberg's almae mater were swept up in the *gleichschaltung* which saw all educational institutions become Nazified, the law graduate joined the SS.

The *Schuzstaffel* (defence echelon) was originally a small bodyguard created by Hitler after his release from Landsberg prison and the resurgence of the Nazi Party that resulted. It immediately had a cachet and distanced Hitler from the brown-shirted SA (*Sturmabteilung*), which, in turn, was developed from the various groups of disaffected soldiery at the end of the First World War. After the 'night of the long knives' in 1934, when its leaders were murdered, the SA became secondary and ended up as little more than a glorified Home Guard during the war. The SS then became a police arm of the Nazi Party under the direction of Heinrich Himmler. It maintained the highest principles of National Socialism, its members chosen for their racial Aryan purity of blood. From a mere 280 strong at the time of the Wall Street crash, by the outbreak of war it had grown to 240,000, divided into sections. The oldest unit and core of the organisation were the Allgemeine SS, composed of full and part-time members, active, inactive and even honorary. They were eclipsed by the time of Venlo by the Waffen SS, its military arm of diehard fanatics.

If the German High Command distrusted Hitler, the feeling was entirely mutual but in the Waffen SS he had men who would obey him without question. A million men eventually, divided into thirty-nine Divisions, they quickly acquired a formidable fighting reputation as soon as war broke out. They were by no means entirely German – at least fourteen other nationalities were represented. The definition of an SS man, set by Himmler, was uncompromising:

> 'The SS man's basic attitude must be that of a fighter for fighting's sake; he must be unquestioningly obedient and... emotionally hard; he must have contempt for all 'racial inferiors' and for those who do not belong to the order; he must feel the strongest bonds of comradeship with those who do belong... and he must think nothing is impossible.'

At the time of Venlo, the Waffen SS had only two Divisions – the *Liebstandarte* Adolf Hitler and Das Reich, both panzer units. Four more were added in 1940. Their collar flashes were the lightning bolts of Teutonic-Norse mythology and a similar

SS was tattooed in runic design on the underside of the upper arm (a problem for surrendering Germans in 1945 who tried to deny any involvement in atrocities).

Himmler, the ex-chicken farmer from Munich, clawed his way up the Nazi hierarchy and made himself the most powerful man in Germany after the Führer. While the *Stellvertreter* Rudolf Hess flew into a confused oblivion in Scotland in May 1941 and while Goering, having failed to deliver in the Battle of Britain, made himself ever more ridiculous and drug-addicted, Himmler took all the reins of police power in his own hands. Obsessive and punctilious, he also had a pseudo-Medieval romanticism about Germany's past and dabbled with the occult. Beneath him, in the various departments, his underlings may have been fanatical Nazis but they were also hard-headed realists who often put their own careers before party. Among these were Himmler's second-in-command, the 'blond beast', the 'man with the iron heart', Reinhard Heydrich and Walter Schellenberg himself. Hitler understood this perfectly well. In fact, he made the weakness, jealousy and pettiness of others an integral part of his system, playing one politician off against another and letting departments fight it out among themselves.

As in Britain, each service of the armed forces had its own Intelligence unit. In Germany, that of the SS was grafted on. This was the *Sicherheitsdient* (SD), led by Heydrich. They were the elite of the elite and it was this department that Schellenberg joined in 1935, earning himself a reputation as a brilliant information-gatherer. In the phrase of the historian Alan Bullock, he became one of the 'technicians of dictatorship'. Himmler had spelled out the SD's role – 'to discover the enemies of the National Socialist concept and... initiate countermeasures through the official police authorities.' This last phrase was misleading and never really applied. The SD was in no way subservient to the Gestapo or any other branch of the police. Instead, it was responsible for the security of the Reich, overseeing other police departments. The tight camaraderie of the Waffen SS did not exist here; as Bullock says, 'The Third Reich was a gangster empire'. Only a very few of the key men (Schellenberg among them) knew the names of the others. The V men were trusted confidantes. The A men were field agents. Z men were informers, as were H men, although the latter acted out of personal, selfish motives. At the bottom of the heap came the U men; the unreliables, whose information could be useful but who had to be watched. In his rank of *Sturmbannführer*, by 1939, Schellenberg mixed with them all.

The methods he used in Germany, both before and during the war, were exactly those he employed in compiling the Special Search List. His snoopers reported on the great and not so good of Nazi Germany, keeping their eyes and ears open for anything that smacked of dissent. Files were kept and anything major reached Heydrich at Headquarters at 102, Wilhelmstrasse in Berlin. The dissidents who were Schellenberg's targets were the same types who ended up on the List G.B. Jews, Communists, socialists, Freemasons, trenchant Christians – all of them were watched, photographed, reported on, first to Wilhelm Frick, Minister of the Interior, then to Heydrich. Heydrich and Schellenberg even took over the clandestine running of Salon Kitty, Berlin's most affluent brothel, in 1939 so that the pillow talk of various men on the inside would be reported back. Rooms were bugged and there were even discreet security cameras, which were switched off when Heydrich made his occasional 'tours of inspection'!

The relationship between the two was usually tense.

Heydrich was paranoid and would have been a[
Schellenberg's description of him in his memoirs. Wh[
generic books on Nazi Germany refer to Heydrich's hand[
face and swashbuckling persona, Schellenberg wrote:

> 'He was a tall, impressive figure... with small, restless
> eyes as crafty as an animal's . . . a long, predatory nose.
> His hands were slender and rather too long – they made
> one think of the legs of a spider. His splendid figure was
> marred by the breadth of his hips, a disturbingly feminine
> effect which made him... even more sinister. His voice
> was much too high ... and his speech was nervous and
> staccato.'

Several times, Heydrich tested Schellenberg, even arranging
for his wife to spend time with his subordinate. Every time,
Schellenberg recognised the ploy and came out squeaky
clean! By 1939, Schellenberg had impressed both Heydrich
and Himmler to the point where he became involved in the
planning and setting up of the *Reichssicherheitshauptamt*
(RSHA), the Reich Central Security Office. This combined
all aspects of police work, including the Gestapo. 'Persons
of interest', as we would call them today, were passed
over to Oswald Pohl, *Obergruppenführer* in charge of the
concentration camps. The various departments of the RSHA,
which feature prominently on the List, were complicated and
there was a certain degree of overlap.

Amt I, concerned with Administration and Law was itself
split into eight sub-units, including budget and training. It was
run by *Oberführer* Dr Werner Best, later Gauleiter/Governor
of Denmark, whose enthusiasm for Hitler seemed to have been
waning by 1940. Once a keen Nazi and legal expert, he became

head of the SD in France that year. Schellenberg liked him.

Amt II was the responsibility of *Standartenführer* Dr Franz Six, who would have been the governor of Britain if the invasion had taken place. He was an economist and he does not seem to have been totally committed to Nazism. Nevertheless, the year after the drawing up of the List saw him commanding the *Einsatzgruppen* in Russia. Amt II specialised in investigating the opposition and its five sub-units looked into ideological issues inside Germany as well as external problems like the British 'imperium'.

Amt III was concerned with the most positive aspects of German life: the cultural and economic. Its leader was *Standartenführer* Otto Ohlendorff, a Hanoverian farmer who became both lawyer and economist. In many ways, his is the strangest appointment in the entire RSHA because he was an early critic of the Nazi Party, finding it too socialist.[40] He was arrested for heckling by the Gestapo in the early Thirties. He nevertheless became an economic adviser to the SD and won Himmler's favour as 'Nazism's knight of the Holy Grail.' Amt III had five sub-units.

Amt IV, often described today as 'the dreaded' Amt IV, was actually the Gestapo, run by *Oberführer* Heinrich Muller, described by Schellenberg as having 'the squarish skull of a peasant'. He had something of a phobia about intellectuals. In the Thirties, the ex-airman of the First World War had served as a police officer in Munich, keeping a special eye on Communists. When Hitler's niece, Geli Raubal, committed suicide in 1931, Muller was paid to hush things up and ensure that no scandal stuck to Hitler himself. Heydrich appointed him to take over the Gestapo and he was a natural to lead Amt IV; its brief was combatting the opposition. Six sub-units dealt with all matters of crushing opponents, including assassination. One of its leading lights was the thug Alfred Naujocks, who had led the SS team that had snatched Stevens and Payne Best. He had also led the bogus raid on the radio station at Gleiwitz, which had triggered the invasion of Poland and he was occasionally referred to as 'the man who started the war'.

Amt V was headed by *Oberführer* Artur Nebe, director of the Kripo (Criminal Police), who was used to dirty dealing of all kinds. Playing the game of political in-fighting to perfection, he threw in his lot with Himmler against Goering. The department handled traditional criminal police work, a great deal of which was screened from the public by Josef Goebbels' propaganda machinery.

Finally, Amt VI was concerned with the foreign situation. Its nine sub-units divided the world into geographical areas (VIG, for example, 'ran' the North West, which was Britain, Scandinavia and the USA). The information retained here would be invaluable to Schellenberg compiling the List because it covered the ideological opposition to Nazism in other countries. Its boss was *Brigadeführer* Heinz Jost, who had had espionage experience in Spain during the Civil War. Amt VI was the *Ausland* department, which Schellenberg himself would take over in 1941. At the time of Venlo, he served in Amt VI (E).

All these departments had their 'honorary' agents; men of wide experience in all walks of life who reported on the attitudes of the German people to various decrees from Wilhelmstrasse and the Führer. Was there such a body of men in England in 1939–40?

★ ★ ★

Frantic work in June 1940 led to the publication of the *Informationshaft GrossBritannia,* known today as the *Gestapo*

Handbook for Invasion. This was the background to the Special Search List itself, which formed a 110-page appendix in the English printed version of 2001.[41] In his memoirs, Schellenberg claimed that he wrote both the *Handbook* and the List and, bearing in mind he had been interrogated by the Allies at the end of the war, it is difficult to see why he would lie about this. After all, if the eagle had landed, he would effectively have been signing the death warrants of nearly 3,000 people. By admitting to his role in the List's creation, he was risking death himself. David Lampe, the only historian in Britain to have partly analysed the List, says Schellenberg was 'an autobiographer in the Munchausen tradition'.[42] It is a good line but it applies to a lot of people who went on to write their wartime memoirs, by no means all of them Nazis! Having said that, there are anomalies between the *Handbook* and the List which ought not to exist if Schellenberg wrote them both. My personal belief is that he wrote some sections, especially the Secret Service chapter and pulled the whole thing together in a hurry and with less attention to detail than he should have given.

Schellenberg wrote his memoirs in the summer of 1951 after his release, on humanitarian grounds, from prison. He was suffering from an incurable liver condition, which would kill him the following year, and he had already undergone a major operation. He was living at Pallanza on the shores of Lake Maggiore and was helped in the work by a young German journalist, Klause Harpprecht. When they met, Harpprecht wrote: 'You had the impression that his large, bright eyes were asking how you liked this . . . former chief of German Intelligence [which he became in 1944] and whether he was still able to impress his surroundings as he had in the past.'[43]

Harpprecht was not a ghost writer but merely catalogued

Schellenberg's reminiscences. In the context of Lampe's comments, both Alan Bullock in 1956 and Richard J. Evans, Regius Professor of History at Cambridge in 2006, agree that, as far as the memoirs can be checked, they are genuine. At no point does Schellenberg distort the truth (although he omits his work on the killing grounds operating in Poland in 1940), nor does he, as many Nazis did, try to apologise or distance himself from the lunacy of the National Socialist mindset.

At the end of July, the month in which the List was drawn up, Schellenberg received new orders, this time concerning the Duke of Windsor. The abdication crisis sent shockwaves around polite society in 1936. Foreign newspapers openly ridiculed the stuffed-shirt mentality of a king who was not allowed to marry a divorcee and keep his job. The British press were hamstrung by etiquette and the laws of libel.

On 19 June, the Duke got out of the South of France as the Italians failed to invade it and went to Spain with his wife and a small entourage. By 3 July they were in Portugal and the next day, Winston Churchill offered him the post of Governor of the Bahamas, which the Duke accepted. The jury is still out on exactly how impressed by Nazism the former Edward VIII actually was. The same polite society who cold-shouldered him in 1936 rallied after the war to claim that the whole thing was a misunderstanding and there are various surviving documents which tend to substantiate that. Equally, there are several that do not.

There is no question that the Germans were interested in 'working on' the Duke via their agents, both in Spain and Portugal, but time was short. Throughout July, telegrams flew between Berlin, Madrid and Lisbon. Ribbentrop talked to Hitler about sending an agent with charm and flair to persuade the Duke to leave Lisbon, not for the Bahamas but for Madrid.

Schellenberg was the perfect choice for 'Operation Willi' as it came to be known. As the historian Alan Bullock wrote many years ago, he worked, 'in a world in which nothing was too fantastic to happen . . . in which lies, blackmail and false papers, treachery and violence were part of the daily routine.'[44]

Ribbentrop was oiliness itself on the phone to Schellenberg – 'Tell me, my dear fellow, could you come over to my office at once? You have time, haven't you?' Ribbentrop's command, straight from the Führer, was that, if the Duke could not be persuaded, he was to be kidnapped and bundled over the Spanish border á la Stevens and Payne Best at Venlo. There were huge differences between the two and it is likely that Schellenberg never took the order too seriously. What, in the end, would be the value of a captive ex-king in enemy hands? No doubt, the SS and Josef Goebbels would use him for propaganda purposes but no one would believe a word he said. Schellenberg's report for Ribbentrop, dated 2 August 1940, has survived. In the event, the idea of kidnap was dropped and Schellenberg's internal telegram was the last word. The Duke would not play ball – *'Willi will nicht'*. By 6 August, Schellenberg was back in Berlin, reporting to a furious Ribbentrop. The altogether more pragmatic (and intelligent) Heydrich, as Schellenberg's boss, urged the List maker to have nothing to do with the champagne salesman who had inexplicably become a Reichminister.

The only other name to emerge in the context of the List is *Sturmbannführer* Walter zu Christian, who claimed that the work was his. Unlike Schellenberg, zu Christian *had* spent time in England. As a boy, he went to Seaford College, near Brighton, which would, had things gone differently in 1940, been part of the initial bridgehead of the Wehrmacht and would probably have become the temporary HQ of someone senior in Army Group A. No records of his attendance there have emerged, however, so perhaps we are once again in Munchausen country! He was certainly in Madrid in the early Thirties, ostensibly working for the Siemens Corporation but actually cosying up to the Fascists whom Francisco Franco would take into a civil war four years later. He may or may not have been spying on the British at the vital strategic toe-hold of Gibraltar but he was recalled to Berlin at the end of 1935, having fallen out with other agents in Spain. He may well have contributed to the *Handbook* and even the List, since he was appointed to Amt VI in 1933; but in all probability, the spadework was done by a number of pen-pushers, working feverishly behind the scenes on the assumption that Operation Sealion was actually going to work. Such men (and women) were cogs in the machine but it is possible, in the work they did, to see them as 'desktop murderers'.[45]

Where did the data come from? We can rule out the idiots sent over in 1940 by Admiral Wilhelm Canaris, head of the Abwehr.[46] They were hopelessly inept, probably all intercepted and had not the time nor the status to feed anything of importance back to the RSHA. Were there spies of any calibre already in Britain before the outbreak of war? Yes and no! David Lampe refers to an anonymous agent who sold matches outside St James's Park Underground Station, sneakily photographing everyone who went in and out of Broadway, the home of SIS and a number of other branches of the Secret Service. SIS knew exactly why he was there – the purpose of Broadway was known to all and sundry – and he was finally arrested on the outbreak of war. Since he was working for the Gestapo, he may well have contributed information directly to Schellenberg.

Two men who were not arrested but who nevertheless spied

for Berlin were an Englishman named Bales and the Prussian old-school aristocrat Baron Robert Treeck. Bales had bought a farm in Bedfordshire and got himself invited to grand balls at the Beaufort Hunt, then *the* gathering ground for the great and good of Baldwin's and Chamberlain's England. Treeck was already there and it is inconceivable that he and Bales did not collaborate. The Baron, an Uhlan officer in the First World War, rode to hounds with British cavalry officers, all of whom no doubt dropped snippets over the stirrup cup long before the MOI was created to tell them to 'keep Mum'. He leased Luckington manor (his neighbour was Stewart Menzies, who would become 'C' under Churchill). Treeck almost certainly worked for Canaris and the Abwehr, an altogether more gentlemanly lot than the SD and the Gestapo. Associated with Beaufort was the Prince of Wales, whose abdication in these years caused such a stir amid rumours of his pro-Nazi sympathies. Who knew what useful tittle-tattle the Duke and Duchess of Windsor dropped within earshot of the Führer, who met them, smiling and shaking hands, at the Freidrichstrasse Station in Berlin on 11 October 1937.

Treeck rented property at 12, Cheyne Walk, Chelsea, in the fashionable politicians' quarter and, to add to his hob-nobbing with the aristocracy and gentry, also joined the prestigious Pytchley Hunt in Northamptonshire. In the late summer of 1939, just weeks before war was declared, Treeck vanished, leaving all his valuables behind. But what, in terms of information, did he take with him?

Because of the lack of quality of the 1940-41 spies and the prosecution of Hermann Goetz four years earlier, it is usually assumed that nothing of major importance was getting back to Berlin. Goetz, the 'flying spy' caused quite a sensation in what was, after all, peace time. He had arrived in Britain in August 1935 with a 'secretary', Marianne Ernig, and had settled in Broadstairs. The couple befriended an airman, Kenneth Lewis, and pumped him for information about his base at RAF Manston on the Isle of Thanet. While Goetz and Marianne popped back to Germany, his Kent landlady discovered secret papers in an outhouse and contacted the police. Arrested on his return (Marianne sensibly stayed in Germany), Goetz stood trial for sabotage – even though he had not actually sabotaged anything – at the Old Bailey in March 1936. He claimed that he was acting independently, having recently been turned down for a job with the German Ministry of Aviation, the RLM. Found guilty, he was sentenced to four years and was released and deported seven months before war broke out.

Just weeks before Schellenberg was compiling the List, Goetz, now *actually* working for Canaris and the Abwehr, was parachuted into County Meath to link up with the IRA in *Plan Kathleen*, a projected amphibious landing by the Wehrmacht in Derry. How realistic these plans are is debatable but the Irish connection was certainly one, as we have seen, that Dennis Wheatley was theorising about in the same period. Goetz found the IRA flaky and spent months on the run, dodging from safehouse to safehouse until the *garda* finally caught him in November 1941. He spent the duration of the war in prison. MI5 knew all about *Plan Kathleen* but just as disturbing, perhaps, was the fact that, at the Old Bailey trial, Kenneth Lewis said he was astonished how much Goetz *already knew* about the RAF.

Nigel West, the espionage expert, points to Abwehr Intelligence dating from 2 September 1940 relating to the defences at Rye and Beachy Head on the south coast. It is possible that the agent working there was a double agent of the

Russians, so that some of the information he was collecting was ending up in Berlin, though bound originally for Moscow.

Most concerning of all was the work of Colonel C. H. 'Dick' Ellis. Much to the amazement of his friends and family, Ellis was accused, in the 1960s, of selling 'vast quantities of information' (James Dalrymple of the *Independent*[47]) to the Germans. Chapman Pincher accused him outright of treason[48] and the Thatcher government (Ellis died in 1975) refused to confirm or deny the allegations. When Walter Schellenberg was interrogated after the war, he said that the SIS was compromised by 'a man named Ellis'. This of course could have been a lie, a genuine error or even a code name but the *Handbook* and the List make it clear that the RSHA knew a great deal that ought to have been secret about SIS, down to car registration plates, home addresses and telephone numbers. In some ways, Ellis was well placed to be 'in the know'. Born in Australia in 1895, he was in England at the outbreak of the First World War and served with distinction on the Western Front. Recruited by the Intelligence Service, he held a variety of diplomatic posts after the war, including, briefly, a Vice Consulship in Berlin in 1923. At the time of Munich, he was brought back to monitor the telephone lines of Ribbentrop's German embassy but they got wise to him and he was transferred to Liverpool to oversee mail censorship there.

At the time of the List, he had recently been made deputy head of the British Security Co-ordination unit, run by MI6 and approved by Churchill, in the Rockefeller Center, New York. He worked with the FBI before Pearl Harbor and with 'Wild Bill' Donovan, the creator of the Office of Strategic Services (forerunner of the CIA) after that. Ellis himself is said to have admitted his complicity with the Germans before the war.

The key point about the *Handbook* and the List is that it

is not *merely* about hush-hush people and their activities. Neither was the information in both contributed solely by German spies. What about the Ausland Organisation and the Fellow Travellers of the Right?

When Hitler came to power in Germany, it was decided to strengthen the Reich's ties to Germans living elsewhere in the world. *Lebensraum* and the invasion of the Sudetenland was, after all, a logical extension of this. The Ausland Organisation emerged under the auspices of Rudolf Hess, as Hitler's deputy and eventually had its tentacles across forty-four countries. In Britain, the head office was in Cleveland Terrace, London but there were subsidiary branches in Birmingham, Liverpool, Glasgow and Belfast. The corollary of this was that every German living and working in Britain was registered with a local Nazi group. Until 1940, and Defence Regulation 18B, those nationals were left alone, so that vast amounts of information could, in theory, have been transmitted back to Berlin. Particularly important were pending patent applications which were translated and routinely sent to the Reich Ministry of Trade, keeping German technology half a step ahead of its British counterpart. Every German in the Ausland movement paid three shillings a month to the Nazi Party. The annual contribution worldwide before the war was a staggering £6 million.

The Auslanders' remit was actually quite difficult. They were not to interfere in any way with the politics of their host nation nor even voice an opinion. On the other hand, the Auslander was a 'front-line fighter' for the Nazi Party (this in peace time, of course). He or she was supposed to read party literature, meet regularly in groups and do credit to National Socialism and Germany.

Hess's brother Alfred ran Department 21 of the organisation, responsible for international commerce, tenders and contracts. Ernst Bohle was the *gauleiter* who ran the outfit on a day-to-day basis. Born in Bradford, Bohle's English was impeccable and he retained his British passport for several years after the outbreak of war.

It could be argued that bank tellers, shopkeepers, waiters and bus conductors, devout Nazis or not, would have little to contribute to the sort of Intelligence Schellenberg was looking for. But that was precisely the point. Look at the information in both the *Handbook* and the List and you will see that it is not technical or even military. It was everyday, the sort of casual information that could be picked up by German students on cycling holidays in Britain (highly popular in the Thirties) and might certainly be stored away for future use.

Of potential significance to the Reich were the Nazi sympathisers, the 'Fellow Travellers of the Right', who were impressed by Hitler's economic miracle before the war and concerned about the threat of Bolshevism. Russia was the political elephant in the room in the Thirties, which accounts in part for Chamberlain's appeasement. Britain and France needed Hitler's Fascism to act as a bulwark against the Red menace from Stalin. From the Prince of Wales (until 1936) through disaffected lords like Lothian, Brocket, Buccleuch and Tavistock, to charismatic politicians like Oswald Mosely and newspaper tycoons like Esmond Harmsworth, there was a sizeable and powerful lobby who would have liked a rapprochement with Hitler. True, many of them preferred Mussolini's brand of Fascism to Hitler's and, with the advent of war, they all toed the British line or were, like Mosely, imprisoned; but the Right Club in London was their spiritual home and several of them travelled to Germany and met Hitler personally. The mad Mitfords were only the tip of the iceberg but the aristocracy, in particular, were accepted in the corridors of power and were, wittingly or not, perfectly capable of letting men like Schellenberg have a peep inside those corridors.

In fact, there is no need to hunt out obscure spies or to accuse the Fellow Travellers of treachery. Much – perhaps most – of the information in the *Handbook* and the List was collected from obvious and legitimate sources. British newspapers, especially the gossip columns; journals like the *Tatler*; organisation booklets like that of the RAC; telephone directories; school lists; university handbooks, all these and more were trawled by Amt IV in their compilation of the List.

History is written by the winners and today, those few publications which mention the List point out its mistakes, its duplications and misspellings. But it *was* a death list, pure and simple. And if 1940 had gone another way, I would be approaching the whole subject very differently. Who knows, I might even be writing it in German.

CHAPTER FIVE

A HANDBOOK FOR THE GESTAPO

Berlin, 1945. Hitler was dead. Admiral Doenitz, his unlikely successor, announced from Radio Hamburg to the battered, shell-shocked Berliners that 'it is my duty to save the German people from destruction by the Bolshevists.'⁴⁹ His last communique to the armed forces, dated 9 May ended, 'In this bitter hour the armed forces remember those comrades who fell facing the enemy. Those dead compel us to work loyally, obediently and with discipline on behalf of our fatherland which is bleeding from innumerable wounds.'⁵⁰

Few people outside Germany felt sorry for the defeated. Europe was a scarred battlefield that would take decades to heal. The dead had not yet been counted but they would run into millions, the result of the bloodiest war in history. And there were no bleeding hearts then to point the finger at the harshness of Versailles, the economic crises of the Twenties or the appeasing weakness of Britain and France, which could be said to have given *raison d'être* to the Nazis. Then, the whole thing was Hitler's fault and he had been backed, unbelievably, by millions of Germans and fellow Nazis who, surely, must once have been decent, honourable people.

In the meantime, while troops were rounded up, deprived of weapons and shoved into makeshift camps, a ghastly prospect opened up. The Red Army had got to Berlin first, found the Führer's partly burned body after his suicide and had helped themselves to whatever took their fancy; that included thousands of women and girls in the shattered capital. It had been the way of armies for ever – to the victors, the spoils; and the bloodiness of the Eastern front meant that it was payback time.

While some Nazis conveniently disappeared, slipping off their swastika armbands and denying all knowledge of atrocities and camps and plain murder, some were caught later and faced the English hangman Albert Pierrepoint at Nuremberg, scene of the great pre-war rallies. Others changed their names and moved west to the mountain hideouts of South America, where nobody asked too many questions.

The bulldozers moved into Germany, shovelling away the rubble that had once been homes, offices, shops. And somewhere, in the debris of May 1945, a document came to light. It was typed, single-spaced and stamped with the badges of the SS and the Reich Chancellery. It was called *Informationscheft Gross Britannia* (The Information Book for Great Britain) and there was no author's name.

The Nazis were obsessed by lists. Even – and perhaps especially – in the death camps, careful notes were kept on inmates, the food they ate, the medical complaints they suffered from, what their bowel movements were. That those people were routinely put to death in the gas chambers and their bodies burned was irrelevant. The Nazis had convinced themselves that they were saving mankind by eliminating the physically and mentally weak, the *Untermenschen*, life unworthy of life. By late 1944, most of them had come to realise that their *weltanschauung* (world view) was not, in fact, shared by the rest of the world and it became necessary to destroy the evidence. Hiding bodies was difficult, although they tried, but paper burns and thousands of tons of the minutiae of the most vicious regime in the world went up in smoke.

The survival of the *Handbook* is therefore all the more important because it gives us the SS's attitudes towards Britain with a far greater clarity than the mere propaganda of the time. While the Wehrmacht and no doubt the Hitler Youth were belting out the 'War Song Against England' –

'We challenge the lion of England,
For the last and decisive cup.
We judge and we say
An Empire breaks up.
This is our proudest day.'[51]

– Walter Schellenberg and his minions in Amt IV were providing essential details for the men who would be running Britain by the autumn of 1940. The Wehrmacht's handbook was all about rivers, mountains, bridges, factories and roads. The SS version was about the soul of a nation.

The General Survey's opening section reads like a geography book, which is essentially what it was, covering size, topography and climate. In terms of the economy, individual districts were marked. The north-west was dominated by the ore-mining area of Cumberland; the north-east centred on Durham and its coalfields, with Middlesborough as the most modern centre for steel production. South Wales had its coal and the docks at Cardiff; the Midlands were packed with small, light industry – knitwear, iron and steel. The cotton industry flourished in Lancashire, with Manchester its 'capital' and Liverpool its port. The biggest shipyards could be found in the Clyde-Firth area of Scotland. The south-east, which the Wehrmacht would reach first, was largely agricultural. London was 'an enormous warehouse'.

The employment figures were woefully out of date, relating to 1931, when the country was still in the grip of icy repression and the pound had collapsed along with the Labour government. The general trend held good, though – Britain had the highest industrial cohort in Europe, mostly in heavy industry and coal mining. Coal and iron ore were plentiful 'in house', as it were, but large amounts of raw material, as well as foodstuffs, had to be imported. This was not a problem, thanks to the vastness of the empire. Although trade was falling, Britain was still ahead of the world here. Germany's economic dislocations in 1924 and 1929 meant that she had lost ground in terms of competition and America, though a serious contender, had not yet caught up. As with the employment figures, this was anachronistic. Germany had briefly overtaken Britain in manufacture before the First World War and American goods and know-how were making their mark at the turn of the century. Without question, however, London was the world's financial capital.

Agriculture, imports/exports, fisheries and transport all had paragraphs to themselves. Forestry was severely neglected, with far less timber than Germany. Only 21.5 per cent of the land was arable, as compared to the Reich's 38.6 per cent. There were over twenty million sheep but other livestock numbers were comparatively low. The fishing industry was the largest in Europe, as might be expected of an island. Only Japan and the USA were larger. In terms of communication, the mail, telegraphy and telephones were all nationalised but the four great railway lines (LMS, LNER, GWR and SR) were private enterprises. Canals had largely been abandoned because of the rail network. Road networks and air routes were 'well developed'. Even so, British roads could boast nothing like Hitler's autobahns; the country's first full-length motorway, the M1, would not be opened until 1959.

The population, which included the Isle of Man and the Channel Islands, was wrongly written up at 46,225,900. It seems odd to break down the various languages spoken but, since a foreign power was about to take over, such things were important. There were three 'proto-languages' of the Celts; Scottish, Welsh and Irish Gaelic. The Irish situation was quite fluid in the Thirties. In the Irish Free State (today's Eire), 'Gaelic is used now with remarkable devotion'.[52] The constitution of the Republic of the Whole of Ireland (December 1937) insisted that Gaelic was the first language, English the second.

The list of principal cities shows a serious lack of understanding by the RSHA. Forty-nine are included for England but some of these were merely parts of a larger conurbation – West Ham, Willesden, Tottenham, etc. – and some were not cities at all – Rondda [sic], Ealing, Hendon and St Helens.

★ ★ ★

The rest of the *Handbook* deals with structures and institutions. We shall visit these again in later chapters as appropriate but an overview now will give us a general pattern of what the Gestapo thought it would have to deal with when the eagle landed.

The British Constitution, earliest and most liberal in the

world, was (and remains) partially unwritten. Germany's constitution dated from 1871 and had, of course, been totally subsumed by the Nazi directives from the Chancellery since 1933. The *Handbook* reminded the Gestapo that, until 7 July 1917, the British monarchy had been called the house of Saxe-Coburg-Gotha – and, of course, still was, however much the Royals might pretend the family name was Windsor. The German connection still glimmered vaguely in the Duke of Windsor, who had abdicated in December 1936 but who had shown an alarmingly cordial attitude towards Fascism.

Interestingly, Schellenberg draws a distinction between Britain's apparent democracy and the fact that 'parliamentary and governmental absolutism prevail'. Constitutional historians, when the *Handbook* came into British hands, sniggered at this – yet another 'amusing' little mistake by the Master Race. In fact, it was not that wide of the mark. The leadership of the country had changed in May 1940 (the last election was in 1935) and there would be no rush to the polls until 1945. The government would have claimed that such an election would have been impossibly disruptive in war time, yet the Americans managed it in November 1864 when Abraham Lincoln won his second term and the Civil War still had six months to run. It was the monarchy – 'really obsolete' – and the bureaucracy that kept the elite in power. Virtually all Churchill's cabinet (even the Labour representatives) were public schoolboys and, of course, there were no women, despite the fact that there had been female MPs since 1919.

The *Handbook* correctly describes the theoretical powers of the king, summoning and dissolving parliament and using the royal prerogative. It goes off track with what it imagined the king could actually *do*. In theory, he nominated the Prime Minister and key governmental posts. He sat as head of the

Privy Council – the 'secret crown council' as the *Handbook* describes it – but the fact was, again, as the *Handbook* says, all real power lay in the hands of the Cabinet. Schellenberg was also aware that there was a state within a state – Churchill's six-man War Cabinet actually called the shots. There are thumbnail sketches of thirty-six key members of government, with their careers to date, their ages and their approximate addresses. So well informed was Schellenberg that he even has Clement Attlee down twice – once as Leader of the Labour Party (A81) and again as (A80) Major, of Stanmore, Middlesex.

Within parliament, the Lords, composed of about 750 hereditary peers, was predominantly Conservative. It was subservient to the Commons (since the constitutional crisis of 1911) but, 'with its vast political connections and capitalist networks, should not be underestimated'. The Commons had 615 MPs and the seating in the chamber meant that physical segregation of the parties was not possible. The Reichstag in Berlin, by comparison, had a semi-circular structure with aisles that separated the various groups.

The Conservatives dominated the Commons too, 'partly ultra-conservative and chauvinist.' One of these groups represented the 'warmongers' around Churchill. Because there was a wartime coalition of parties, there was no Opposition to criticise government decisions – hence Schellenberg's contention that 'the leader of "His Majesty's Most Loyal Opposition" is actually paid by the government'. Schellenberg knew that Attlee's Labour Party was itching to 'address peacetime social injustices' but he doubted whether much would come of it because of the social rigidity of its leaders, having 'mainly attended feudal public schools.'

And of course, the *Handbook* is absolutely accurate when it says, 'An Enabling Act at the beginning of the war has allowed the government to impose military law on the entire country, which, in its dictatorial application, defies all democratic principles.'

The British legal system mystified the Germans. Based as it was, on precedent, it had never subscribed to the Roman law that operated everywhere in Europe. Again, the Nazi code had swept away the rule of law in Germany and in the occupied countries, so that comparisons made no sense. The cost of legal proceedings in Britain appalled the Germans – this made it 'almost impossible for the less affluent classes to gain their rights in court'.

Central and local government is dealt with, with the roles of the Home Office ('Ministry of the Interior') and Ministry of Health outlined. The *Handbook* seems vaguely horrified that local government was largely allowed to do its own thing. In Nazi Germany, there was a rigid vertical system via the *Gau* (regions) down to the *Zelle* (apartment blocks), with Party snoopers at every level.

Vitally important to the Gestapo – and to the Wehrmacht – was an understanding of the British armed forces. The country was divided into six military districts and there was the dual system in the army of the Regulars and the Territorials. Schellenberg noted that the Dominions were not obliged to join Britain's war (in practice, by 1940, they all had), which would provide an extra one million whites and three million 'coloured' able-bodied men. The figures that the *Handbook* gives were for peacetime only (133,000 Regulars, a Reserve of 149,000 and 187,000 TAs), although conscription had added considerably to that. The Royal Navy, which is not accorded the healthy respect that the *Kriegsmarine* actually had for it, had a strength of 125,000 pre-war, all serving under the auspices of the Admiralty in London. The major naval bases are listed, from Scapa Flow to Portsmouth. The air force gets more coverage in the *Handbook*, perhaps because it was seen as the biggest single obstacle to invasion. The navy, after all, was scattered over the globe, whereas both Bomber and Fighter Command were island-based. In the spring of 1939, the RAF had 123 Squadrons, 1,750 aircraft and the same number again in Reserve. The total strength was 125,000 and there were 80 airbases being built rapidly by that time. The Luftwaffe dwarfed this but there is no smugness in the statistics as laid down. There were three defensive areas with Coastal Command run by the navy.

In terms of education, the universities are singled out in the *Handbook* as 'enemy cultural institutes'. The List itself is full of philosophers and lecturers who had dared to criticise the Reich, or Fascism in general; these places were their bolt-holes and breeding grounds. Oxford, Bristol and London were particularly active in this context. The Oxford Pamphlets, which had been published during the First World War, were revived in the spring of 1939 in which various academics attacked Germany. One of the seven mentioned appears on the List – Robert Kuczynski (K165), whose speciality was *lebensraum*. Oxford and London were working in collaboration with Duff Cooper's Ministry of Information (Harold Nicolson's offices were in the Gower Street buildings of University College) and Bristol was 'under Churchill's protection', perhaps because the Prime Minister was Chancellor of the University. Various cultural institutions are treated with contempt. The Cobden Club in London was attempting to prove the superiority of British culture over that of Germany, claiming arrogantly that all science simply stopped in the Reich in 1933. Although Amt IV clearly did not have up-to-date information (the figures it quotes are from

1914-18), there were neutral countries that 'benefited' from the bias of British speakers on their lecture circuits. Those speakers distributed a total of 25,000 pamphlets, tracts and books (no doubt of the type that had been ceremoniously burned by the Nazis when they came to power in Germany). 'The Institut Français in Kensington,' warns the *Handbook*, 'requires special attention.' So did the Academic Assistance Council, at 12, Clement's Inn Passage, Clare Market, WC2; this was a society of émigré Germans whose leaving of the Reich might well have explained the Cobden Club's views! Another centre of propaganda was the Information Bureau in the Council House of the City of Birmingham – it 'gets little public attention' but, clearly, that would change once jack boots thudded along Corporation Street.

The public schools and the Boy Scout Movement are singled out as centres of trouble. Many of the schools had 'important anti-German material' in their archives. Accurately, the *Handbook* explains that barely one per cent of all children attend these schools but that they provide eighty per cent of all important political and social positions. It was all about money but breeding mattered too – Eton was 'sold out' until 1949! Schellenberg then lists key politicians whose careers he had studied carefully: John Hankey (Chancellor of the Duchy of Lancaster)[53]; Halifax, H14 (Foreign Office); Eden, E6 (War Office); Oliver Stanley (War Office); and Duff Cooper, D114 (Ministry of Information) were all Old Etonians, as were Robert Vansittart (foreign-policy adviser) and Lord Linlithgow (Viceroy of India). Churchill himself (C49) was a product of Harrow. So was Samuel Hoare (Air Ministry). Leslie Hore-Belisha, B91 (War Office) went to Clifton College in Bristol and John Simon, S74 (Lord Chancellor) to Fettes in Edinburgh. 'It is here,' sneered Schellenberg, 'that the future English gentleman is educated, the gentleman who has never thought about philosophical issues, who has hardly any knowledge of foreign culture and who thinks of Germany as the embodiment of evil, but accepts British power as inviolable.'

The Boy Scouts come under scrutiny rather as the Trade Unions do later in the *Handbook*. In the Reich, the country's youth had been forced into the strait-jacket of conformity. Both the *Hitler Jugend* and the *Bund Deutscher Mädel* (League of German Maidens) swore absolute obedience to the Führer. Robert Baden-Powell, whose name is on the List at B6, could never hold such a position in the eyes of the average Boy Scout or Girl Guide. Wrongly, the *Handbook* believed that 'a half-Jew, Mr Martin' ran the movement in 1940. He also ran the Passport Office, the international branches of which were actually Claude Dansey's Z System of agents and had been destroyed since Venlo. The Scouts were 'a disguised instrument of power for British cultural propaganda and an excellent source of information for the British Intelligence Service.' There was evidence of collaboration between the Scouts and the Free Youth Movement in Germany. Schellenberg may or may not have known that in the early weeks of the First World War, Boy Scouts were routinely sent out to find the names and addresses of Germans living in Britain and were encouraged to report them to the authorities.

At first sight, the inclusion of important museums in Britain makes little sense. After all, the *Handbook* was not a cute little guide for the casual tourist. The clue is in the second sentence – '[the museums] contain documents and works of art from German history, in which the German Reich must have a special interest.' There is a rich irony here. Had the eagle landed, Hermann Goering would no doubt have plundered the museums and galleries for his own extensive art collection.

From October 1940, a task force, headed by the Nazi ideologist Alfred Rosenberg, cleared various institutions of iconic works of art, which, officially, the Nazis believed to be 'degenerate', and stashed them at various sites in the Reich. The value of paintings from France alone was an estimated $1 billion.

The media merits special attention in the *Handbook* because it was the most obvious anti-Nazi aspect of British defiance. In the Reich, all media came under the direct control of Josef Goebbels' Ministry of Enlightenment and Propaganda, which shut down opposition publications and created a wealth of propaganda, from Leni Riefenstahl's *Triumph of the Will* to Viet Harlan's *Ju Suss*. While Schellenberg was very accurate about the various newspapers, down to the size of their circulation, he is nevertheless scornful of the level of journalistic ability of their editors. 'The advertising business,' the *Handbook* says, 'is dependent upon commercial clients with offers of insurance, crossword puzzles and competitions etc. The editorial content is secondary.' Most papers were what, today, we would call tabloids, aiming at a working-class readership. The Sundays were particularly popular and, we are assured, 'The English, and especially those who live in the cities, read papers only in the morning.'

'Lord Rothermere, Lord Northcliffe's brother, with his friendly attitude towards Germany... is an exception among the press tycoons.' His empire ran the *Daily Mail*, *Daily Mirror*, *Evening News* and *Sunday Dispatch*. Independent newspapers included the *Observer*, the *Manchester Guardian* and *The Times*. Several Fascist publications are listed but their circulation, even before the outbreak of war, was tiny. Mosley's *The Blackshirt* was one of these, along with *The British Union Quarterly* and *The Fascist*, edited by Arnold Leese.

When Schellenberg contended there was no press law in

Britain, he was thinking of the relationship between the media and the government. The laws of libel held good and journalists infringed them occasionally, as they still do today. By and large, there was full co-operation between the papers and the Ministry of Information, although the new and very popular *Picture Post* went out on a limb of its own. Fiercely patriotic, it raised its own Home Guard training school and, in August 1940, printed an article which must have given Harold Nicolson and Duff Cooper apoplexy. It was called 'How to Invade Britain' but turned out to be Napoleon's plans from 1804! Furious at the Nazi-style censorship of the MOI, it printed three identical black squares with the captions still in place as though photographs had been allowed. Two months after the war began, it told its readers, 'We get twenty pictures showing the German side of the War for every one showing the British. Is this War? Is this Democracy? Is this common sense?'[54]

Schellenberg knew perfectly well that the BBC was listened to in the Reich – Marie Vassiltchikov was not the only Berlin resident glued to her wireless set – and he merely states the corporation's structure and key directors, together with the transmitters around the country. As with Gleiwitz on the Polish border, the Wehrmacht would have made a beeline for those had 1940 gone differently.

Religion takes up twenty-one pages of the *Handbook*. Hitler's own relationship with the Reich churches was complicated. He was once a Catholic choirboy in Linz and there is a story that he was saved from drowning by a priest when he was very young. Many of his speeches refer to God in a variety of ways, while at the same time encouraging the German people to see him as the new Messiah. In kindergartens across the Reich, little tots prayed to Adolf Hitler as the creator of all that was good. Priests, both Protestant and Catholic, who crossed the state in any way would end up alongside their congregations in the camps. The structure of the leading churches in Britain is described in the *Handbook*, using terms 'High', 'Low' and 'Broad' and funding is covered. The terms of the Lambeth Conference of 1930 are spelled out, though very few people in Britain even knew that such a conference took place. The Conference was the seventh in a series that began in 1867 and was presided over by Cosmo Lang, the Archbishop of Canterbury, whose London address was Lambeth Palace. Much was discussed but most of it revolved around unity of faiths, abortion and contraception. The Conference praised the work of the League of Nations.

The Anglican church in particular, the *Handbook* contends, was 'an instrument of British imperial political power'; Protestantism's other manifestations – Methodism, Calvinism and Presbyterianism – barely get a look in. Schellenberg was clearly scornful of the Catholics. They were mostly 'people of Irish descent' and there was a high percentage of them in the Foreign Office and the Privy Council. He particularly had it in for Cardinal Archbishop of Westminster Arthur Hinsley, who 'is one of the most notorious anti-German agitators in the Catholic Church.' He had advocated the setting up of an 'anti-parachute defence organisation under the name of "sword of the spirit"'. Astonishingly, the fighting archbishop's name is not on the List.

The Ministry of Information was using religion to whip up anti-German sentiment. The Religions Division was set up at the start of the war. 'Taking possession of this department's material,' Schellenberg wrote, 'would be absolutely necessary.' It was also necessary to grab the reels made by the Missionary Film Committee and to ask searching questions of the Church of England Council on Foreign Relations and the Student Christian Movement.

Inevitably, considering Fascism's opposition to it, Communism in Britain is a key section in the *Handbook*. Including Socialism, the Trade Unions and, especially, the illegal Marxist groups of German émigrés, it runs to eighteen pages, with the names and addresses of important individuals.

Several names on the List come under the category of émigrés, the people who ran from the Reich in 1933 or soon afterwards simply because it was Nazi and they valued their freedom or their lives too much. These groups were subdivided into: the Jewish organisations, responsible for most of the press agitation against Germany; the pacifists who 'fight Germany under the cover of ideology'; and the Left, including Trade Unions. Names and addresses follow, in some cases complete with telephone numbers. Mention is made of the categories set up under Regulation 18B: Category A were arrested at once; Category B were registered as aliens but were not imprisoned; Category C lost their usual peacetime rights but were otherwise left alone. Why? 'The principal aim was to try to integrate this group into the national defence system and, if desired, into the armed forces.' Although he would not have been aware of the precise details, Schellenberg may have been thinking of the very specific task along these lines being carried out by Captain J. C. Masterman, who, at Latchmere House in London, was already 'turning' German agents to work for British Intelligence.

Hitler's antipathy to the Freemasons is well documented. He had spoken out against them in *Mein Kampf* in 1924 as the servants of the Jews (the one group follows the other in the *Handbook*) and slammed them for their 'mistaken teaching of the equality of all men.' Today, thanks largely to pseudo-medieval fiction, the Freemasons are everybody's conspiratorial bogeymen. That was not Hitler's objection. Herman Rauschning (R14) quoted him in a book written before the List was compiled: 'An order, that is what [the Nazi Party] has to be . . . Ourselves or the Freemasons or the Church – there is room for one of the three and no more . . . We are the strongest of the three and shall get rid of the other two.'[55]

Accordingly, in 1933, the ten grand lodges in Germany were dissolved, their leaders disappearing into the camps. Their libraries and works of art were grabbed by the Gestapo and exhibited by Josef Goebbels at an Anti-Masonic Exposition four years later. The same liquidation took place in each of the countries the Germans invaded – Austria, Czechoslovakia, Poland, Holland, Belgium and France. Britain would have followed suit, especially since Schellenberg wrote, 'England is the country of Freemasonry,' and then proceeds to write a highly distorted 'history' of the order, linking the king, the aristocracy and their underlings throughout the Empire: 'What concerns us is that in its ideological orientation and its political effectiveness – as long as it lasts – it is a dangerous weapon in the hands of Britain's plutocrats against National Socialist Germany.'

The links with the Jews were obvious – the notion of being 'chosen' gave the British their insufferable arrogance as the rulers of the greatest empire the world has ever seen. All the known lodges appear on the List.

Bearing in mind Hitler's detestation of them, the Jews only occupy eleven pages in the *Handbook*. The Nazis were convinced that the Jews were responsible for virtually every war in history, not to mention economic and even physical disasters. They had led Europe into the First World War, making fortunes for themselves in the process and were behind Churchill now, holding out against all reason in the summer of 1940. They had already been eliminated from German civil life with the Nuremberg laws of five years earlier. From November 1938, when *Kristallnacht* had seen synagogues burn and the pavements glitter with broken glass, thousands had been rounded up and sent to the camps. Vast numbers of Jews – perhaps three million of them – had added to the Reich's 'Jewish problem' after *Fall Weiss* in September 1939. By the time Schellenberg was drawing up the *Handbook* and the List, the Madagascar Plan emerged. It was simple; eliminate all the Jews from Europe by taking them to the island off East Africa. They had been bleating for years about a homeland – here was one for the taking. The project was still in the planning stage and it depended on Germany's ability to command the sea around the island. Once Britain was defeated, of course, it would be all systems go. And because that never happened, there would be some in Germany in the years ahead who actually had the arch-hypocrisy to blame the Holocaust on the British!

Schellenberg estimated there were 300,000 Jews in Britain but he suspected the number was higher. Suspect historical figures had been too generous in the past – Richard the Lionheart and Oliver Cromwell, for example. And since Benjamin Disraeli had been prime minister in the 1870s, the position of powerful Jews was assured. And they were still there – Philip Sassoon and Hore-Belisha in Chamberlain's government. Churchill was known to be a Zionist and he was not alone. Needless to say, huge swathes of the British economy were in Jewish hands, especially the banks. Jews dominated the media; one of the BBC's directors was Godfrey Isaacs. Ivor Montagu and S. Bernstein made anti-German films. Thirty-five Jewish organisations are listed in the

Handbook, along with addresses and key members, many of whose names appear, naturally, on the List.

With a brief six pages on the country's economy – much of which, of course, Schellenberg believed was Jewish-backed – the *Handbook* moves on to its last phase: the police and the Intelligence services. In the Reich, of course, both of these were subsumed into the RSHA, with close co-operation that kept the totalitarian lid on the whole regime. In Britain, it was not like that: 'Comparisons with the German Criminal Police [Kripo] cannot be made because of the entirely different – and for us inexplicable [!] – organisation and activities of the British police.'

Perhaps because of his own calling, it was the Special Branch of the Metropolitan force that interested Schellenberg most. He noted that, from 1936 onwards, an increasing number of London's policemen expressed an interest in learning German and he could not wait to get his hands on the superlative fingerprint collection (run by Superintendent Fred Cherrill) on the third floor at Scotland Yard. The CRO index was essential too, although Schellenberg's criminals were very different from the ones the Yard was looking for. Special Branch records were vital to secure, as well as the register of aliens at 28 Bow Street.

The last section of the *Handbook* is devoted to twenty-three pages (the longest section) on the Intelligence Service. These men were Schellenberg's immediate enemies; the opposition in the great game of espionage. Peter Fleming, writing in the 1950s and surrounded by the men, like himself, who had beaten the Nazis, found this section 'novelettish' and 'marred by inaccuracy and pedantry'. In that, he was not prepared to give Schellenberg any credit – history as written by the victors. On the contrary, the man who engineered Venlo was extraordinarily well informed about the structures and personnel of departments that were supposed to be hush-hush at the time and were so for years after the war. The name of the chief of SIS – Stewart Menzies – was not known to the *British* public until 1966; Schellenberg knew it in 1940 as the new 'C' took up his post. He also knew that the name was pronounced in the Scots way – Mingies.

What, for Schellenberg, characterised SIS was the laidback, devil-may-care amateurishness of men, largely public school, occasionally of private means, who dominated the Intelligence field. And he had a grudging admiration for them – their 'unscrupulousness, self-discipline, cool calculation and ruthless action'. He had problems with definitions and the exact meaning of department names and codes. 'Stevens and Best,' he wrote, 'may have told the truth, at least subjectively, when they claimed that there was an SIS but not a Secret Service.' He likened SIS to a Freemasons' Lodge – shapeless, anonymous and given over to false mysticism. The departments are named, along with their addresses and heads. Robert Vansittart, for instance, formerly Speaker of the Commons, friend of Churchill and general government adviser, was forty-nine years old and lived at 44, Park Street, Grosvenor Square.

Schellenberg knew about Bletchley Park but not exactly what went on there. Bletchley has received an unprecedented coverage in the last few years, with numerous books, articles, a television series and even a film devoted to it. It was the headquarters of the government's code and cypher school, focusing on the German Enigma machine and cracking the encrypted codes used by the Nazi military. Experts believe that this brilliant 'Ultra' work shortened the war by two years, perhaps more. He knew about Broadway. Number 54 was the headquarters building of SIS and it was from here that Dr R. V. Jones, Director of Intelligence, did his level best to upset the Luftwaffe's navigation aids. It would take a direct hit from the Luftwaffe on the night of 14 October 1940. Schellenberg had at his fingertips the middle managers of the various departments – Slocum and Bowlby ran personnel. Captain Russell of the Naval Section operated out of the sixth floor at the Admiralty. A retired colonel called Geoffreys used to work in the Cipher Department. Admiral Lipenny of the Industrial Section was retired from the day job too. Obviously, because Captain Payne Best had been so obliging, the man's colleagues were fixed in the forefront of Schellenberg's mind. There was Kenneth Cohan, Keith Krane, Robert Craig. 'Hinchley-Cook [H134a] wears glasses, is robust, fresh-faced... and speaks German fluently in a mix of dialects from Saxony and Hamburg.' *Picture Post* had been enormously helpful, back in November 1938, with its detailed article on the Secret Service. You really could not make it up!

* * *

All that was needed now was the Luftwaffe to smash the RAF; for the *Kriegsmarine* to hold off the navy for long enough to get the Wehrmacht ashore. Then the List could be dusted off from the boxes and the filing cabinets. It could be distributed to the various Amte of the RSHA. And the killing could begin.

CHAPTER SIX

CIRCLES OF GUILT

Throughout the Special Search List, the word *täterkreis* features prominently. Like many German portmanteau words, it is surprisingly difficult to translate. Some commentators have used the phrase spy-ring but this wanders too far off the point for our purposes. After *täterkreis*, various names are listed. These are the people linked by politics and mindset to be anti-Nazi and represent one of the most sinister aspects of Nazism and the SD in particular. It shows guilt by association. If one name in the *täterkreis* could be opposed to the Reich, the chances are they all could.

There are 133 *täterkreis* and that of Stevens/Payne Best stands out like a sore thumb and must have given Schellenberg huge satisfaction. After Venlo, as we have seen, MI6 lay in ruins and had to be rebuilt but the two agents were a mine of information for the SD and they seem to have co-operated to an alarming degree. Sigismund Payne Best was born in Cheltenham, studied in London and went into business briefly and read Economics and Musicology at Munich University at the same time that Adolf Hitler was starving in Vienna trying to get into art school. Payne Best's German was superb and he served in the First World War as an Intelligence officer with GHQ's Wallinger bureau, an agency linked with Belgian resistance. In 1917, he was in Rotterdam, liaising with the Belgians and he fell foul of Richard Tinsley (T38), MI6's local chief, code-named, perhaps a little obviously, 'T'. Tinsley was perhaps the most successful spymaster in the field during the war but Payne Best was a prickly subordinate and he was caught in bed with the wife of a Belgian resistance leader. He was recalled to London and replaced by Lieutenant Ivone Kirkpatrick, who would be prominent in the Ministry of Information by the time the List was drawn up. It was all, of course, Payne Best contended, a 'fix' by Tinsley.

After the war, Payne Best set up a pharmaceutical business in The Hague but his dandified figure, complete with spats and a monocle, made him something of a caricature. Most people just assumed that he was a spy. In 1938, as tension built across Europe, Payne Best was recruited into Claude Dansey's Z organisation. In some ways, it was a marriage made in heaven. Both men were hugely arrogant, believing in an omnipotence that neither of them actually possessed. The Z system had the cover of the Passport Control Office and, as with Payne Best, an alarming number of people knew all about it. For an organisation whose motto was *Semper Occultis* (always secret), this was something of a joke. It was in this context that he met Major Richard Stevens.

Looking as pompous as Payne Best in the most commonly found photographs, with a Hitlerite toothbrush moustache, he had worked as an Intelligence officer in India until 1939. A master of languages – he spoke Arabic, Hindustani, Malay,

Greek, French, German and Russian – he had no specific training for information-gathering in Europe, where he was sent on the outbreak of war. It was this casual, laid-back, almost amateur behaviour which characterised all British Intelligence services early in the Second World War and which Schellenberg found frustrating and amusing in equal proportions. The historian Hugh Trevor-Roper, whose reputation was inevitably destroyed by his belief in the veracity of the 'Hitler Diaries', wrote of Schellenberg, 'Like so many Germans, he was an admirer, a despairing admirer, of the British Intelligence Service – an organisation of which he knew very little....'[56]

In fact, as the *Handbook* and List make clear, he knew a great deal. Most accounts claim that the Nazis were envious of SIS, yet the tone of the *Handbook* is one of mocking contempt. When the List was drawn up, Payne Best was imprisoned in Sachsenhausen concentration camp in Berlin. Also known as Oranienburg, it was a known centre for political prisoners and a training centre for the SS. Never a death camp, executions nevertheless took place, either by hanging or shooting, until the installation of a gas chamber in March 1943. Incarceration here cannot have been a walk in the park but Payne Best had the protection of the *Totenkopf* SS who ran the camp and was allowed civilian clothing, a library and access to a radio. Schellenberg was looking after his informants very well!

The public-show trial of Stevens and Payne Best as instigators of Elser's Beer Hall outrage never happened. Had it done so, they would certainly have been executed. Schellenberg had advised against it – he knew they were not involved and could count on their freely offered information. It was Stevens, not Payne Best, who knew the names of all SIS station chiefs in Europe but it is Payne Best who put his head over the parapet in his autobiography *The Venlo Incident*, which is a frankly embarrassing piece of self-servery. He admits to being not very brave – even the dentist's chair terrified him – and he knew what consummate torturers the SS were. The book is full of bonhomie and charm. He liked his captors at Sachsenhausen and they liked him. Schellenberg, of course, was the exception. Payne Best found him arrogant and stupid, with all the irony that that conveys in the context of the German 'false flag' sting at Venlo. Schellenberg had made an idiot of him and Payne Best was clearly not the forgiving type.

He purports to being very concerned about May, his wife, without knowing, after the gunfight outside the Bacchus, how or even where she was. This does not prevent her personal details appearing in Schellenberg's List (B129), however – 'Best, born van Rees, Maria Margareta 9.1.92'. She lived, as far as Schellenberg knew, at 3, Hartford Rd, Hampstead. Who else but Payne Best could have told him that? Stevens' wife is there too, along with his valet. Moya, nee Godfrey, is described as a writer, living in London. Amt IV E4 were interested in her. And in the valet; he was Hasting, H55 (probably Hastings) and nothing more is recorded about him.

As is to be expected, most of the names in the Stevens/Payne Best network are Dutch. These men and women would have taken the opportunity to get out of the Netherlands as soon as it was realised, after 10 May, that the Wehrmacht could not be stopped. There are twenty-seven other names in the Stevens/Payne Best *täterkreis* and one thing is certain: had the eagle landed, all those people would be dead. Nigel Jones, writing an introduction to a 2009 edition of Payne Best's book, explains that the former prisoner leaned on Stewart Menzies, head of SIS at White's Club in London and threatened all kinds of whistle-blowing if he was not allowed to publish. Jones concludes, 'the author deserves our sympathy – and our respect.' No, he does not. Did no one in British Intelligence notice that the man's Christian name was Sigismund?

A49 was Andriessen, a senior banker with the Bankfuria Piersen Company of Amsterdam but there must have been more to him than that because Schellenberg's own department, Amt IV E4, wanted a word. B9 was Guillaume Edouard Bagnay; everybody wanted him but especially, for reasons now lost, the Munster police. John Curnbull is such an unusual name that he was probably Turnbull – the typo an inevitable result of secretaries working at top speed in crowded SD offices in the summer of 1940. The wanted were scattered far and wide in Britain. Whereas most of the List lived in or had addresses in London, some did not. Aneta Demmer was a journalist in the fraught world of wartime propaganda, always a dangerous operation, and was living first in The Hague then in Mitchells Road, Ventnor, in the Isle of Wight. She was only twenty-four and a widow, her husband presumably a casualty of war. And it can hardly have just been Schellenberg's department that were on the lookout for D124 Commander (the List says 'Leutnant') William 'Biffy' Dunderdale. The man was a friend of Ian Fleming, then in Naval Intelligence, and one of a dozen or so claimed as being the stereotype of the future James Bond. He was the head of MI6 in Paris until living there became a trifle risky. Larger than life, with a Rolls Royce, handmade suits and Cartier cufflinks, Dunderdale was a typical war-time agent, fond of fast women and fast cars. A celebrated raconteur, he served SIS superbly for years. He remembered later only being asked to kill someone once: 'It was suggested that I would render the country a great service if I nudged a certain individual into the English Channel. Unhappily, the man concerned was not on the [night] train [to Paris] so there was no one to nudge.'[57]

Had Schellenberg known that Dunderdale was among the code-breakers at Bletchley Park, he might have been all the more anxious to catch him.

Spies listed in the Black Book often turn up under different names. So, thanks to Stevens and Payne Best, Adrianus Vrinten's cover as 'Emmering' was blown. He had lived at Loon-op-Zud in Holland and was a British agent working out of Rotterdam. E36 was Edo Fimmen, the seamen's leader, perhaps recruited by Guy Burgess, then working for Section D of SIS in London. The man organised courier services and supervised the transportation of anti-Reich agents and refugees. The fact that he was a Communist as well (as of course, by this time, was Burgess) made him doubly likely to end up on the List. No one seriously believed that the Russo-German honeymoon could last for long. And they were all after Fimmen – Schellenberg's Amt IV E4, as well as A1b and A5. G101 is another typo. 'Grant' is almost certainly Colonel Laurence Grand, the tall, elegant chain-smoker with a rose in his buttonhole. He ran Section D of British Intelligence and was Burgess's boss, constantly on the lookout for 'unorthodox people with good brains'. The List describes him as the leader of the Sabotage department at SIS (D stood for Destruction). Theo Hespers was a one-time youth leader from Munchen-Gladbach and had now turned anti-Nazi resistance fighter. Lionel Loewe, L120, was a British Intelligence officer from The Hague. So was Christopher Rhodes (R50), of Gosport, Hampshire, who was one of Claude Dansey's boys in the Passport Control offices in the Netherlands. Gustav Straetmann (53), must have been more than a ship's radio operator, which is why the SD were interested in him. He had last been heard of in Maastricht. They did not come much more highly placed than fifty-year-old Raleigh Temperley (T12), the British military attaché in the Netherlands. Politicians at this level were natural targets. The product of the public schools and Oxbridge, their charm and diplomacy only went so far in dealing with the Nazi threat and many of them made their feelings clear long before the actual balloon went up. Albert Voorbough (V42) was lesser fry, merely listed as 'secretary', a catch-all term to cover a multitude of anti-Nazi sins.

There is, inevitably, considerable crossover between the *täterkreis* networks and the List names themselves. We cannot, in the present work, enumerate all 130 but some stand out as deserving research.

One of these is an anomaly. He is at the heart of a *täterkreis* but his name is omitted from the list. Why is not clear, since he was clearly an enemy of the Reich. His name was Karel Machacek and he was the son of a railway station-master in the Austro-Hungarian Empire, which became the new state of Czechoslovakia when Machacek was four. He read Medicine at university and became involved with Sobel, a Czech youth movement pledged to democracy and patriotism. In the allegedly peaceful takeover of the country, Machacek's university came under attack. Three of his friends went down in a hail of bullets; others were marched off to the camps. Despairing of any help for his eviscerated country, Machacek joined the French Foreign Legion, traditionally home to the lost and the dispossessed. By the time that Schellenberg was writing the list, Machacek had landed in Liverpool. As a medical student himself, he believed that medics were of more use than foot soldiers and persuaded President Benes to pressure the British authorities into allowing such students to continue their training at British medical schools. As a qualified doctor, he went on to involve himself briefly with the exiled Czech ministry in London and then trained as a pilot, flying with 311 Czechoslovak Squadron.

Frantisek Moravec was another Czech on the run. He had fought for the Austrians in the First World War and had been captured by the Russians in one of their rare successes on the Eastern Front, in 1915. After the war, he served with the Czech Legion, an impressive unit which earned everybody's respect. By 1937, he was head of the Legion's Intelligence department. On 14 March 1939, he and ten comrades flew secretly to London's Croydon airport with news that an invasion of Czechoslovakia was imminent – it happened the next day. By the time the List was compiled, Moravec was head of Intelligence for the Czech government in exile, based at Portchester Gate, London. His 'neighbour' in Addington, Buckinghamshire, was Edouard Benes (B98), the Czech president. Moravec was *precisely* the type that Schellenberg was looking for. Not only had he passed considerable sensitive information on the Nazis to MI6, he now ran a resistance group called the Three Kings, who co-operated with Churchill's new boys on the espionage front – the Special Operations Executive. In the List he appears twice, as M172 and 173 and his London address is given as 53, Lexington Gardens, Kensington, which is almost certainly an error. Lexham Gardens was the Czech HQ.

Among the network, presumably the ten who had escaped with him to Croydon, were S40 Karel Sedlacek and C54, Vladimir Cigna, both staff officers. Cigna has his address as Lexan Gardens, again a typo for Lexham, as above. He was forty-two in 1940. Sedlacek's names are misspelled on the List. His British address is not given but he was known to have been living in Brussels at some point.

The elegantly named Wolfgang Gans Edler, Herr zu Putlitz (P139) came to London in 1924 to learn English. By 1935, when the Anglo-German naval agreement was signed and before Hitler started flexing his international muscles, he was First Secretary in the German Embassy in London. He had also met the journalist Jona von Ustinov and it makes sense then to deal with them as a pair. They were both recruited by MI5 and strongly anti-Nazi. Both men might well feature in a later chapter in this book, since they were both spies, but it seems logical to look at them under the *täterkreis* label. U10 Ustinov had offered his services to Robert Vansittart, as chief adviser to the Foreign Office. The secrets that zu Putlitz dug out of the German Embassy in the 1930s were worth their weight in gold. He confirmed the pro-Nazi stance of Wallis Simpson, busy wrecking the royal family in 1935/36; the future spy, Ann Wolkoff was her dressmaker. He was feeding Churchill, via Ustinov and Vansittart, the factual reality of Luftwaffe numbers. Then von Ribbentrop was made ambassador and the Embassy became a madhouse. Desks and wastepaper bins were checked every night and it may be more than a coincidence that zu Putlitz found himself reassigned to The Hague in May 1938. From here, and operating very carefully, he fed back on Czechoslovak events to Ustinov.

In April 1939, with the war still months away, zu Putlitz uncovered the fact that Italy intended to invade Albania. The Duce had done this sort of thing before, trying to recreate Rome's African Empire in Ethiopia. Then the League of Nations had done nothing, despite an impassioned appeal from the emperor, Haile Selassie. Now, with Albania, Halifax at the Foreign Office refused to believe it. Two days later, it became reality. Two weeks after the invasion of Poland, zu Putlitz and his lover, driver Willy Schnieder, fled to London. 'The whole situation,' wrote Guy Liddell of MI5, 'had got rather on his nerves and... he felt he could not go on.'[58]

We have an unusual take on Klop Ustinov in this period because it was written by his son Peter in his autobiography, *Dear Me*. He remembers his father as a dapper little 5ft 2in who dressed in the German fashion in the early years but became decidedly British later. Interestingly, Rudolf von Ribbentrop, son of the German ambassador, was brought to school each day in a white Rolls Royce and was a classmate of the younger Ustinov. Peter was aware, as an only child, of his father's fluctuating fortunes. The problems seemed to disappear after Klop applied (in Welsh, to confuse the Germans!) for British citizenship and he wangled, as did zu Putlitz, an authentic-looking passport. Young Peter, in his teens and as aware as the next well-connected schoolboy about the mounting tension in Europe, noticed strange, secretive people turning up at their flat in 134, Redcliffe Gardens, SW10 – 'English colonels with so little to say that their very appearance seemed like a uncrackable code; foreign gentlemen who darted menacing looks at each other, then quickly pretended they hadn't.'[59] On one particular night, the father sent the son to the pictures – something that *never* happened on account of the outrageous cost of the cheapest seats (9d). At the top of the stairs (the Ustinov flat was four storeys up and there was no lift), a procession of gloomy old men in top hats and homburgs shambled past him. One of them, young Ustinov would realise days later when he read the papers, was Major Richard Stevens, whom the papers said had been arrested at Venlo. I would suggest that all the others on that staircase had their names on the List and Walter Schellenberg would have given his right arm to meet them.

Enter Sigrid Lilian Schulz. Unlike most of the *täterkreis* names, hers is not on the List in its own right; why is unclear. She was born in Chicago in January 1893 and the family moved to Berlin eight years later. As a bilingual, Sigrid was a natural for journalism and worked for Colonel Robert McCormick, owner of the *Chicago Tribune*. Repelled by Nazism, she steeled herself and interviewed both Hitler and Goering in the 1920s.

A superb writer and investigator, she worked with fellow correspondent William Shirer for the Montreal Broadcasting System in 1938. He said of her, 'No other American correspondent in Berlin knew so much of what was going on behind the scenes as Sigrid Schulz.' She would have made (and perhaps did make?) an excellent double agent, reporting on Nazi attacks on German churches and the growth of concentration camps while smiling benignly at Josef Goebbels at press conferences! She used the pen name John Dickson and often, for her own safety, wrote from Oslo or Copenhagen.

William Shirer got a phone call from her on 1 September 1939: 'At six a.m., Sigrid Schultz – bless her heart – phoned. She said "It's happened". I was very sleepy – my body and mind numbed, paralysed. I mumbled "Thanks, Sigrid" and tumbled out of bed. The war is on!'[60]

Sigrid stayed in Germany to report the early triumphs of the Wehrmacht in the war but was not, as a woman, allowed near the Front. Hurt in an air raid, she was wisely back in Chicago by early 1941.

One of the over-the-top characters on the List, and with her own modest *täterkreis*, is Maria Budberg (B249 and M195). She was born in Sakewska, in the Poltava region of the Ukraine, was a baroness known widely as Moura and she was a British secret agent. Often referred to as the 'Mata Hari of Russia', the problem, both for anyone working with her and for us researching years later, was summed up by an MI5 agent in the 1930s – 'she can drink an amazing quantity, mostly gin'. How much validity any statements she may have made to the

Gestapo, had they caught her, would have been debatable. Her own story is so full of inconsistencies, unlikely coincidences and 'dodgy' people that she makes the real Mata Hari seem quite boring.

The wife of a Tsarist diplomat based in Estonia, Moura was sitting on the powder keg of the twin revolutions that rocked Russia in 1917. During the second, the Bolshevik takeover, her husband, Count Benckendorff, was murdered by a peasant. Moura fled to the Russian Embassy in Berlin before returning to St Petersburg to attempt to sort out her family's property. In the chaos of revolution, she met Robert Bruce Lockhart (L115) at the British embassy there and they began a passionate affair. When he was transferred to Moscow, she followed and both of them were arrested by Lenin's agents on a charge of espionage. The Lubianka had a fearsome reputation as a prison where people habitually disappeared. The rumour ran that she offered the commandant sex in exchange for her release. Bruce Lockhart's followed soon after and he was recalled to Britain.

Moura now began her next conquest. Starting as a secretary for the celebrated writer Maxim Gorky, she soon became his mistress and met both Lenin and Stalin through him. In 1933, she moved to London. Gorky was old and ill (he died in 1936) and she had already met H. G. Wells (W55), another literary lion whose skin, according to Moura, smelled like honey. London adored her; she was the star of the White Russian community, glad to have got out of the Bolshevik nightmare with their lives (and often a surprisingly large amount of money). As if to underline her heroism, Hollywood made a movie about her in 1934, *British Agent*, with the urbane Leslie Howard as Bruce Lockhart and Kay Francis as 'Maria Elena'. There was a lot of shooting in night-time snowy streets and soft-edged love scenes in dark cells. No doubt Moura loved it.

So why is she on the List at all? Clearly, Schellenberg regarded her as a spy but the jury is still out. Such was the woman's duplicity and carefully crafted air of mystery that she *could* have been an agent, a double agent or even a triple agent. Like so many people in the *täterkreis* and the world of espionage generally, she knew *everybody* and could just as well have been a spy for White or Red Russia; Communist or Fascist. Ideologically, she was hollow. Her one cause seems to have been Moura Budberg and she was faithfully constant to that.

★ ★ ★

But the oddest inclusion in the List's *täterkreis* is Arthur John Maundy Gregory. Typically, the name appears both ways round but always with an extra 'r' – Maundry. The man was a consummate con artist at the heart of the 'cash for honours' scandal, which had helped bring down Lloyd George in 1922. The superlative trickster, Gregory established himself in offices in Parliament Square, literally yards from the seats of power. He lived at 10, Hyde Park Terrace and delighted in arranging urgent telephone calls when he was out dining clients. 'Number Ten for you, sir,' the maitre d' would intone; the client was impressed. At the height of his influence (Gregory, too, knew everybody) he was charging £10,000 for knighthoods, £30,000 for baronetcies and £50-100,000 for peerages. He was very much the 'go-to' man for anybody who wanted instant class and recognition in a world that seemed to be trembling on the verge of oblivion. The General Strike had rattled Britain's elite, the Red Menace was constantly on the move and there was a brave new world on the horizon that not everyone wanted to be part of.

It all came crashing down for Gregory in February 1932.

Not everyone was taken in by the opulence – he toyed with a huge diamond during business meetings – or name-dropping. A young Liberal MP, Colin Coote, summed him up perfectly – 'Gregory could not, by any possibility, live up to his trousers.'[61] He was arrested by Scotland Yard on charges under the Honours Act after complaints by a completely innocent – and rather naïve – client. He was found guilty and sent to Wormwood Scrubs, where there must have been very few people he wanted to hob-nob with.

The link with espionage is as fleeting as that of Budberg. He carried a three-page curriculum vitae with him at certain times making outrageous claims about his own credentials and contacts as well as his exploits. He claimed to have run a thousand field agents in counter-espionage during the First World War but the reality was very different. Totally unsuited to physical activity, he applied to British Intelligence several times, both during and after the war. Internal memos about him have survived – 'Don't want him' and 'No thanks' are the politest of them. Instead, Maundy Gregory served as a private in an infantry regiment for the last year of the war. At thirty-nine, he was almost too old for active service anyway.

He *had*, as a man with links to no less than forty-one London hotels, a list of people whose comings and goings would have been of interest to the authorities. He supplied Basil Thompson, Head of the Metropolitan Police's Special Branch, with a list of sixteen names of Germans in 1917, presumably because he believed them to be spies.

From the Scrubs, Gregory sailed for France, drifting from hotel to hotel until his money ran out. Friends in England (the names on his *täterkreis*?) sent him a monthly allowance of cash and 'Sir Arthur Gregory' acquired a huge fur coat and a little Pomeranian dog called Monsieur le Beau. Gregory himself spoke not a word of French but still managed to charm everyone he met.

When war broke out, he clearly had plenty of time to go home but he was still wanted on various fraud charges and perhaps thought he could use his considerable wiles on the Germans. As it became increasingly obvious that neither the French nor the British Expeditionary Force could stop the Wehrmacht, Gregory hid in a hotel at Chateauneuf du Faon in Brittany. As 'M. de Grégoire', he kept exclusively to his room. When he came out to use the bathroom, he bandaged his face, claiming with grunts that it was toothache that was making him both invisible and incomprehensible.

Technically, he *should* have been on Schellenberg's List because his ruse was not discovered until November 1940. Already seriously ill, his deportation to various camps was halted at the Val de Grace military hospital and he died there in September 1942. By that time, the List and all the other plans for the invasion of Britain were dead in the water and the world had moved on.

CHAPTER SEVEN

THE INNER SANCTUM

When details of the List first became public in Britain, several people (who had not seen it because it was not printed in its entirety until 1969) claimed to have been in the 'top ten'. They assumed, with some justification, that the 'Most Wanted' would be in rank order, probably with Churchill as public-enemy number one. It was not like that but, inevitably, it was the politicians in whom the RSHA was most interested and, in dealing with them first, I am following the order of precedence of topics as set out in the Gestapo's *Information Handbook*. For clarity's sake, I have divided the politicians into: home-grown – the leading British politicians of all parties; the vice-consulary functionaries – with whom the Reich had often dealt personally; and the foreign governments in exile.

Unsurprisingly, the Cabinet is represented in force but by no means are all members covered. Of the thirty-six listed (as of 13 May 1940), sixteen are missing. The Dominions held little interest for Schellenberg. Had the eagle landed, the

Empire would have withered and scattered, so the office held by Viscount Caldecote, who had been governor of Hong Kong since 1935, was irrelevant. So was Scotland – Ernest Brown, who had been Labour Minister under Stanley Baldwin – could slumber on in his Edinburgh offices. Andrew Duncan at the Board of Trade would find his office swallowed up by whatever economic system the Reich GB intended to set up. Harold Ramsbotham at the Board of Education would have no role – the complete indoctrination of the nation's youth would be a priority once the military conquest was over. Malcolm MacDonald need not fret over the nation's health at that Ministry; the Reich had its own systems; Strength Through Joy and the euthanasia programme, still under wraps in 1940 and known mysteriously as T4, after the address in Berlin (Tiergarten 4) where such operations were routinely carried out. The Minister of Transport was John Reith and, since he was also director of the BBC, his omission from the List is rather odd. Lord Woolton at Food and Nutrition could carry on making his meatless pies for as long as he could; bratwurst and sauerkraut were on their way to replace national fare. J. H. Shakespeare, Minister for Overseas Trade, would have no role once Britain fell. Shipping, Public Works and Pensions caused no ruffles on the mainland of Europe – all would be subsumed. The Attorney-General, Donald Somervel; the Solicitor-General, William Jowitt; and the Paymaster-General, Lord Cranborne, would all find themselves on the scrapheap of history.

The people who mattered, who *were* on the List, were those who held key positions or were individuals who had crossed the Reich in British propaganda once too often. Winston Churchill appears as *Ministerprasident* (Prime Minister) with his address at Chartwell Manor, Westerham, Kent; Amt VI A1, the Ausland Security Service under Dr Gerhard Filbert, wanted to get to know the 'warmonger' better. July was a grim month for Churchill. He made the decision to destroy the French fleet – his most difficult in the war, he would write later. He rejected Hitler's peace overtures, however half-hearted they may have been and was still holding out a vague hope that there would be some kind of rising against Hitler from within the Reich. The only positive move – and that would not become apparent for months – was the creation of the Special Operations Executive, intended to 'set Europe ablaze'. At that stage, Churchill had only just got the matches out. And his party still did not trust him fully.

That was partly because of Neville Chamberlain, C37 on the List. He is referred to, correctly, as former Prime Minister with an address in Edgbaston, Birmingham. Oddly, his London residence is still given as 10, Downing Street and that very much made the point. Discredited as he largely is today, Chamberlain still had his following as the List was being compiled and he was in the War Cabinet, however vague his new title of Lord President of the Council might sound. Churchill had divided his command into three committees; the War Cabinet, the Ministry of Defence and Home Affairs. Since he dominated the first two and left the third to Attlee, it could be argued that his control was absolute. His friends saw this as pragmatic politics; his enemies as an example of his paranoia and megalomania. Even Hitler let his ministers get on with the job. As things stood, Chamberlain was like Banquo's ghost, a stark reminder of a recent past that could have been very different. In fact, he was already seriously ill with the cancer that would kill him and underwent an operation in August. It did no good and he resigned at the end of September. He was dead two months later.

John Simon was Lord Chancellor in May. The nearest that Schellenberg could come to this role in Nazi Germany was 'similar to a Minister of Justice', but the man had moved on by July and was now Chancellor of the Exchequer. 'He will be quite innocuous [there],' Attlee had correctly said. Simon was not popular at any level of government. An alumnus of Fettes, the Edinburgh public school, a graduate of Wadham College, Oxford and a Fellow of the exclusive All Souls, he had been called to the Bar in 1899 and been returned as liberal MP for Spen Valley in 1922. He had been Foreign Secretary briefly under Ramsay MacDonald and Home Secretary at the time when Mosley's Blackshirts had gone on the rampage in the East End. He was cold and aloof, difficult to work with. Harold Nicholson called him 'a toad and a worm'. Above all, he was forever tainted by the appeasement of the 1930s and a crony of Chamberlain's, according to Hugh Dalton, 'the snakiest of the lot'. He never made it to the War Cabinet.

Viscount Halifax was another of Churchill's rivals, outnumbered by him on the crucial debates of 8/9 May. At the time, Beaverbrook had written, 'Chamberlain wanted Halifax [to replace him]. Labour wanted Halifax. Sinclair [Air Minister] wanted Halifax. The Lords wanted Halifax. The King wanted Halifax. And Halifax wanted Halifax.'

On that last point, Beaverbrook was wrong. Halifax was not made of the sternest stuff and he did not want the job. Born to the aristocracy with a missing left hand and withered arm, Halifax looms over all his contemporaries in photographs at well over six feet tall. He was deeply religious and a crafty politician, giving rise to Churchill's phrase for him – the holy fox. The product of Eton, Christ Church Oxford and All Souls, Halifax had stood as Conservative candidate for Ripon in 1910 and served with the Yorkshire Dragoons in the First World

War. He ended up, after a succession of relatively dead-end government posts, as Viceroy of India, clashing with Nehru, Gandhi and the growing clamour for independence. He met Hitler in 1937 and almost mistook him for a footman, nearly handing him his coat! He also hunted foxes with Hermann Goering, who christened him 'Halalifax'. 'Halali' was the German for 'Tally Ho'.

Halifax's position in the 1930s was not totally for appeasement but he was a doubtful re-armer. As the List was being written, he was still very interested in various German peace-feelers via the Papal nuncio in Bern and the efforts of various Finnish ministers. Churchill of course had already scuppered that as early as 28 May: 'If this long island story of ours is to end at last, let it end only when each of us lies choking in his own blood upon the ground.'

On the List, Halifax is described as *Politiker*, with his London address (88 Eaton Square), Garrowby, York and Hickleton Hall, Doncaster.

Clement Attlee's Tory enemies would have been delighted to see him referred to as 'Führer' but nothing could be further from the truth. He had been called to the Bar in 1908 after reading Law at University College, Oxford. He joined the Independent Labour Party in the same year, lectured at the London School of Economics (with its Left leanings) and worked at Toynbee Hall in London's East End with Beatrice Webb (W29) of the Fabian Society. Despite the awkward fact that his brother Tom was a Conscientious Objector in the First World War, Attlee was the penultimate man to leave Gallipoli, the disastrous Turkish campaign ill-conceived by Churchill in 1915. He was still called 'the Major' for years after the war – and, of course, is included as such on the List. He had a succession of posts in the Twenties and Thirties, supporting George Lansbury (L22), the pacifist Labour leader. Although he was anti-rearmament, Attlee was incensed by Munich and was happy to serve under Churchill, spearheading the Lord President's committee for home affairs. There was no such role as Deputy Prime Minister in 1940 – although Attlee is frequently called that today. Even so, that was, effectively, his position and he had access in that capacity to all three of Churchill's committees. He and the Prime Minister were the only two of the War Cabinet to serve right through the war. His office in May had been Lord Privy Seal, which Schellenberg dismisses contemptuously as 'an insignificant court appointment and honorary office'.

Lord Lloyd (L112), Eton and Trinity College, Cambridge, was a diehard Tory from the Quaker family who had established the High Street bank. The deaths of both his parents in 1899 meant that he never took his university degree but moved into the family financial business instead. Turned down by the snooty family of the woman he loved, he toured the East and ended up as unofficial honorary attaché in Constantinople. In the First World War, he was commissioned in the Warwickshire Yeomanry, landing with the Anzacs at Gallipoli in 1915 and later liaising with T. E. Lawrence in his extraordinary guerrilla war in the Sinai desert. With a captaincy and a DSO, he turned his attention to politics after the war and found himself at loggerheads with Gandhi as governor of Bombay. Lloyd put the pacifist leader in prison for six years.

Unsurprisingly, he opposed the Indian home rule movement and was highly suspicious of Hitler's rise to power and what followed. In May 1940, Churchill made him Secretary of State for the Colonies and later, leader of the House of Lords. He died of myeloid leukaemia at the Marylebone clinic in 1941.

The Secretary of State for India, as he was when Churchill took over the reins of government, Leo Amery's (A43) address is given as King Charles St, Whitehall. He had been born in Gorakpur, India, before Victoria had been made Queen Empress and it annoyed him that Churchill had so little time for India or its thrust for independence – 'he knew as much of the Indian problem as George III did of the American colonies'. He and Churchill went way back; they were at Harrow together. Balliol and All Souls followed, together with a spell as a war correspondent for *The Times* in the Boer War. The First World War had seen him as an Intelligence officer in the Balkans. Despite a variety of government posts, he found himself, like Churchill, in the political wilderness in the Thirties. He opposed appeasement, especially Chamberlain's notion of returning Germany's pre-First World War colonies, and was highly vocal at the overthrow of the Prime Minister. Parodying Oliver Cromwell, he said, 'You have sat too long here... Depart, I say and let us have done with you. In the name of God, go!' Chamberlain (eventually) did.

But Amery's undoubted patriotism was forever tainted by the bizarre behaviour of his son John. A bankrupt at twenty-four and guilty of running guns to Franco at exorbitant prices in the Spanish Civil War, he would go on to make radio broadcasts from Germany in 1942 and to form the ineffective British Free Corps, a Fascist unit also calling itself the Legion of St George. Captured by the Allies, John Amery was hanged for treason at Pentonville. Back in the heated debates of May 1940, Leo Amery had shouted across the House to Arthur Greenwood, 'Speak for England, Arthur.' His own son most assuredly did not.

The First Lord of the Admiralty, now that Churchill had vacated the post, was Albert Alexander (A35), as different from the Prime Minister as it was possible to be. The son of a blacksmith, he had left school at thirteen and become involved in local Labour politics. Unlike many socialists, Alexander supported the First World War and joined the Artists' Rifles. He saw no active service and became MP for Hillsborough, opposing Churchill in the General Strike of 1926. He was anti-Fascist and anti-appeasement but he also opposed the coalition government of 1939. He was the only Labour politician ever to hold the Admiralty post but he was completely overshadowed by Churchill; he had no access either to the War Room or classified information, the source of bitter animosity later when the Prime Minister appeared to be guilty of corruption and of dragging his feet in making his war aims clear. The List gives his address as Victoria Street, London.

Anthony Eden would have made a fine trophy for Schellenberg. E6 was described as War Minister with an address in Fitzharding Street. He was the glamour boy of the Conservatives in the Thirties, with an immaculate moustache, fashionable, slicked-back hair and what Harold Nicolson described as 'beautiful eyes'. The son of a baronet from County Durham, he attended Eton where he excelled as a sportsman. Fluent in French and German, he nevertheless, out of professionalism, used a translator when he met Hitler in 1934. They had nearly met before, when both men faced each other across No Man's Land on the Western Front in 1918. At nineteen, Eden was the youngest adjutant in France and, two years later, the youngest brigade-major in the British army.

Fascinated by the Middle East, Eden's heart lay in foreign policy and his political career took off in 1923. He was anti-war, like many of his generation, and put a great deal of hope in the League of Nations, the ultimately useless international body pledged to maintain world peace. As Foreign Secretary in the mid-thirties, he failed to impress Mussolini, who called him 'the best dressed fool in Europe' with his trademark

Homburg hat. Ultimately, Chamberlain's appeasement became too much and Eden resigned in February 1938.

The outbreak of war saw him as Secretary of State for the Dominions and he was not in the War Cabinet. Chamberlain's overthrow saw him elevated to War Minister but what looked in the years ahead to be a rock-solid alliance between Churchill and Eden was not so apparent at the time. His marriage was not a happy one and he suffered from a stomach ulcer throughout his parliamentary career. No doubt the hectic events of the summer of 1940 made this worse.

'Sir Archibald Sinclair' was '*Führer der Liberalen Partei*' – the Leader of the Liberal Party – according to the List (S85). In fact, by July 1940, he was much more than that. With a Scots father and an American mother, 'Archie', as he was universally known, had attended Eton and the Royal Military College at Sandhurst before service in the Life Guards in 1910. He had been Churchill's second-in-command when the ex-First Lord of the Admiralty took up a post in the trenches of the Western Front in 1916. He followed his boss back into politics, becoming Churchill's personal military secretary until 1921.

Sinclair was a fierce Liberal at a time when the party was in serious decline. Its swansong was under Lloyd George and Asquith and the arrival of the Labour Party would effectively squeeze Britain into a two-party state. There were only twenty Liberal MPs in the Commons by the 1930s and, like Churchill, Sinclair was in the wilderness.

The arrival of Churchill at Number Ten changed all that. At first, Sinclair did not have a place in the War Cabinet but Churchill needed the tiny rump of the Liberals (of which he had once been a member) on his side and Sinclair was a staunch supporter. There is no doubt that, as the war progressed, both Sinclair and Eden stood closest to Churchill, even if both were prone to feel the rough edge of his tongue. The List refers to him as 'a representative Peer of Scotland' and gives his address as Adastral House, Kingsway WC2. By the time Schellenberg was compiling it, Sinclair was Air Minister, up to his eyes co-ordinating the various fighter-command defences in the Battle of Britain.

Ernest Bevin appears on the List as B131, 'Minister (*Einkreisungspolitiker*) *Gewerkschafter*'. In some ways, the Minister of Labour was the oddest man out of Churchill's clique. He had little formal education and his West Somerset brogue was so strong that he was often misunderstood in cabinet meetings. Did he say 'You and I' or was it 'Hugh and Nye', referring to Gaitskill and Bevan, his Labour colleagues? He was a Baptist lay preacher and the founder of the country's largest union, the Transport and General Workers'. He was to the right of the Labour Party, regarding Communism (as, of course, did Hitler!) as a Jewish plot. He also opposed Fascism and appeasement, believed the strike to be a weapon of last resort and introduced the Holidays with Pay Act in 1938. Under Churchill, he was given enormous powers as Minister of Labour, diverting 48,000 conscripts to the vital coal industry as 'Bevin Boys'.

The List's D114 was Alfred Duff Cooper, '*Informiesminister*' – Minister of Information. The man and the post would have held high priority for the RSHA; they were the equivalent of Josef Goebbels' Ministry of Enlightenment and Propaganda. In that sense, the whole notion of propaganda as an organised entity with a government department was alien to British culture. There had always been propaganda, of course, but it was vague and uncoordinated, drip-fed via the bias of newspapers and the incoherent ramblings of extremist groups, Right and Left in the 1920s and 1930s. When the Mass

Observation Unit carried out its surveys during the war, it was the Ministry of Information that came in for the most flak. It was 'Cooper's snoopers' who made defeatism a crime. Times were grim and people were not even able to moan about it. The clichés that are fondly remembered now – 'Careless talk costs lives', 'Be like Dad – keep Mum' – all originated with the MoI and were less popular at the time. 'The first casualty of the war is truth,' American senator Hiram Johnson (misquoting Aeschylus) had said in 1917 and censorship meant that the public were not being told the truth. It dented morale rather than strengthened it.

Schellenberg would have been amused to know that Duff Cooper shared people's views by and large. Whereas Goebbels *was* Enlightenment and Propaganda, Duff Cooper moaned, 'The presence of so many able, undisciplined men in one Ministry was bound to lead to a great deal of internal friction… I was never happy there.'[62]

It did not help that Duff Cooper did not like journalists (unlike Goebbels, who just told them what to print) and he was constantly at odds with the three Service departments and the Foreign Office.

Duff Cooper was, nevertheless, regarded as foremost among the warmongers under Churchill. Born to a fashionable West End doctor's family, he emerged from Eton and New College, Oxford as a gambler, drinker, poet and womaniser, basing himself on one of his heroes, the eighteenth century Whig leader Charles James Fox. He won the DSO with the Grenadier Guards in the First World War, where most of his close friends were killed. Despite his marriage to society beauty Diana Manners, daughter of the Duke of Rutland, Duff Cooper continued to have affairs. Diana was stoic –'They were the flowers, but I was the tree.' He held a series of posts in the Conservative governments of the 1930s before Churchill offered him the new Ministry of Information.

Another new department was the Ministry of Economic Warfare. It is a maxim that each war a country fights costs more than the last and a war the length and breadth of the Second World War was ruinous; Britain has never truly recovered from it. Heading this department was D6 on the List, Hugh Dalton, *'Wirtschafter Universitat London'*. A lawyer born in Neath and educated at Eton and King's College, Cambridge, Dalton had served in the Army Service Corps and the Artillery in the First World War. He was Labour MP for Peckham in 1924 and was probably the most intellectual of the socialist lobby at the time. He turned the Labour Party from a pacifist support group to one of armed deterrence by 1938 and loathed the dithering of Chamberlain.

Dalton took up the post of Economic Warfare Minister on 15 May in the helter-skelter first week of Churchill's coup and, on 22 July, perhaps as Schellenberg was drawing up the final stages of the List, he was put in charge of the Special Operations Executive, specifically SO1, a collection of fascinating misfits tasked with 'words', the black propaganda which Schellenberg was pledged to defeat. It was early days, of course, and the *exact* ploys of SO1 are still overlaid with all kinds of confusion. Long classified, their efforts were finally revealed with the long-awaited Freedom of Information Act under Tony Blair, only for it to be realised that umpteen files have disappeared. No doubt Dalton – and Schellenberg – would not only have understood but approved.

The scowl of the pugnacious Max Aitken, Lord Beaverbrook, still stares at us from the black and white photographs of 1940. A Canadian by birth, the List's B65 had begun his career as a financier and businessman in Halifax, Nova Scotia. In Britain, he became an MP for Ashton-under-Lyne, receiving a peerage in 1918 and taking on the undemanding role of the Duchy of Lancaster. His heart lay in business however and by the late Thirties, he owned the *Daily Express*, the *Globe* and the *Evening Standard*, making him *the* press baron of his day. As such he made enemies, especially in various editorials in the *Express* once the war was underway. The paper was selling 2,239,000 copies a day by 1937, despite the pro-appeasement stance of its boss – 'There will be no war,' he assured his readers at the time of Munich. He did, however, produce war-winning propaganda, appointing writers Francis Willis and cartoonist David Low (L137), who also featured on the List.

Churchill, aware of the man's business flair, appointed Beaverbrook Minister for Aircraft Production, in which he exceeded even Kingsley Wood's output, raised from 80 aircraft a month to 546! As *Time* magazine put it weeks after the List was completed, 'Even if Britain goes down this Fall, it will not be Lord Beaverbrook's fault... This is a war of machines. It will be won on the assembly line.'

Like Attlee, Herbert Morrison appears twice on the List, once with his middle name – Stanley – and once without. M178 has him as '*Stadtpräsident* v. London' and M179 as 'Minister' living at 55 Archery Road, SE9. A policeman's son from Stockwell, Morrison had been blind in the right eye since he was a baby. He had been a Conscientious Objector, along with many socialists in the First World War and became Labour MP for Hackney in 1919. He was Minister of Transport under the first Labour Prime Minister Ramsay MacDonald and leader of the influential London County Council in the same year that Adolf Hitler made himself Führer for life. He largely created London's green belt and controlled the capital's transport system.

Churchill made him Minister of Supply and the Morrison shelter, an indoor cage version of the outdoor Anderson shelter, was named after him. He had spearheaded the attack on Chamberlain in the May debates that saw the Prime Minister fall. Churchill never warmed to the man – their politics were poles apart – but he acknowledged his usefulness, not just in the work he did (he became Home Secretary in October 1940) but as a senior member of the Left to keep the coalition alive.

And there the list of cabinet ministers ends. There is no Kingsley Wood, Chancellor of the Exchequer, although he is listed in the *Gestapo Handbook*. He was a friend of Chamberlain's, but not an appeaser and his work at the Air Ministry wore him out. His first (unremarkable) budget as Chancellor was delivered in the month that Schellenberg was writing the List. Perhaps the RSHA were prepared to let the man live; after all, he had famously stated in the opening weeks of the war that the Ruhr should not be bombed because it was private property! John Anderson is not on the List either. He would become Home Secretary by September – the Anderson shelter named after him.

Schellenberg may or may not have known the divisions of ideology and petty rivalries that existed within Churchill's cabinet. The point was that, in a democratic society, these were the men who called the shots and ran the country. And, increasingly in the summer of 1940, it looked as though their days were numbered.

CHAPTER EIGHT

'THEY ALSO SERVE . . .'

Below the men of cabinet rank came a number of B-Listers. The oddly typed 'Sir Cadogan' (C2a) was Alexander Cadogan, Old Etonian and Oxford historian. A backer of Eden in the Thirties, he was hugely experienced in the Foreign Office, having been present at the Versailles conference. It is doubtful whether Schellenberg knew how critical he was of the government, as Permanent Under Secretary of State for Foreign Affairs. 'It can't be said,' he wrote in his diary, 'that our "policy" so far has been successful. In fact, we haven't got a policy; we merely wait to see what will happen to us next.'[63] Such talk, if uttered in public, would have cost him his job and perhaps even a spell in gaol.

On the fringes, but oddly at the centre of events, were Robert Boothby and Brendan Bracken. Long before he became a notorious roué, mixing with the Kray brothers in the 1960s, Bob Boothby (B188) was Churchill's parliamentary secretary. Eton, Magdalen, Oxford and the Brigade of Guards gave Boothby the entrée to

Conservative politics as MP for Aberdeen in 1924. He launched the Popular Front in 1936; a loose alliance of Labour, Liberal and Communist supporters who, bizarrely perhaps, threw in their lot with the anti-appeasers among the Conservatives. Boothby was a junior minister at Lord Woolton's Ministry of Food in 1940. He had a long affair with Dorothy Macmillan, the wife of Harold, the future Prime Minister, and was a notorious bisexual. In certain circles, even in his university days, he was known as the Palladium because he was 'twice nightly'! When he visited Germany in the Thirties, he allegedly said 'Heil Boothby' in response to the traditional Nazi greeting.

Brendan Bracken (B199) was a very different character. A builder's son from County Tipperary, he was 'Churchill's Irishman' and 'the Tory thug'. He stands out in the photographs of the time with his tightly curled auburn hair and sharp suits. Expelled for bad behaviour from his Jesuit school, he wandered in Australia for a while before settling down to academic success at Sedbergh. He became MP for North Paddington in 1929 and became Churchill's *chela* (the Hindi word for disciple). Bracken's problem was that he felt he had to play down the Irish connection if he was to succeed in English politics. The Easter rising of 1916 was a recent memory and the IRA an active, and in wartime potentially dangerous, force. He could be economical with the truth in other areas. He put it about that his brother had been killed in the Norway campaign of 1940, whereas the man was alive and well in Ireland, continually pestering Bracken for money! He joined Churchill's Other Club in the Pinafore Room at the Savoy hotel and pushed his boss to replace Chamberlain in May 1940. Churchill made him a member of the Privy Council. The List has him down, vaguely, as *'Direcktor, Abgeordnetr'* (deputy) with an address at 8, North St, SW1.

B261 Lord Burghley was David Cecil, part of an illustrious family that had ruled Britain since the first Elizabeth's day, two centuries before Germany was born. Cecil himself attended Eton and Magdalene, Cambridge, where he famously ran 380 yards in 42½ seconds as the Great Trinity clock was striking.[64] A star of the 1924 Olympics, he was the best hurdler in England. His address on the List is given as St James Court, Buckingham Gate but he actually had no active role in politics, resigning on the outbreak of war and taking up the rank of Staff Captain in tank supply.

Sir Stafford Cripps (C103) was ambassador to Moscow and properly belongs perhaps to the next section of this chapter. He would not become a key figure in the cabinet until the following year. A Wykehamist and chemistry graduate from University College, London, he had driven a Red Cross ambulance in the First World War and, called to the Bar in 1913, became the highest paid lawyer in the country between the wars. He founded the Socialist League in 1932 and opposed re-armament and appeasement in equal measure. Seven years later, he found himself being expelled from the Labour Party for dabbling with the Popular Front.

One of the oddities in the List's political section is Lord Dawson of Penn (D27). His description is 'Mitunterzeichner der engl. Rundunkbotschaft an das deutsche Volk im Jahre 1939', whereas he actually was the royal family's doctor. Why a physician should have been broadcasting to the Reich in the year that war broke out is unclear. We know from his diary that he hastened the end of George V in 1935, pumping cocaine and morphine into his veins. This would still be regarded as a decidedly controversial move today (although of course not uncommon in the medical fraternity) but his reason for doing so, it was said, was that *The Times* would carry the news to the British people, rather than a lesser publication later in the day!

Then there was the family connection, which RSHA had not missed. Edwin Duncan-Sandys (D122) held no particular brief in 1940; in fact he was oddly pro-German in the Thirties, believing that Britain's future lay with her colonies. He had fought in Norway in the year of the List and had won an important case for parliamentary privilege three years earlier, which led to the rewriting of the Official Secrets Act. The sole reason he appears on the List is that he was married to Diana Churchill and was, therefore, the son-in-law of the Prime Minister.

The Minister without Portfolio was Arthur Greenwood. He lived at 23 Old Queen St, SW1 and was a competent, if uninspiring, Labour politician from Leeds, the son of a painter and decorator. As Minister of Health in the Thirties, he had aided slum clearance and improved widows' pensions. He happened to be in a key position twice in the period of the List. First, he was deputising for Attlee on 2 September 1939 as the country was panicking over the invasion of Poland. In the lengthy, often bitter debates of the cabinet responding to various German peace offers in the first half of 1940, it was Greenwood's vote (and Anthony Eden's) that swayed the response in Churchill's favour – no surrender; no compromise.

Harold Macmillan (M16), cuckolded so brazenly by Bob Boothby, was the son of the publishing house of the same name. Home taught before Eton and Balliol, he was wounded as a captain with the Grenadier Guards and it took four years for his damaged hip to mend. Out of twenty-eight Balliol men, he and only one other survived. Dorothy Cavendish became his wife before taking up with Boothby in 1929 and Macmillan was advised by all and sundry to put up with it if he wanted a serious political career. Divorce had a whiff of unacceptability about it at the time and the whole thing probably contributed to Macmillan's nervous breakdown in 1931. 'Chips' Channon, inveterate gossip and man-about-town, found him the 'unprepossessing, bookish, eccentric member for Stockton-on-Tees'. At first a supporter of Chamberlain, Macmillan was outraged by Munich and helped bring the Prime Minister down in the May debates, singing a hearty rendition of 'Rule Britannia' in the House along with Colonel Josiah Wedgwood. On 29 May, he was Permanent Secretary to the Ministry of Supply under Beaverbrook.

Harold Nicolson was accurately described in the List as writer and politician, with his address as 4, King's Bench walk, but there is no mention of his country home at Sissinghurst, Kent. He was Labour MP for West Leicester in 1935 but, as we have seen, Churchill personally requested him to 'help Duff at the Ministry of Information' in the May of 1940. His diaries and letters are a fascinating source of the inner workings of Whitehall in the period of the List, although, of course, he had no idea of its existence. A committed Francophile, he made two trips to the country, the last in March before it fell. He disliked Charles de Gaulle, the arrogant and insufferable leader of the Free French, but admired him for his leadership. As Schellenberg finished the List, Nicolson wrote to his wife, Vita Sackville-West:

'I have always loved England. But now I am in love with England. What a people! What a chance! The whole of Europe humiliated except us. And the chance that by our stubbornness we shall give victory to the world!'

John Sankey is dismissed in the List as 'Jurist' and 'Fabian Society', with its address at 13, Albert Place, W8. A product of Lansing College and Jesus, Oxford, he was called to the Bar in 1892, a KC by 1909 and, as Baron Sankey of Moreton, Lord Chancellor under Ramsay MacDonald. It was he who created the notion now enshrined in British civil law of 'beyond reasonable doubt', then referred to as the 'golden thread'. In the year of the List, he drew up the Declaration of the Rights of Man, backed by the *Daily Herald* and the National Peace Council, of which Sankey was chairman. Before more modern reworkings on human rights, it was the 1940 Sankey version that was universally accepted. Of its key eleven points, the Nazis would have accepted none of them.

What strikes a slightly odd chord in the List today is the number of Left wing politicians mentioned, by no means all of them directly in politics. We have to see this in context. The arch enemy of the Reich, despite the transparent duplicity of the Molotov-Ribbentrop pact, was Communism and it was often difficult to tell where hard-line Communism ended and softer socialism began. The socialist elements of the Nazi Party's original twenty-five points had long since disappeared. The *Gestapo Handbook* was aware that Labour leaders were often the product of the same public schools and universities as their Conservative counterparts but they could not speak for the rank and file. The Labour Party had not impressed in its two outings in power but it was very much the second party in Britain, the Liberals in sharp decline. The roots of socialism in Britain lay in the response of the working class to the social and economic injustices of the nineteenth century and, perhaps because of that, Victorian politicians and activists found themselves on the List.

Megan Lloyd George (L111) was not *quite* a Victorian. She was the youngest child of the former Prime Minister and was already appearing in public at the age of eight. She became the first female MP for Wales, representing Anglesey in 1929, a seat she held until long after the war. Exactly why she should be there – her far more famous father is conspicuously absent – is not clear. She became a member of a Radical Action group but that was not until the year after the List. Perhaps Megan was the result of a harassed secretary beavering away in a sweltering Berlin office on a Friday afternoon!

Almost as inexplicable is P14, Sylvia Pankhurst. Her whole family are, of course, forever associated with female emancipation, the Independent Labour Party and women's rights. The Nazis had no patience with any of this. Women in the Reich were expected to know their place, producing children for the next thousand years and being given medals for it. On the rare occasions when they *were* given power, they were terrifying. In her diary of January 1941, Missie Vassiltchikov wrote, 'when they have big offices, German women can be quite difficult, as their femininity somehow recedes into the background.' Nobody could be more impressive than Josef Goebbels' pet filmmaker Leni Riefenstahl. And that is before we shy away from the careers of Irma Grese and Ilse Koch, the murderers of Auschwitz and Buchenwald respectively. Against them, the youngest Pankhurst, for all her mother's daring exploits bordering on terrorism before the First World War, seems a pussy cat. Votes for women were won in 1928 and Sylvia had less to fight for. She had opposed the First World War and supported the International Women's Peace Congress at The Hague in 1915. She was a committed Communist to the extent that MI5 were monitoring her from 1936. In the year of the List, Sylvia was busy compiling one of her own. She sent the names of active Fascists at large in the country to Viscount Swinton, who was looking, on Churchill's behalf, into the existence of a Fifth Column in Britain. She pointed out that anti-Fascists were in gaol. Swinton's dismissive comment in the margin of her letter reads, 'I should think a most doubtful source of information.' The List has Sylvia as secretary of the Matteotic Women's League so, not only had she sinned against the Reich by her Left orientation but she openly supported an avowed opponent of Mussolini. Giacomo Matteotti was an Italian Socialist MP who not only denounced Fascism in the Chamber of Deputies but wrote inflammatory books against it too. He was stabbed to death in August 1924 during a botched kidnap attempt – Mussolini's role in the murder was never established.

Swinton might have been more impressed by a trio of feisty ladies determined to grab international politics by the scruff of its neck. A79 led them; she was Catherine, Duchess of Atholl and Marchioness of Tullibardine, with a town house in Elm Park Gardens, SW10 and the family seat of Blair Castle in Perethshire. Kitty Ramsay, as she had once been, was educated at Wimbledon High School and sat on the public-health committee, which one day would form the National Health Service. She was also private secretary to the Board of Education in the Twenties and Scottish Unionist MP for Kinross and West Perthshire. In 1931, she slammed the failure of the Russian revolution with her book *The Conscription of a People* and resigned her parliamentary seat as a protest against the 'national socialist tendencies of the [Baldwin] government's domestic policy'.

R12, Eleanor Rathbone, was the daughter of a social reformer and devoted herself to the Liverpool slums, despite her own Oxford University background. She wrote articles for the Suffragette cause and, during the First World War, ran the '1918 Club', a support group for the wives and dependants of soldiers, which is still running today. She argued for family allowances, opposed the government's policy in Ireland and, as MP for the Combined English Universities, pushed for free milk for children hit by the Depression. Her reputation was formidable – junior ministers and Foreign Office civil servants hid behind columns in the House to avoid her wrath. Her cousin was the best of the actors who ever played Sherlock Holmes; Basil Rathbone.

The third of the trio was W80, Ellen Wilkinson. Born in Manchester to a cotton broker and his wife, she was a bright and outspoken girl who won a scholarship to Manchester University. A staunch socialist and supportive of women's suffrage, she joined the Trade Union movement; her opponents accused her of 'unreasonable guerrilla warfare'. By 1921, she was an avowed Communist and represented Middlesbrough from 1924, writing a brilliant account of the 1936 Jarrow March – *The Town That Was Murdered*.

All three of them went to Spain in 1937, reporting on the atrocities of the Civil War. *So* partisan was the former Kitty Ramsay that the British press dubbed her the 'Red Duchess'.

Beatrice Potter went *way* back. W29 was married to another Socialist social pioneer, Sidney Webb (P25). Beatrice was an extraordinary woman, who went 'underground' in the 1880s, taking on menial work in the sweatshops to report on prostitution and poverty. No doubt her experiences here of the only existing political parties – Conservative and Liberal – doing almost nothing for the poor led her towards the Labour Movement as a viable alternative. Both she and Sidney were both active Trades Unionists and spent two months in the USSR in 1932, choosing to turn a blind eye to Stalin's excesses. Economic theorists and staunch members of the Co-operative movement, the pair produced an excellent history of British

Trades Unionism. Webb himself had set up the School of Economics with Fabian Socialist funds and was a founder member of the Coefficients, a monthly Left-wing dining club. He was MP for Seaham in 1922 but resigned from mainstream politics eight years later because of ill health. Writing extensively on poverty, and establishing the famous Clause IV on public ownership of industry for the Labour Party, it must have come as something of a shock to his followers when he was made Baron Passfield in 1929. It is under this name that he appears on the List. The Webbs' influence in 1940 was negligible. Likewise, T35, Ben Tillett, the tough, tiny orator who led the London dockers in their demand for their 'tanner' (2½p) in 1889. All that was a long time ago; Tillett, at eighty, was no longer a firebrand and it is a surprise to find him on the List at all.

But the strangest entry from the Left must be George Lansbury, grandfather of the actress Angela. He was dedicated to peace and appeasement and resigned from the Labour Party in 1935 when he felt it was being too belligerent. He met Mussolini on a tour of Europe in 1937 and found him a bizarre 'mixture of Lloyd George, Stanley Baldwin and Winston Churchill'. As President of the Peace Pledge Union, he was nominated for the Nobel Peace prize in the year of the List. Respected, stubborn and lovable, there was one problem with Lansbury's entry – he had died of stomach cancer on 7 May 1940. His ashes were scattered at sea – 'I desire this,' his will had said, 'because although I love England very dearly, I am a convinced internationalist.' The closest that Schellenberg could get to him was when the Luftwaffe flattened his home at 39 Bow Road in the Blitz.

★ ★ ★

The List is littered with a galaxy of Consuls, Vice Consuls, Chargés d'Affaires, Envoys and Attachés who were essentially 'our men in' various countries. They were often at the sharp end of diplomacy and, in the days before leaders of countries picked up the phone and talked directly to each other, were probably taking a huge chance. 'Don't shoot the messenger' is still a common phrase today – Shakespeare is full of beleaguered leaders from Richard III to Macbeth slapping such men around the head, venting their anger on the luckless individual with the bad news. So, when Neville Chamberlain spoke to the nation on 3 September 1939 – 'This morning, the British ambassador in Berlin handed the German government a final note' – he was talking about Neville Henderson (D101 on the List), who had to beard Ribbentrop in his den. Henderson was an appeaser; most diplomats developed an affection for the country which hosted them. In Henderson's case, he had served in France, Yugoslavia and Argentina before taking up Berlin in 1937. He believed, as did much of Europe, that Hitler could be controlled – 'If we handle him right, my belief is that he will gradually become more pacific. But if we treat him as a pariah or a mad dog, we shall turn him finally and irrevocably into one.' The man was ill with cancer throughout the Munich crisis and returned to London for treatment. He clashed with Cadogan at the Foreign Office, desperate to keep rearmament a close secret.

The whirlwind events of early September 1939 are confused. Convention dictated that diplomatic staffs, on the outbreak of war, were allowed to leave their host country but, in Henderson's case, this was Nazi Germany, the gangster empire where they did not play by the rules. According to *The Times* of 4 September, Henderson and his staff passed their affairs to the American Embassy and prepared to leave. Some accounts say that they were arrested by the Gestapo and allowed to go on the 7th in a closely guarded train. In the meantime, Henderson's opposite number, the German Chargé d'Affaires, Dr Kordt, passed his paperwork to the Swiss embassy in London and left for Victoria, crossing to Rotterdam by steamship. 'British and German diplomacy,' said *The Times* in a masterly piece of under-reporting, 'was severed'. Henderson's subsequent book, *Failure of a Mission: Berlin 1937–39*, was published in the same year as the List. In it, he spoke highly of many of the Nazi high command, especially Goering, but, like most people, he had little time for Ribbentrop. Henderson was given no more assignments before his death in 1942.

Most of the diplomats on the List are today forgotten. They were almost exclusively the product of the public schools and Oxbridge and were, almost by definition, multi-lingual. One or two, perhaps, deserve a special mention. A82, Werner Aue, of Albion Villas, had been the British Vice Consul in Antwerp. He was one of eighteen people on the original List that had a photograph appended, which implies that he was, perhaps, *very* wanted; alternatively, it could mean that he was so bland and unknown that a photograph was necessary to track him down. Had he been found, the Hanover police would have shot him.

George Ogilvie-Forbes (O11) had served as Counsellor in Iraq in the mid-Thirties, in Spain during the Civil War, and ended up in Berlin by 1937. He had been a captain in the Scottish Horse in the First World War and extended his diplomatic brief considerably by helping a number of Jewish children to escape west on the *kindertransporten*. By 1940, he was with the British legation in Norway, for as long as the country held out.

Another diplomat who stands out was Robert Smallbones

(S102). With an Austrian parent and an Oxford degree he was a natural for the consular service which he joined in 1910. He had effectively ended slavery in Portuguese West Africa (today's Angola) and was an outspoken critic of the Czechoslovakian government's treatment of minorities. 'Bones' was described in the *Jewish Chronicle* as 'the diplomat who faced down the Gestapo'. As Consul-General in Frankfurt until 1939, he visited internment camps, demanding the release of Jews. He provided space in his official residence for refugees and told his noisy daughter Irene to use her whip on any Nazi agents who came snooping. It is estimated that he saved up to 48,000 Jews by October 1939 and he was posthumously given a Hero of the Holocaust medal. On the outbreak of war, he and his staff sailed on the SS *Avila Star* for Brazil.

★ ★ ★

It is difficult to know where to place His Serene Highness Ernst Rudiger Camillo, Fürst von Starhemberg (S7 and 8), if only because he represented no dispossessed government, merely a social class outmanoeuvred by the bullying 'democracy' of the Nazis. Why the man should be listed twice, one above the other, is unclear. S7 gives his political role – 'Leiter d. osterr. Heimwehr' – and S8 refers to him as 'brit. *Flugeroffizer*' (British pilot). The prince was born at Eferding, Austria in 1899 and represented the Catholic and Conservative Party in the Bundesrat. A Right-winger, as most Austro-German aristocrats were, von Starhemberg became disillusioned with the Nazis after the abortive Beer Hall Putsch and became leader of the Heimwehr, a party which won only eight seats in the elections of 1930.

When Engelbert Dollfuss became chancellor of Austria in 1934, he asked von Starhemberg to create the Fatherland Front, an amalgam of minority parties which were broadly Fascist. On 25 July of that year, Dollfuss was shot in the throat in a badly bungled Nazi-orchestrated coup and allowed to bleed to death. Von Starhemberg briefly ran the country in the hysterical aftermath. Even when Kurt Schuschnigg became head of state, von Starhemberg was kept on to achieve some sort of cohesion and to keep Austria independent of Nazi encroachment.

The two men inevitably clashed in May 1936 and the prince travelled first to Switzerland and then to Britain. He served with both the Free French and British forces during the war, which he abruptly left in 1942 to spend thirteen years in Argentina. Fascism seems to have haunted von Starhemberg – when the dictator Juan Peron came to power in 1955, the dispossessed aristocrat went home to Austria to die.

★ ★ ★

'Miniature Europe in London' was how the Glasgow *Herald* summed up the unprecedented diplomatic situation during the war. Eventually, there would be eight governments in exile based there, along with at least two deposed heads of state and one officially sanctioned Resistance movement headquarters (the Netherlands, based at first in the Dutch Reformed Church at 7, Austin Friars). That total had not been reached in the summer of 1940. Belgium's Prime Minister, Hubert Pierlot, did not arrive until late October, the Luxembourg government a month later. Norway's King Haakon and Crown Prince Olav were based at the Norwegian Embassy in Kensington Palace Gardens but they were often the guests of George VI at Buckingham Palace and also had a suite at Claridge's. Their prime minister, Johan Nygaardsvold, met with his cabinet at Kingston House North in Prince's Gate. The Poles split their command. President Wladyslaw Raczkriewicz (R2) lived at 43

Eaton Place; his army commander, Wladyslaw Sikorski (S64) at 47 Portland Place. Edward Benes, the Czech president, had his headquarters at 26 Gwendoline Avenue, Putney (as the List confirms) and his Intelligence service was at Portchester Gate in the Bayswater Road. It was here that the assassination of Reinhard Heydrich would be planned in May 1942.

The position of the Free French was anomalous. WHY NOT LOCK UP GENERAL DE GAULLE? had been the mischievous title of an article written by the young Michael Foot in the *Evening Standard*. He was referring to the often ridiculous and arbitrary practice of rounding up and interning foreigners which was a feature of the first year of war. Bearing in mind how difficult de Gaulle was, it was probably a question Churchill often asked himself! Technically, as the British government had never broken off diplomatic relations with Marshal Petain's Vichy France, it could not recognise the Free French. Even so, they were given full diplomatic status and were based at 1, Dorset Square. The RSHA wanted them all but especially, perhaps, they wanted Charles de Gaulle.

G13 is referred to, rather contemptuously, as 'former French general'. He was born in Lille in 1890, of a devout Catholic family which had once owned extensive lands in Normandy and Burgundy. Fascinated by military history, as a boy he had read Froissart's *Chronicles* by the time he was ten and inevitably attended the prestigious military academy at St Cyr when he was called 'the great asparagus' because of his height – he was 6ft 5in. He was a platoon commander of the 33rd Regiment in the First World War, wounded at Dinant and his commanding officer was the same Marshal Petain who would go on to run the Vichy government in Hitler's war. His wound had meant that he had to wear his wedding ring on his right hand for the rest of his life. With a formal, stiff disposition, de

Gaulle came to be known at the front as 'the constable' and, as a prisoner of war, wrote his first book, as well as making five unsuccessful escape attempts.

After the war, de Gaulle served with the French military mission to Poland in the war with Russia that ended in 1921 and he was awarded the Vistuti Militari cross, Poland's highest award for valour. He served with the army of occupation in the Rhineland in 1924 and was a lieutenant colonel six years later. Interestingly, his book, *Toward a Professional Army*, sold only 700 copies in France, still fatally wedded to outdated Napoleonic tactics as the country's military were, but 7,000 in Germany. Even Hitler was said to have read it.

At the outbreak of war, de Gaulle was still only a colonel because of his irritating habit of annoying his superiors. He was impressive as a tank commander in the German invasion of France but a lack of air support meant that he had to fall back to the coast along with everybody else. On 5 June, the beleaguered Paul Reynaud made de Gaulle Under Secretary of State for National Defence and War, co-ordinating with Gort's BEF. He opposed surrender and advocated a move of the French government to Algeria. Two weeks later, with France beaten and Vichy in place, de Gaulle and a team of staff officers flew to London with 100,000 francs. On the 18th he broadcast to the French people via the BBC, exhorting them not to give up; that a 'free French' movement was building across the Channel, waiting for its chance to liberate the country. His time in London was hardly peaceful. Abrasive and arrogant, he upset most of the people he worked with, having little but contempt for the 'Anglo-Saxons' who had taken him in. It could have been worse. He had been tried by court martial in absentia in France and sentenced to death by Vichy on 2 August.

Edouard Benes (B98) is accorded his full courtesy title on the List – Doctor of Philosophy, ex-President of the Czech Republic. The Prague police, inevitably, had marked his card but he would have to answer to no less than three Amte of the RSHA. Schellenberg was not sure of the man's exact date of birth (it was 1884) but such things were unimportant in the scheme of things. Benes was born in Kozlay in what was then still Bohemia in the vast, ungovernable Austro-Hungarian Empire. He read Law at Charles University in Prague and attended the Sorbonne, obtaining his doctorate in 1908. During the First World War, he became one of the leaders of an independent Czech movement: a Resistance organisation confusingly called the *Maffia*. He sat on the Czech National Council in Paris and, with Tomas Masaryk, formed the formidable Czech Legion of 1,500,000 fighting men. With the creation of Czechoslovakia at Versailles, Benes became Foreign Minister and was well known as a prominent speaker at the League of Nations.

When the Sudetenland crisis emerged, Benes obviously opposed Hitler's fatuous and blatant takeover. Excluded from the Munich talks by the bullying of the Germans and Italians, Benes was forced to resign by October 1938. Soon after the List was compiled, the President moved from Gwendoline Avenue for safety during the Blitz and ended up in the abbey at Aston Abbots near Aylesbury. Benes himself appears twice, the second entry referring to him as chairman of the Czech National Liberation Committee. His wife Hanna follows him on the List, every bit as much of a political firebrand as her husband.

On his staff was M83, Jan Masaryk, described as Czech envoy and foreign minister in London. He was the son of Tomas, the first president of Czechoslovakia in 1918 and had received a scrappy education in the USA, where he had worked for a time as a drifter. He had fought for the Austro-Hungarian army in the First World War and become the Czech Chargé d'Affaires in Washington the following year. By 1925, he was ambassador to Britain and was still there at the time of the Sudetenland, over which he resigned his post in protest. The government's response was hardly Chamberlain's finest hour but it was in keeping with the general tenor of appeasement then in vogue. Masaryk was appointed Foreign Minister by Benes and made regular broadcasts to his home country courtesy of the BBC. He often stayed with Benes at Wingrave or Aston Abbots. Later in the war, he told an amusing story to Harold Nicolson. Before the war, Konrad Henlein, leader of the Sudeten German Party, had come to see Masaryk at the Czech Legation in London. With him was an SS thug. 'My friend here,' said Henlein, 'accompanies me wherever I go.' Msaryk whistled up his Aberdeen terrier and said, smiling, 'My friend here accompanies *me* wherever I go.' The Czechs laughed. The German did not.

Jan Masaryk was found dead in 1948 in the courtyard outside his residence in Prague. He had committed suicide by jumping out of the bathroom window. 'Mr Masaryk,' a shrewd commentator said at the time, 'was a very neat man. So neat that he carefully closed the window behind him as he jumped.' Masaryk, like so many others, was a victim of 'Uncle Joe' Stalin and by 1945 it was clear that Czechoslovakia had just swapped one vicious totalitarian master for another. Edouard Benes perished in the same year as Masaryk. Schellenberg's gripe against Masaryk was that he was supporting 'the highly treacherous organisations and operations in the protectorate, as well as arranging unscrupulous agitation and horror propaganda.'[65] Pots and kettles.

Uniquely, the Czech émigré organisation has a separate section in the *Gestapo Handbook*. Before the war, the Czech links were purely cultural, with the Foreign Institute at 26, Gloucester Road, London and 26, Ann Street, Jersey in the Channel Islands. Johann Sramek (S144) was Prime Minister, but he was effectively eclipsed by Masaryk. The cabinet ministers were: Jan Becke (B74); Naromir Necas (N9); Stefan Osusky (S87 and 88); Eduard Outraya, who appears three times (O41, 42 and 43) in his various roles as industrialist, financier and politician; Herbert Ripka (R70) described as an editor; Juraj Slavek (S100); Rudolf Viest (V23) and the ex-commander-in-chief of the Czech Legion in France, General Sergei Ingre (I7).

In the exiled Polish section of the List, Wladyslaw Raczkiewicz had a long, proud history of patriotism. His grandfather had fought the Russians as long ago as 1863 and his own law studies at St Petersburg University had been interrupted by the Tsar's dreaded secret police, the Ochrana, on account of Raczkiewicz's Polish patriotic fervour. He had nevertheless fought for Russia in the First World War and, with the outbreak of revolution in 1917, joined the 1st Polish Army Corps. As a politician, he was four times Minister of the Interior between the wars and was governor of Pomerania when *Fall Weiss* hit home. The existing president, Moscicki, threw the Polish hot potato in Raczkiewicz's direction and resigned. Raczkiewicz appointed Sikorski as his prime minister and army commander and fled to Paris to continue the war from there. He was later personally welcomed to London by George VI, who assured him of his support and loyalty.

Equally welcome was K126, Stanislav Kot. Born in Ruda, then part of the Austro-Hungarian Empire, he studied History and Philosophy at the University of Lvov and obtained his doctorate in 1911. Fluent in several languages and widely travelled, he published the *Polish News* weekly from 1919 and, by the following year, was professor at the Jagiellonian University in Krakow, ultimately the author of fifty-four books. In 1933, he was sacked for trying to protect the autonomy of the university and joined the Right wing of the People's Party. At the time of the List, he was Minister of Internal Affairs of the exiled government.

Thousands of Poles had already reached Britain before the fall of France, and the air force, in particular, far more experienced than the RAF, cut a swathe through hordes of admiring British girls as they cut similar – and more deadly – swathes through the Luftwaffe as the List was being compiled. Already President of the Poles Abroad organisation, Raczkiewicz was stoic and dignified as a man with no country. But it was Sikorski who was larger than life and we are left with the sense that he was the *real* target of the RSHA: three Amte had signed up for him.

Wladyslaw Sikorski was born in Tuszov in Galicia, then part of the Austro-Hungarian Empire, and was the son of a teacher. He studied engineering at Lvov polytechnic and became involved in various paramilitary groups. He ended up a colonel at the end of the First World War but, a rebel to the last, was imprisoned briefly for refusing to take the oath to the Habsburg emperor. By 1918, he was busy reorganising the Polish army in the war against Russia in the Ukraine and was promoted to general. In the Twenties he held key government posts but fell foul of Josef Pilsudski, Field Marshal in 1926, and spent years writing military theory. Like Winston Churchill, he foresaw the rise of an ambitious and belligerent Reich. Pilsudski's venom permeated the appointments system and, even after the man had gone (he died in 1935) and *Fall Weiss* was a reality, Sikorski found himself unemployed. He escaped through Romania to Paris, where he linked up with Raczkiewicz and received the appointments he would hold for the next three years. His warnings about Russian duplicity fell on deaf ears, despite the fact that the USSR could be said to be Britain's enemy until Operation Barbarossa changed the European dynamic. Like de Gaulle, Sikorski was never an easy man to get on with and he was killed in a plane crash on 4 July 1943 near Gibraltar. Perhaps there was, in Schellenberg's eyes, some kind of God.

CHAPTER NINE

'ENEMY CULTURAL INSTITUTES'

In the year that Hitler came to power, an extraordinary motion was put before the Oxford Union, the university's debating chamber – 'that this House will in no circumstances fight for its king and country.' It was carried by 275 votes to 153. Kenelm Digby, who proposed the motion, came out with one of the most fatuous pieces of nonsense ever heard in Oxford: 'It is no mere coincidence that the only country fighting for the cause of peace, Soviet Russia, is the country that has rid itself of the war-mongering clique.'

Even allowing for the dodgy rhetoric of a country *fighting* for peace, it is difficult to see how wider of the mark of reality Digby could be. Within six years, Stalin would gleefully join Hitler in dismembering Poland and was already, by the year of the debate, responsible for the deaths of six to eight million kulaks (land-owning peasants) in the Ukraine.

Middle England, especially the generation who had actually

fought the First World War, unlike Digby's, which had not, was outraged. The *Telegraph* snarled:

> 'There is no question that the woozy-minded Communists, the practical jokers and the sexual indeterminates of Oxford, have scored a great success... Even the plea of immaturity, or the irresistible passion of the undergraduate for posing, cannot excuse such a contemptible and indecent action as the passing of that resolution.'[66]

The mayor of Oxford was ashamed. Cambridge threatened to pull out of the boat race. Every man who voted for the resolution was sent a white feather, the Victorian symbol of cowardice. Churchill joined in the horror, referring to 'that abject, squalid, shameless avowal ... It is a very disquieting and disgusting symptom.'[67]

It was made all the worse by the fact that the universities of Melbourne, Toronto and Cape Town all said they *would* fight for king and country, putting the mother country to shame.

It is not clear whether Walter Schellenberg knew of the debate but, in 1933, the Nazis made little capital out of it, if only because they were busy consolidating power in Germany itself. The journalist Patrick Leigh Fermor, later to be involved in the Cretan resistance in the war, was eighteen at the time and believed that 'England was too far gone in degeneracy and frivolity to present a problem'[68] for the Reich, should it ever come to an invasion.

And that was Schellenberg's problem. It is very likely that most, if not all, of the 275 'Bolshies' of 1933, *did*, in fact, serve king and country six years later, if only because, by virtue of conscription, they had little choice. Schellenberg and the other writers of the *Gestapo Handbook* considered the British educational establishments – the public schools and the universities – as their enemies.

The *Handbook* refers to 'about 150 public schools', the best known of which are Eton, Harrow and Winchester. In a debate on his war aims in January 1941, Churchill used the Latin phrase *primus inter pares* (first among equals). There were cries of 'Translate!' in the Chamber. '"Certainly I shall translate," – then he pauses and turns to his right – "for the benefit of any Old Etonians who may be present."' Churchill, of course, was an old Harrovian. It would be surprising if there were any schoolmasters from those schools on the List, even though Schellenberg understood perfectly well that this tiny cohort of boys went on to dominate politics and fill the corridors of power.

The universities were a different matter, especially since they housed the enemies of the Reich, the Jewish academics who had been kicked out of Germany by Hitler's decree of 1933. This was merely a step towards the Holocaust, excluding Jews from public sector employment, which included the universities. President Hindenberg insisted that there should be exceptions. Any First World War veteran or child of such a veteran would not forfeit their posts. On his death the following year however, the law was applied to everybody. The most famous of all the Jewish academics who left Germany – Albert Einstein – is not on the List. He jumped before he was pushed, emigrating briefly to Britain before moving on permanently to the United States. Of the identifiable academics on the List,[69] 88 per cent are German refugees, all of them Jews. They often got their new posts in Britain through contacts among the international scientific community and they were funded either by the Rockefeller Foundation or William Beveridge's

Academic Assistance Council. In a few cases, the universities paid for these extra lecturers themselves – Leeds had its own system, as did Somerville, Oxford. The word *privatdozent* occurs many times in the List. It was a qualification enabling a lecturer to teach to degree level, tested by means of a dissertation and did not necessarily carry a salary.

The charge has often been made that science effectively stopped in the Reich after 1933 and certainly the self-inflicted 'brain drain' of the new laws did the cause of German academic rigour no good at all. In terms of the war effort, it allowed the Allies to gain the initiative in the production of the atom bomb, both in Britain (where the research was carried out under the code name of 'Tube Alloys') and in the United States, where it became the Manhattan Project.

Why did Schellenberg target these academics on the List? Some were brilliant scientists, so perhaps the intention was to use them on military projects. It was precisely what the Americans were to do after 1945. Werner von Braun was the most famous of the Reich's rocket scientists whose services were sought for the American space programme of the 1950s. Von Braun had built the V2 rockets, which had brought a new Blitz to British cities in 1944-45; there were those who wanted the man hanged at Nuremberg. Alternatively, it may be that the inclusion of those people on the List is purely vindictive. By 1940, the action against Jews was far more vicious than it had been in 1933; the *Einsatzgruppen* had butchered thousands in Poland, for instance. Not content with removing them from their livelihoods, perhaps the Reich now wanted them dead. It is difficult to see what value to a blinkered, Teutonic-oriented state an expert on classical Greek poetry, like the sixty-year-old Dr Paul Jacobsthal (J8), would have. He had obtained his doctorate at Bonn in 1912 and had taught at Marburg University. During his enforced exile at Christ Church, Oxford, he studied the Celts.

The author of *Displaced German Scholars* probably thought he was highlighting a political and racial evil when he published a list of such people in Britain in 1936. All he was actually doing, of course, was providing a useful blueprint for Schellenberg to use four years later on a list of his own.

We cannot examine all ninety-eight of those refugees for reasons of space but some clearly stand out. C35 was Dr Ernest Chain, last heard of by Schellenberg at Oxford. He had obtained his doctorate in biochemistry and physiology and, in Britain, by 1934, had come across Alexander Fleming's paper on penicillin. He and Howard Florey worked on it, taking 125 gallons of broth to make a single tablet. In the year of the List, Chain discovered penicillinase, an enzyme which made penicillin inactive. The three men between them have saved millions of lives worldwide.

Dr Peter Drucker (D104) is one of many on the List who is dismissed as 'emigrant'. Part of Vienna's cultural elite, he obtained his doctorate in public and international law at Frankfurt University in 1931 and he was headhunted two years later by Josef Goebbels' Ministry of Enlightenment because of his talents as a writer. His first article, however, was openly critical of National Socialism and it hastened his departure to Britain in the same year. The List has him in London but, by 1937, he was already in the United States, an investment adviser writing for the *Financial News*, which would become the authoritative *Financial Times* soon after. Two years later, he warned of the Hitler-Stalin alliance and predicted the Holocaust. J. B. Priestley (P124) said of Drucker's *End of Economic Man*, written in the year war broke out, 'At last there is a ray of light in the dark chaos.'

Dr Werner Falk (F5) was skiing in Oberguyl when Goebbels took over the Institute where he taught. He was no stranger to violence, having witnessed the street fighting of the Kapp Putsch in Berlin soon after the First World War and facing the anti-Semitism of pupils and teachers at his school there. He went first to Switzerland then to Britain, changed his first name to David and became a lecturer in New College, Oxford by 1938. It is unlikely that a lecturer in ethics would have found any useful employment in the Reich.

One of the few women[70] in the academic section of the List was H122, Dr Mathilde Hertz. With a doctorate from Munich in biology and comparative psychology, she had taught at the Kaiser Wilhelm Institute of Science in Berlin, specialising in the behaviour of bees. Unusually, Mathilde was allowed to go on working after 1933 because of the personal intervention of the renowned scientist Max Planck. Even so, she was safer elsewhere and was researching in Cambridge two years later. An unhappy woman, always in the shadow of her physicist father, Heinrich, long dead, she stopped working by 1937 and disappeared from public life.

The case of Dr Heinrich Kuhn (K171) highlights a curious anomaly that could only be found in wartime Britain. A physicist from Breslau, Kuhn obtained his doctorate in 1926 and the fact that he was a Christian cut no ice with the Reich authorities; his father was a Jew and that was enough.[71] With an Assisted Council grant of £400 a year, Kuhn became a nationalised British subject in 1939 and, in the year of the List, joined the Tube Alloys team, working on nuclear weapons manufacture. Why? Because Chamberlain's and Churchill's government considered it unwise to allow foreigners to work on radar; they could not get the necessary security clearance!

One of the most unusual names to crop up in this section of

the List is that of Nicholas Pevsner (misspelled in the original paperwork). Today, Pevsner's name has an almost hallowed ring to it as the doyen of English historic architecture. That was not how it was in 1940. P118 was the son of a Jewish fur haulier from Leipzig who obtained his doctorate in 1924 for work on the baroque merchant houses in the city. He was assistant keeper at the Dresden Art Gallery in the late Twenties and lectured at Gottingen University until the Reich took away his livelihood. In Britain, he became a research Fellow at Birmingham University, moonlighting by buying textiles, glass and ceramics for the London showrooms of Gordon Russell.[72] The bizarre thing about Pevsner was that he was more German than the Germans. In 1933, he backed the Reich's move against decadent art[73] and wrote, 'I want this movement to succeed. There is no alternative but chaos... there are worse things than Hitlerism.'[74]

Some of the academics fleeing Nazi Germany were overtly political. R109 was Dr Arthur Rosenberg, an ancient historian and archaeologist who took his doctorate in 1911. In the First World War, he had worked with the German army's press bureau and in the political upheavals afterwards had joined the Independent Social Democratic Party, one of dozens of alternatives to the Kaiser's government. By 1920, Rosenberg was a committed Communist working for the Comintern[75] and, bearing in mind his own Jewish background, denounced the Dawes Plan of 1924 as a conspiracy between American capitalists and international Jewry! In 1933, he moved first to Switzerland and then to Britain, where he taught History briefly at Liverpool University. By the time the List was drawn up, Rosenberg was already lecturing at Brooklyn College, New York.

Because of the temper of the times, Leo Spitz (S160) had

reinvented himself slightly by 1900, becoming Leo Szilliard. Initially from Budapest, he had fought in the Austro-Hungarian army in the First World War. In Berlin by 1920, he impressed Albert Einstein and Max Planck with his work at the Institute of Technology. With a doctorate in 1922, he worked largely on X-rays and made several patent applications with Einstein throughout the decade. Arriving in Britain in 1933, he worked at the laboratory in St Bartholomew's Hospital, London before moving to the Clarendon Laboratory in Oxford. He worked on nuclear chain reactions, proving the eminent British physicist Ernest Rutherford wrong, before moving to the United States to become involved in the Manhattan Project. In 1945, he organised a petition urging President Harry S. Truman not to use the bomb on Japan that Szilliard himself had helped create.

Several of the displaced academics with a medical background ended up working at the Maudsley psychiatric hospital in Denmark Hill, London, attached to King's College. The greatest psychologist of his day, however, although on the List, was not among them. He was F114, 'Freud, Sigmund, Dr, Jude' and he had been dead for nine months. Although many of his ideas are disputed today, there is no doubt that Freud was the 'father of psychoanalysis'. He had read Medicine at the University of Vienna, winning prizes galore. When told that his books were among those famously burned by Hitler's order on 10 May 1933, he wrote, 'What progress we are making. In the Middle Ages they would have burned me.' Even so, Freud seems to have underestimated the ruthlessness of the Reich and stayed in Austria, even after the Anschluss. Urged by the international community to get out, he eventually did in May 1938. He reached Victoria Station, London on 6 June. All four of his older sisters would die in the camps in the years ahead. Freud made his home at 20, Marefield Gardens, Hampstead and died of cancer of the jaw, his end hastened by mutual agreement by his doctor and fellow refugee, Max Schur.

One of the great ironies in the events of 1939-40 is that the very people already threatened by the Reich and who had fled its tentacles, found themselves, however briefly, on the receiving end of the British government's paranoia. At the outbreak of war, there were an estimated 60,000 Germans and Austrians in the country (three times the pre-war figure). In September, under three categories, A, B and C, they were rounded up as 'enemy aliens' and sent before tribunals. Most were released but scares continued. In May 1940, all 'B' class men and women were rounded up in anti-Fifth Column hysteria. There were suicides. 'Collar the lot,' shrieked the *Daily Mail* and Beaverbrook's *Express* was not far behind. When Italy joined the war that month, it was their turn to vanish from Britain's streets. In Leeds, an organ grinder hung a placard from his machine that read, 'I'm British and the monkey is from India.'[76] Some of those on the List, eminent scientists, historians and scholars, ended up on the Isle of Man. Others were put behind barbed wire in Heyton, Lancashire or in derelict cotton factories in the same county.

Three thousand Germans living in Britain were arrested on 16 May 1940 and a further 24,000 were picked up throughout the summer. The vast majority were anti-Nazi and large numbers of policemen and troops were tied up controlling them. There was a deep irony that while an anti-Fascist ballet was being performed in South America backed by the British Council, the choreographers and set designer were behind bars in the Isle of Man. Here, there were so many intellectuals that 'universities' sprang up, with classes on art, music and sculpture. The Dadaist Kurt Schwitters (not on the List) made statuettes from leftover porridge!

The issue was debated in the Commons in August and the MP Victor Cazalet (C31) said:

> 'Frankly, I shall not feel happy, either as an Englishman or a supporter of this government, until this bespattered page of our history has been cleaned up and rewritten.'[77]

Penguin published an exposé Special: *The Internment of Aliens*. Eventually, the page was cleaned up and the academic refugees were allowed to get on with their lives as best they could.

The List also has a crop of homegrown academic troublemakers as far as the RSHA was concerned. B16 was Philip Noel-Baker, in the B's on the List because of the usual confusion with the order of double-barrelled surnames. He could easily appear in other categories, although Schellenberg has him down as 'Professor'. The son of a Canadian Quaker, Noel-Baker was President of the Cambridge Union in 1912 and a superb athlete, performing at the Olympic Games that year. In the First World War, he began by driving a Friends' Ambulance, then became a Conscientious Objector. He taught international relations at London University in the Twenties, worked with the League of Nations and spoke at the World Disarmament conference in 1932-33. As a Labour MP from 1936, he spoke against the monstrosity of aerial warfare – 'The only way to prevent atrocities from the air [like Guernica] is to abolish air warfare and national air forces altogether.' It was an unrealistic proposition and it had been tried before; in the Middle Ages, the Papacy had sought to ban crossbows because they were too accurate! Noel-Baker had links to two women also on the List – Megan Lloyd George we have met already; she was his mistress. The other was W116, the novelist Virginia Woolf, a friend of his wife.

C87 was Edward Conze, damned by Schellenberg on two counts. First, he was descended from Freidrich Engels, who had co-written *The Communist Manifesto* with Karl Marx in 1848 and secondly, he was a Communist himself. Born in London when his father was German vice-consul there, he had obtained his doctorate from Cologne in 1928 and carried out his post-graduate work on theosophy and astrology at Bonn and Hamburg. He could speak fourteen languages fluently by the age of twenty-four. In Hamburg, he witnessed at first hand the unacceptable face of the Reich, battling with the street-gangsters of the SA. From 1933 onwards, he lectured in London and Oxford universities, converting to Buddhism during the war. In 1939, he published two provocative books – *Why War?* and *Why Fascism?*

Julian Huxley came from a family that had dominated British philosophy for nearly a century. His grandfather was Thomas Huxley, Darwin's champion in the evolution debates against the Church of England in the Oxford of the 1860s. His great uncle was the Victorian poet Matthew Arnold and *his* father was Thomas Arnold, busy turning upper-class thugs into 'Christian gentlemen' at Rugby School in the 1840s. Julian was H120, a product of Eton and Balliol, Oxford, with a passion for zoology and bird-watching. He joined British Intelligence in 1916 and became a Fellow of New College, Oxford after the war. By 1929, he was Professor of Zoology at King's College, London, visiting the USSR in 1931 and carrying out work in Africa for the Colonial Office. For seven years, he ran both London Zoo and its sister establishment at Whipsnade, setting up a Pets' Corner for children, then considered an avant-garde and controversial move. Interestingly, he was Vice-President of the British Eugenics Society at the time of the List, believing that it was right to remove the most hopeless cases from the human gene pool. His book *We Europeans* (1937) outlined his views but stopped short of the sort of euthanasia programme that the Nazis were employing two years later.

More political was L26, Harold Laski. He was born in Manchester to a Jewish cotton merchant who was also a leading Liberal. He attended the prestigious Manchester Grammar School (which Schellenberg would have been unlikely to list as a 'subversive' school), married a Gentile and repudiated his Jewish faith. He failed the medical for war service in 1914 and wrote for the socialist *Daily Herald* under George Lansbury. Lecturing in the 1920s at Yale, Harvard and McGill University in Montreal, Laski had a vast list of contacts. The jury is still out on his teaching ability. He never used notes and dazzled his students with his brilliance. On the other hand, he picked on individuals (rather as anti-Semitic teachers did in Germany before Jewish children were excluded from schools altogether) and at one point hit a boy so hard around the head that it made his ears bleed. Laski became a Marxist and wrote for the Left Book Club, pushing for American involvement in the war long before Pearl Harbor. George Orwell described him as 'a socialist by allegiance and a liberal by temperament'. He turned down various seats in parliament but joined the Socialist League in 1932 and the Popular Front four years later.

P18 was Bernard Pares, an old Harrovian who went on to Trinity College, Cambridge. A Russian history specialist, he taught in schools, spending his holidays touring Napoleonic battlefields all over Europe. He became Reader in Russian History at Liverpool University in 1906 and was in touch with various members of the Duma, the Russian parliament trying to come to some sort of rapprochement with the absolutism of Tsar Nicholas II. In the First World War, he was appointed official observer to the Russian army and ended up supporting Admiral Kolchak and his White Russians in their attempt to wrest control from the Bolsheviks under Lenin and Trotsky. He was banned from returning to Russia until 1935. Officially retired by 1939, Pares continued to advise the government on the Russian mindset throughout the war.

Robert Seton-Watson (S51) was born in London of Scots parentage. One of the richest men on the List – his father made a fortune out of trade with India – he attended Winchester and New College, Oxford, where he got a first in History. He wrote for the *Spectator* from Berlin, Vienna and the Sorbonne before visiting Hungary in 1908. Here he became a passionate supporter of ethnic minorities in the vast Austro-Hungarian Empire and a friend of Tomas Masaryk. He helped the man escape to Britain to avoid arrest by the authorities. Seton-Watson's pro-Czech stance was not popular at home and his enemies got him drafted into the Royal Army Medical Corps in 1917, where he spent most of his time scrubbing hospital floors. He went as a private individual to the treaty discussions at Versailles and was unimpressed by people like Lloyd George, Georges Clemenceau, the French Prime Minister and Woodrow Wilson, the American President, calling them 'the pygmies of Paris.' He set up the School of Slavonic Studies in London and got Masaryk a job there. Notoriously disorganised, his students loved him but they knew he was likely to lose their work! A passionate opponent of appeasement, he wrote *Britain and the Dictators* in 1938 and by the time of the List was attached to the Press Bureau at the Foreign Office. In a move that would have pleased Josef Goebbels, Seton-Watson was not allowed to publish anything of his own during the war.

Undoubtedly, the icing on the cake for Schellenberg would

have been the doyen of philosophers, then as now, R134, Bertrand Russell. Mercilessly lampooned by Alan Bennett in *Forty Years On*, the man was seen as part genius, part buffoon for much of his life. Born into an aristocratic family (his father was Viscount Amberley), one of the many dicta he lived by was taken from Exodus 23:2 – 'Thou shalt not follow a multitude to do evil' – which could have been applied to several million Germans in the 1930s and 1940s. He was one of the elite Apostles at Cambridge when he read Mathematics at Trinity and his first book was *German Social Democracy*, written at a time when the Kaiser ruled. He taught at the London School of Economics and became a member of the Webbs' culture group, the Coefficients. It was while he was tutoring at Cambridge that Ludwig Wittgenstein became one of his students. Russell tolerated the man's mood swings in the belief that he was a genius; whether the pair discussed an old school enemy of Wittgenstein's – Adolf Hitler – is unknown.[78]

The First World War brought out the conscientious objector in Russell. He was dismissed from Trinity for his views and spent six months in prison in Bristol in 1916. Four years later, reinstated in academe, he visited Russia and was not impressed either by the revolution or its leader, Vladimir Lenin. In China, he became so ill that the Japanese newspapers reported his death. His mistress, Dora Black, said, 'Mr Bertrand Russell, having died according to the Japanese press, is unable to give interviews to Japanese journalists.'[79]

In the Thirties, with a marriage and divorce behind him at a time when such things were just not done in the aristocracy, the new Viscount Amberley backed the cause of Indian independence as a friend of the nationalist V. K. Krishna Menon. More relevantly to this book, he continued his pacifist stance by opposing rearmament. In 1937, he wrote:

'If the Germans succeed in sending an invading army to England we should do best to treat them as visitors, give them quarters and invite the commander-in-chief to dine with the Prime Minister.'

What Russell failed to understand was that there would be *no* prime minister in the event of an invasion; just a *gauleiter*/governor, who would probably have been Dr Franz Six. The *Einsatzkommando* would have had Russell for breakfast.

★ ★ ★

The *Gestapo Handbook* singled out the International Boy Scout movement largely because it was international and had already 'contaminated' German youth by its established links with the German Free Youth movement. Worse, from the RSHA point of view, the German Youth Front, composed of émigré youth leaders, also had ties with the Scouts and they were all linked to British Intelligence. So not only did the Scouts – and possibly Girl Guides, which Schellenberg does not mention at all – play a part in the propaganda/indoctrination aspect of youth culture but young people were actively being recruited and perhaps even working for SIS.

All this sounds far-fetched but it was born of the German experience. The Hitler Youth movement and the League of German Maidens had been set up in 1933 and, in theory at least,[80] every child over the age of ten had to belong. Indoctrination was the life-blood of the Reich. National Socialist ideas alone could prevail – rebels were either exiled, in the camps or dead. The RSHA could not envisage a youth organisation that did not subscribe to a totalitarian idea. Similarly, Rudolf Hess's *Ausland* organisation and other clubs and societies before the war were busy collating all kinds of information about

Britain that found its way into the *Handbook*; children made impressive observers and, if encouraged by adults, could be relied upon to spill the beans. In both world wars, British scouts stepped up to the plate, carrying out emergency tasks which would horrify today's social services. In 1914, they knocked on doors looking for enemy aliens. In 1940, they plane-spotted and reported the existence of incendiary bombs.

Only three names on the List can be identified as Scout leaders. The 'half-Jew, Mr Martin', who was also head of the Passport Office and who ran the International Bureau in London, is M80. Despite the English-sounding name, he is listed as 'emigrant'. E. S. Martin produced the annual books for Scouts, which promoted the organisation's (non-political) ideals. Martin had been succeeded, according to Schellenberg, by John Wilson, the former chief of police in Calcutta, but, unless he is the uncategorised H. J. Wilson of 13, Barnstaple Mansions, Rosebery Avenue, EC1, he is not on the List at all. 'A certain Mr Lunt,' Secretary of the Bureau, appears as 'R. T. Lund...25, Buckingham Palace Road'. Schellenberg saves most of his opprobrium, however, for the creator of the Scouting movement, B6, Lord Baden-Powell. The son of an Oxford geometry professor, Baden-Powell claimed to have developed his survivalist, orienteering and woodcraft while hiding from teachers at Charterhouse! An expert at reconnaissance, Baden-Powell joined the 13th Hussars in India before service with the regiment in Africa. Here, using deception and fake minefields, he became the hero of Mafeking during the Boer War, in which Germany, while staying neutral, had backed Britain's enemies. As Inspector General of Cavalry in 1903, he was devoting more time to the Boy Scout movement, which was designed to improve the moral fibre of the younger generation, a sickly lot much given to smoking. Perhaps Schellenberg did not know Baden-Powell's views or else the international threat of the Scouts overrode it because the Chief Scout read *Mein Kampf* in one sitting and pronounced it 'a wonderful book, with good ideas on education, health, propaganda, organisation etc.' He did balance that, however, with a classic putdown line – 'ideals which Hitler does not practise himself'. For Schellenberg, Baden-Powell 'was run as an agent against Germany in the last war' and the dissolution of the Austrian Boy Scout movement proved his links with British Intelligence. No doubt Schellenberg would have been delighted with recent biographies of the Chief Scout, which have questioned the man's sexuality and implied that he often cross-dressed. That would not have surprised the puritans of the RSHA at all.

★ ★ ★

There is a curious appendix in the *Gestapo Handbook* relating to museums. As centres of learning, I have included them in this chapter, although they arguably fit nowhere. We have already seen that the Reich was complaining that the British Museum, in particular, had many important examples of German art, 'generally the very best that could have been obtained or stolen'. South Kensington was nearly as guilty and the Guildhall had medieval finds from Scandinavia which was by 1940, neutral Sweden apart, in the hands of the Reich. The New Burlington gallery was particularly at fault because it had held a 'degenerate art' exhibition of exactly the sort of 'rubbish' that Hitler was trying to remove from Germany. The universities, especially Oxford and Cambridge, had their own fabulous collections and these, as well as the Royal Society of Arts, the International Society for Contemporary Music and the Library of the Royal Academy of Arts, had been using international funds to oppose Germany, if only by appropriating German art and artefacts. There was a light on the horizon, however – in Edinburgh, the National Museum of Scotland in Queen Street was run by 'Director Edwards [who] is said to have been sympathetic to Germany'.

The poet John Masefield, himself the product of a public school,[81] described cultural visits[82] made between the wars by German scholars as a preliminary to theft, rather as a bank robber 'cases the joint' to assess how easy it will be to access the valuables. The poet G. K. Chesterton had an interesting view on German *academe*. 'There is something about them [German scholars] that is prehistoric. Even their learned professors... are often prehistoric. I mean that, learned as they are, they seem never to have heard of history.'[83]

CHAPTER TEN

THE FOURTH ESTATE

'Truth, my dear professor, is one of Hitler's victims.' So wrote the List's T14, Gabrielle Tergit-Reifenburg, in one of her anti-Fascist novels. Her real name was Elise Hinschmann, born to a Jewish family in Berlin and once a regular contributor to the *Berliner Tagblatte*, one of Germany's best-known newspapers. She became famous overnight with her 1931 novel *The Folk Singer of the Kurfurstendamm* but, two years later, was on the run from the Third Reich. She was typical of the new journalists of her generation, writing from a feminist standpoint that would have been unthinkable even thirty years earlier.

Schellenberg's List is littered with the categories *schriftseller* (writer), *redakteur* (editor) and *journalist*. The range is actually very wide, from the respectable academics who might well have appeared in Chapter Nine to the traditional hacks of Fleet Street, hammering away on upright typewriters in their dingy offices at the hub of London's newspaper world.

The media did not have the same relentless hold on the public that it has now. In the 1930s, there were very few televisions. Not everybody owned a radio. And there were many who read a newspaper now and again, rather than as a daily routine – even though the consensus is that the British were a nation of newspaper readers.

The war changed all that. The snoopers of the Mass Observation Unit, working in unison with the Ministry of Information, discovered that pre-war readership of dailies had rocketed once the war began. The papers were physically smaller, with a limit on pulp and newsprint, and the facts were not always strictly accurate to avoid a lowering of morale. A London daily, for example, like *The Times* or the *Telegraph*, dropped from twenty-four pages to ten – and they were doing better than many of their tabloid counterparts. Sports pages virtually disappeared, crime news was cut[84] and the kiddies' pages became a thing of the past.[85] Huge numbers of reporters and photographers were hived off into war work; because of censorship, there was little for the camera boys to photograph. Amateurs tried to fill their ranks – lads exempt from war service or earnest matrons intent on doing their bit. Local papers suffered even more – one editor had a total staff of four, aged between fourteen and eighteen.[86]

Even in 'free' Britain – and Schellenberg must have been well aware of this – censorship meant that a paper could be closed down by the government at a moment's notice. Similarly, individual journalists were careful not to fall foul of editors. 'Letters to…' were largely unchallenged – the *Daily Herald*, the *Daily Worker* and the *Daily Mirror* regularly carried the views of the Left, even when, potentially, the USSR was the enemy. News, however, was sacrosanct. The navy, in particular, was paranoid about giving away its ships' positions, especially in

1940, and blinkered blue-pencillers combed everything, even removing mentions of the *Marie Celeste* and performances of *HMS Pinafore* in case such items gave 'comfort to the enemy'. As a result, the public were blissfully unaware of radar (then called radiolocation) until June 1941. Knowing of its existence might have made people feel a *little* safer in the Spitfire summer. Some journalists were defiant and tried to push the boundaries, along the lines that the fourth estate still uses – 'the public's right to know'. Those specifically referred to by Goebbels (men whose names appear on the List) proudly called themselves 'the Goebbels Club'. They probably realised that they were in the rifle sights of Himmler's *Einsatzkommandos*.

The censorship problem extended beyond Fleet Street to other writers of all shapes and sizes. 'Everything in our age,' complained George Orwell (surprisingly, perhaps, not on the List) 'conspires to turn the writer... into a minor official, working on themes handed to him from above and never telling what seems to him the whole of the truth.'[87]

The problem, as Gabrielle Tergit-Reifenburg was aware, was that the truth was objective. The truths of Hitler, Goebbels and Schellenberg were not those that Orwell was talking about. So who were the hard-bitten hacks from Fleet Street that Schellenberg was gunning for in the summer of 1940? Arguably, the grandest old men in this context were Wickham Steed (S12) and Hannen Swaffer (S152). Steed was nearly eighty by the time the List was compiled but he was still writing cutting-edge articles months earlier. Once *The Times*' foreign correspondent, he had a wide knowledge of European politics. He hated Germans and Jews equally, one of that generation of anti-Semites that we shall meet in a later chapter. He described the First World War as 'a dirty German-Jewish international financial attempt to bully us.'[88] As a champion of Yugoslavia and Czechoslovakia (he was a friend of Tomas Masaryk), he endorsed the 'truth' of the *Protocols of the Elders of Zion* until they were proved to be a forgery in 1921. In his day, especially writing for Lord Northcliffe's newspaper empire, Steed's influence was immense. He was the bane of younger journalists, who felt bound to defer to him. Even so, the new *Times* owner, J. J. Astor (A77), fired him because the paper was losing money. WHENCE HITLER AND WHITHER? was one of his articles in 1939, along with THE MEANING OF HITLERISM and OUR WAR AIMS. He was convinced as early as 1934 that the Germans were carrying out secret experiments in airborne biological warfare. An awed and confused government began to stockpile vaccines, just in case Mr Steed was right.

The tall and cadaverous Hannen Swaffer was the terror of young journalists too. As a cub reporter himself, he was once banned by a local theatre because his critiques were too damning. He once referred to Noel Coward (C96), one of the most popular entertainers of his generation, as a 'non-existent talent'. Despite his natural Left-wing leanings, Swaffer wrote for the *Daily Mail* and the *Express*. He was 'Mr Gossip' in the *Sketch*, 'Mr London' in the *Graphic* and helped set up the *Daily Mirror*, a paper originally intended for a female readership. He shared many of the racist trends of his generation and, on the List, is described as writing for the *Herald*, the Left-wing paper associated with George Lansbury. The *Manchester Guardian*, establishing itself in the 1940s as the leading serious socialist news outlet, said of Swaffer, 'he raised professional egoism to a fine art.'[89]

Henry Brailsford is not well known today. He was B204 and lived at Belsize Park Gardens, NW3. He was the most prolific Left-wing journalist of the first half of the century and was the foreign correspondent for the *Manchester Guardian*, specialising in the Balkans. He joined the Independent Labour Party in 1907 and resigned from his job with the *Daily News* when it failed to back the Suffragettes. He wrote for the *New Statesman* and *Reynolds' News* and was an outspoken critic of both Hitler and Mussolini. His anti-militarist *Property or Peace* in 1934 spoke for a generation disenchanted by war.

Claude Cockburn, also known under the pen name of Frank Pitcairn, was C70. The son of a consul-general, he had worked for *The Times* in Germany and America. He also contributed to the Communist *Daily Worker*, the paper closed down by the Home Secretary, Herbert Morrison, in January 1941 under Defence Regulation 2D, brought in at the time of the List. Much of Cockburn's information was supplied by Robert Vansittart of the Foreign Office, who was a major doubter of Britain's success in the summer of 1940. Cockburn's actual political sympathies are difficult to fathom. He worked with Harry Pollitt (P97), the Labour leader, and produced a Communist rag, which may have been funded by the USSR, called *The Week*. On the other hand, he was associated with the Cliveden Set, the aristocratic layabouts who were believed to be part of the pro-German clique, at least until the war began.

James Garvin (G12) came from a working-class family in Birkenhead. By the turn of the century, he was editor of the *Eastern Morning News* and the *Newcastle Evening Chronicle*. He also wrote for the *Telegraph* on the national level and found himself headhunted by Lord Northcliffe for the *Mail*. He turned this down but worked on the *Observer*, making it both profitable and influential. A friend of 'Jackie' Fisher, the First Sea Lord, and Winston Churchill, he lost a son in the First World War and never quite got over it. He prophesied accurately that Versailles would only stir up feelings of revenge in Germany. To buy time, he believed in both appeasement and re-armament and backed Churchill for Prime Minister in the fraught weeks of May 1940.

An unusual entry on the List is G135, John Gunther. Despite the German-sounding name, the man was born in Chicago, working for the *Daily News* both there and in London. He worked in every European country except Portugal and described the work of inter-war journalists with a ferocious simplicity – 'We were scavengers, buzzards, out to get the news, no matter whose wings got clipped.'[90] Gunther wrote a series of 'Inside' books on European politics, which may have been a little too perceptive for the RSHA.

Another American on Fleet Street's books was B166, Ralph D. Blumenfeld, from Wisconsin. Born before the Civil War ended, Blumenfeld's father was an immigrant from Nuremberg who sailed for a new start in life in Europe's Year of Revolutions, 1848. The son worked on the *Chicago Herald* in the 1880s and came to Britain in 1887 to cover Queen Victoria's Golden Jubilee. Both the *Observer* and the *Sunday Times* made him offers but, in the end, he wrote first for the *Mail* and then the *Express*. Single-handedly, he changed the face of British journalism by using the American system of putting news, not advertisements, on the front page. Although he was editor of the *Express*, he became increasingly side-lined by the bustling Beaverbrook, a control freak in everything he touched. Blumenfeld was a critic of socialism and active in the Conservative Party, the chairman of various newspapers and the writer of a series of radio programmes up to 1935. A stroke in the following year effectively ended his career but it may be that Schellenberg believed that he was still influential behind the scenes. That said, there is nothing particularly anti-Nazi in the man's behaviour or career.

One of the most unusual – and famous – denizens of

wartime Fleet Street was the cartoonist David Low. If a picture paints a thousand words, Low was one of the most prolific 'writers' of all time. His incisive and dramatic destruction of the dictators of his day caused fury in Berlin, Rome and Moscow and are standard fare in British school textbooks today. A New Zealander, he was taken out of school by his fussy parents, who believed he was over-working, and he produced his first cartoon in 1901 at the age of eleven! He lampooned various Antipodean politicians, one of whom, the Australian Prime Minister Billy Hughes, called him a bastard to his face. Headhunted by Henry Cadbury, who was part-owner of the British *Star*, he moved to London in the Twenties, where Max Aitken, the future Lord Beaverbrook, gave him a contract. In 1937, Josef Goebbels complained that Low's work was damaging Anglo-German relations. Ever one to oblige, the artist adapted his running comic strip *Hit and Muss* (Hitler and Mussolini) to become *Hit and Muzzler*. The irony would not have been lost on Dr Goebbels. It is an interesting take on the mood swings of a nation that a perspicacious, honest man like Low should have been regarded, even by the British press, as a warmonger in the days of Chamberlain's appeasement. When he read of his own inclusion on the List, he said he was not surprised. He had the Nazis on his list too!

★ ★ ★

The politics of the period before the war meant an inevitable polarisation between Right and Left and this was reflected in the writers and writings of the time. Inevitably, those who made the List were socialists or Communists and many of them wrote for Victor Gollancz's Left Book Club. Gollancz and his wife, Ruth, are G75 and G74, respectively. She is described as 'leader of the Left Book Club' whereas he is merely 'publisher', both with an address at 14, Henrietta Street. Ruth was a Slade School-educated artist, an active Suffragette and one of the country's first qualified female architects. Victor was Jewish; several family members were Rabbis. A product of New College, Oxford, he had served with the Northumberland Fusiliers, without seeing action, in the First World War. An inspirational teacher, he taught at Repton in 1916 and published pacifist literature throughout the Twenties. By the end of that decade, he had hitched his wagon to the Left. George Orwell said of him, 'Gollancz is, of course, part of the Communist-racket.' In 1936, he founded the Left Book Club, which offered a monthly book for half a crown,[91] and a newsletter. The Club held an annual rally and, at one point, boasted a total membership of 57,000. Forty books were produced before 1940, all on socialist themes and written by well-thought-of polemicists. Stafford Cripps and Harold Laski ran the club, along with John Strachey (S51), the most widely read Marxist-Leninist of his day. Both Gollancz and Strachey would become disenchanted with the USSR once the existence of the Molotov-Ribbentrop pact became known.

A galaxy of Left-wingers wrote for Gollancz but their works generally did not sell. Apart from those only available to the Left Book Club, there was little demand for political works, which was odd in those turbulent decades when politics was becoming lethal. The single volume that did well and was streets ahead of anything else in terms of readership demand was *Mein Kampf* in the English translation; everybody wanted to know what was going on in the Führer's head.

The Gollanczes were not the only literary couple on Schellenberg's List. Leonard Woolf (W115) was a member of the elite Apostles group at Cambridge, along with several others inscribed in the Black Book. He met Virginia Stephen (W116) while on leave from the Indian Civil Service in 1912. Together, they became the heart of the Bloomsbury group, meeting in each other's houses or at the 1917 Club in Gerrard Street, Soho. As a Labour party supporter and Fabian Socialist, Leonard wrote for the *New Statesman* and *International Government*, proposing an international agency for the preservation of world peace. The Woolfs set up the Hogarth Press, publishing Virginia's novels and, among others, the poems of T. S. Eliot. Virginia was the more famous of the two, largely because of her fiction output. A serious depressive, she had a nervous breakdown following the death of each of her parents and, despite the fact that Leonard was Jewish, she shared the widespread anti-Semitism of her class and time. 'I do not like the Jewish voice,' she wrote, 'I do not like the Jewish laugh.' She did not like Christians either - 'My Jew has more religion in one toenail – more human love in one hair.' Despite that, she embarked on a lesbian relationship with Vita Sackville-West, the novelist wife of Harold Nicolson. A staunch anti-Fascist, her 1938 novel, *Three Guineas*, was an indictment of the Right. On 28 March 1941, after years of suffering with what we now call a bipolar disorder, Virginia Woolf filled her coat pockets with stones and walked into the River Ouse near her home. They did not find her body for nearly three weeks.

The literary lions are remembered today for things other than their political bias but it is for that reason that they are on the List. E. M. Forster (F81) was another Cambridge Apostle and a Conscientious Objector in the First World War. *A Passage to India* made him famous but he wrote articles for the BBC throughout the 1930s. Schellenberg would not have known about his homosexuality – Forster had a long-standing relationship with a married policeman, Bob Buckingham, which was not made public until long after the war. Aldous Huxley

(H209) joined his brother Julian on the List. A Balliol man, he had been turned down for war service in 1914-18 because of near-blindness in one eye. He taught George Orwell at Eton, where his lessons were a shambles as far as discipline went. His work at a chemical plant in the Twenties gave him his raw material for *Brave New World* and he wrote for both *Vogue* and *Vanity Fair*. None of this would have merited his inclusion on the List but his pacifist novels, like *Eyeless in Gaza*, as well as his membership of the Peace Pledge Union, did. By the time of the List, Huxley had moved to Hollywood with his wife and son, becoming involved in meditation and transcendentalism, which were not usually Nazi preoccupations!

H. G. Wells, of 13, Hanover Terrace, Regent's Park, resolutely refused to carry his gas mask during the war (it is doubtful whether Schellenberg would have known that). His middle-class background – he was a draper's apprentice in the 1880s – gave him the inspiration for *The History of Mr Polly* but it was in the new field of science fiction that Wells would become world famous. *The Time Machine* and *The War of the Worlds* still have a huge readership today. His extra-marital affairs were notorious – apparently, the long-suffering Jane Wells was accepting of this – the List's Moura Budberg being one of many. He was also a Fabian Socialist, writing, in 1940, *New World Order*, in which he prophesied a single world state. His concept was one of armed peace – 'England belonging to England and Germany to Germany.' He disliked the Jews because he believed their election as 'the chosen people' made them out of step with the rest of mankind. Having met Josef Stalin in 1934, he also thought British criticism of the dictator unfair.

Perhaps the oddest literary 'great' was Lytton Strachey (S52)[92], if only because he had died eight years before the

List was compiled! His frail physique led to bullying at his school at Leamington College and, quite possibly, at Liverpool University too. He fared better among the like-minded souls at Trinity College, Cambridge, where he joined the Apostles and lived in an atmosphere of what he called 'higher Sodomy'. A reviewer for the *Spectator*, he achieved overnight fame with his *Eminent Victorians* and was financially secure after the publication of *Queen Victoria*. A Conscientious Objector in the First World War, although his various physical ailments would have made him unfit for service anyway, he was once asked what he would do if he found a German trying to rape his sister. 'I should come between them,' was Strachey's answer. He died of stomach cancer at the age of fifty-one.

Perhaps the least loveable of Schellenberg's entries is J34, Cyril Joad. He was an old friend of Harold Nicolson since their Labour days in the 1931 New Government and Nicolson found Joad's relentless pacifism 'refreshing'. A brilliant Oxford scholar, the man's conscientious objection in the First World War led him not to honourable prison, or driving Red Cross ambulances but to hiding in Snowdonia! An early feminist, he abandoned that position after his own divorce and stated flatly and often that women had 'inferior minds.' He nevertheless had several mistresses, all referred to as Mrs Joad, and was kicked out of the Fabian Society for sexual misconduct at a summer school in 1925. An opponent of Nazism, he nevertheless became the key speaker in the notorious King and Country debate. He opposed much that was modern – overhead electricity cables, ribbon development and what he called 'destructive tourism'. He is probably on the List because of his membership of the National Peace Council 1937-38 and not because of his rather more cranky interests of ghost-hunting and naturism. Unsurprisingly, when he applied for a job with them, the Ministry of Information turned him down.

Of all the areas in the List, the literati/journalist section is where most women appear. Most of them were motivated by feminism (women over twenty-one finally won the vote in 1928) and by pacifism (several had lost fathers, husbands and brothers in the First World War). Neither of these ideas found favour in the Reich. Vera Brittain (B227) of 19, Glebe Place, SW3 was the daughter of a paper manufacturer from Newcastle-under-Lyme. She read English Literature at Somerville, Oxford before serving in the First World War with the nurses of the Voluntary Aid Detachment. Her fiancé and brother were both killed in the trenches. Throughout the 1920s, she was a regular speaker at the League of Nations, the Peace Pledge Union and the Anglican Pacifist Fellowship. Because she married the politician George Caitlin (C31) she appears twice on the List.

Another alumna of Somerville was F150, Margery Fry. A Liberal and Quaker, she became the first warden of the female students' wing at Birmingham University and joined the Howard League for penal reform. In 1921, she became one of the country's first female magistrates and was a governor of the BBC by the time the List was compiled. Other than her broad pacifist stance, it is difficult to see why she is on the List at all.

With so many high-profile names not appearing on the List, it is hard to see why Naomi Mitchison, nee Haldane, M150, another Voluntary Aid Detachment nurse from the First World War, who lived at Hanover Court, Hammersmith, is there at all. The niece of Viscount Haldane, she had been the only girl at her Oxford prep school and married barrister Gilbert Mitchison in 1916. They had an open marriage – the sort of Bohemian behaviour which was, officially at least, anathema to the puritanism of the Nazis. Most of Naomi's ninety books related to relationships and were commissioned by Victor Gollancz. A work on rape and abortion, however, was too much for the mores of the time; even Gollancz could not be persuaded to take it. As a Fabian, Naomi visited Soviet Russia in 1932 but became disenchanted by the Left by the time of the List. She worked for Tom Harrisson's Mass Observation Unit by 1940 and was not at all sure that the famous Cockney *sang froid* would actually survive a sustained Blitz.

Margaret Thomas, Viscountess Rhondda, had faced the Germans before. She had been on the *Lusitania* during the First World War when it was torpedoed and sunk by the Kaiser's U-boats. A painfully shy debutante with no small talk, she found the upper-class girls' rituals of 'the season' (essentially a marriage market) appalling and took up politics instead. A member of the Women's Social and Political Union by 1908, she smashed the windows of Herbert Asquith's car during the general election two years later and went to prison. At her businessman father's death, Margaret inherited his title and thirty-three companies. She divorced her husband and set up house with Helen Archdale, producing a short-lived, Left-wing, feminist magazine, *Time and Tide*, in the Twenties. It is not easy to see why Lady Rhondda is on the List, except that she knew *everybody* in government and business circles.

Far more political was T48, Dona Torr. The daughter of a canon of Chester Cathedral, she read English at University College, London and became the librarian of the socialist *Daily Herald*. The 1926 General Strike pushed her further Left and she translated various works by Marx and Lenin, even working as translator at the Fifth Communist International in Moscow, largely conducted in German. She wrote for the publishing house of Martin Lawrence (the 'ML' was deliberately chosen to reflect Marx and Lenin). She commissioned the historian Christopher Hill to write his epic book on the Cromwellian revolution in the year that the List was compiled and founded the Marxist Historians Group in 1938.

U11 was Freda Utley, whose father was a Fabian Socialist and a friend of George Bernard Shaw. A graduate of King's College, London, Freda became a Communist, like Dona Torr, because of the miners' martyrdom in the General Strike. She married a Russian Jewish economist and travelled with him to Siberia, China and Japan. Their life in Moscow in the Thirties left her disenchanted with Stalinism and most of her books railed on the ambitions of imperialist Japan, virtually ignored in Britain at the time. She returned home in 1936 without her husband. He had been taken away in Moscow one night and it was not for many years that she discovered he had been shot by firing squad for leading a hunger strike in prison. She supported Chamberlain at Munich because she believed that the USSR was a far more dangerous enemy than Hitler.

Nancy Cunard could have made a career of any kind for herself, given the mores of the time, because her father owned the shipping line of the same name. C111's parents may have been wealthy – her mother was an American heiress – but Nancy was the product of a broken home and she was sent to a variety of boarding schools in Britain, France and Germany before marrying, briefly, in 1916. In post-war Paris in the Twenties, she had a fling with Aldous Huxley and became involved in the Bohemian art world of the Left Bank – modernism, surrealism, Dadaism; Nancy embraced it all! She pioneered the 'barbaric look' in jewellery, based on African tribal designs, which fascinated her, and she set up her own publishing house, the Hours Press, in Normandy. Here, she encouraged unknown writers like the playwright Samuel

Beckett and became caught up in the racial politics centred on Jim Crow and the lynchings of blacks in America at the time. Her new lover in 1928 was a jazz musician, a performer of what the Nazis called 'degenerate, nigger music'. When her mother learned of this, she asked incredulously, 'Is it true that my daughter knows a Negro?'[93] Nancy published black poetry and her espousal of the case of the Scottsboro boys, accused of raping a white girl on a train, led to her receiving death threats.

She was anti-Fascist, anti-Mussolini and anti-Franco, writing a series of articles for the *Manchester Guardian* during the Spanish Civil War, which led to her visiting the Front and being horrified by what she saw. Her widely circulated questionnaire on the war, however, backfired. Bertrand Russell and E. M. Forster refused to contribute and George Orwell wrote to her:

'Will you please stop sending me this bloody rubbish... I am not one of your fashionable pansies like Auden or Spender. I was six months in Spain, most of the time fighting. I have a bullet hole in me at present and I am not going to write blah about defending democracy or gallant little anybody.'[94]

It is not certain how Nancy took it!

An altogether less straightforward writer was F1, Dora Fabian, a doctor of philosophy from Berlin. Exactly why she is on the List is uncertain. Not only was she dead by 1940, it is possible that she was murdered by the Gestapo. Born Dora Heinemann to a Left-wing lawyer and his wife, she married SPD member Walter Fabian in 1924. Already active in liberal politics before that, Dora obtained her doctorate in economics and political science from the University of

Gneissen four years later. Immensely outspoken and critical of the Weimar centrist parties, she gravitated to the Left and set up the Socialist Workers Party. She warned German women of being duped by the Nazis into voting for them, calling them *stimmrich* (voting beasts), being only too aware of National Socialism's attitudes to females. She attended the astonishing Nazi rallies of the 1930s to study the crowd and was rather unnerved when an SS man hoisted her onto his shoulders with the words, 'Party comrade, I'm certain that you would like to see our Führer better.'

In March 1933, Dora was arrested in Berlin. Released after a few days, she travelled to Prague, Zurich and Geneva before arriving in London by September. She was allowed to stay in Britain until May 1935 as long as she could maintain herself financially. She worked as a translator – her English was excellent – for the pacifist and anti-Nazi Otto Lehrmann-Russbuldt (L59). Encouraged by fellow refugee Mathilde Wurm, she collected a considerable amount of material on women in the Nazi state. Fellow Listee Ellen Wilkinson (W80) remembered that Dora's flat was burgled twice during 1934 and that the German Embassy knew all about her.

On 4 April 1935, Dora and Mathilde were found dead in their flat in Great Ormond Street. It was a classic 'locked-room mystery' so beloved of crime writers of the time. The inquest concluded that the cause of both women's deaths was Veronal poisoning and that this was a double suicide. Dora was depressed, friends recalled, and was running out of money, which might have meant her having to leave the country. On the other hand, both women had been supplying information to the anti-Nazi agent Roy Ganz, who was investigating the fellow travellers of the Right. This was 1935, the year of the Anglo-German Fellowship, the year in which a naval agreement was reached with Hitler, the year in which a gullible government was beginning to pin its foreign policy hopes on appeasement. Did the Gestapo find Dora Fabian and put an end to her meddling once and for all? And did the British government keep quiet about it? If so, it would not be the last time.

★ ★ ★

Inevitably, many of the journalists and writers on the List, like the politicians and academics, are refugees fleeing from the Reich's reaches. Many of them are Jewish, the reason for their leaving occupied Europe in the first place. Markus van Blankenstein (B155) had been the editor of various Dutch newspapers before May 1940, especially the influential *New Rotterdam Courant*, highly critical of Nazi foreign policy since the Rhineland. By the time he appeared on the List, he was broadcasting from London for Radio Oranje, trying to keep up the morale of his people under the German yoke.

An unexplained oddity is B220, Rudolf Breitschield. Born in Cologne, he obtained his doctorate at the University of Marburg and became the editor of various middle-class Liberal papers before the First World War. He represented Germany in the League of Nations but voted against the Enabling Act of 1934, which made Hitler dictator for life. When he denounced Constantin von Neurath, Hitler's foreign policy guru, as a terrorist, Breitschield realised it was probably time to get out of his own country. He went via Switzerland to France but ended up in Vichy and could not get out. He was arrested in 1941 and died in Buchenwald later in the war. The List, however, has him in Britain in 1940 but, since there is no address, it may be that the inclusion is an error.

There is no mistake about Lion Feuchtwanger, even though

his stay in Britain must have been short. F28 was the son of an Orthodox Jewish margarine manufacturer and studied literature and philosophy at the University of Munich before taking his doctorate at Berlin. A theatre critic, he founded *Der Spiegel* in 1908. Invalided out of the First World War, his experience there turned him into a Communist but he made his living as a playwright and historical novelist, working with Bertolt Brecht on his earlier projects. What made Feuchtwanger's name, however, was *Jud Suss* (the Wandering Jew), written in 1925. There was a deep irony here – in the year that Hitler set up the SS, *Jud Suss* prophesied the Holocaust. In 1934, Denham Studios in Britain turned the book into a film starring Conrad Veidt. Not to be outdone, the Nazis made their own version, suitably bastardised, in the year of the List. When Hitler came to power, Feuchtwanger was on a lecture tour in the States. His house was ransacked and his extensive library stolen. His name appeared on another list of the Nazis – the *Ausbergerungsliste*, a litany of German citizens deprived of their citizenship. His books joined thousands of others burned in the wanton destruction of 10 May 1933. Himmler described Feuchtwanger as 'public enemy number one', a line from the novelist's own *The Devil in France*. On the outbreak of war, Feuchtwanger was imprisoned in Camp des Milles but escaped and was smuggled out, allegedly in women's clothing, to Spain, Portugal and, eventually, the United States, where he settled in Los Angeles. Schellenberg has him living in Henrietta Street, WC6 but, since this is also the area dominated by the Gollanczes and the Left Book Club, it may be that it was only a *poste restante* for Feuchtwanger.

H70's early life reads like something from a fairy story. Helmut Herzfeld (Anglicised on the List to John Heartfield) was, like David Low, a caricaturist. Born in Berlin to socialist parents, he was abandoned in the forest by them when he was nine! He studied art in the Bavarian Arts and Crafts School in Munich and changed his name to the English version during the First World War because he was appalled at the anti-British sentiment current throughout Germany. He became a Dadaist in 1917, painted flats for Brecht's productions and at the end of the war, joined the German Communist Party, the KDP. On Hitler's assumption of power, the SS broke into Heartfield's flat. At only 5ft 2in he could squeeze out of the window and hide in a rubbish bin nearby. From there, he walked to Czechoslovakia and has the 'honour' of appearing on the Czech Special List too!

Egon Kisch (K54) served as a corporal in the First World War but had already worked on the *Bohemia* newspaper in his native Austria. With a naturally rebellious streak, he was imprisoned briefly for criticising the war in 1916 and deserted before the conflict finished. He became a member of the Austrian Communist Party and made his reputation in Berlin under the Weimar government as a gritty, daring journalist. He was arrested the day after the Recihstag fire. On 27 February 1933, a Dutch Communist, the rambling, incoherent Marinus van der Lubbe, was arrested for trying to burn down the German parliament. Regarded today as an inept stitch-up by the Nazis, it served as an excuse for an all-out attack on the Left and Kisch was caught up in it all. There was a fascinating 'counter-trial' held in London at the same time as van der Lubbe's, organised by German and Czech émigrés in the capital. Kisch asked permission to attend this but the Nazi authorities refused to let him leave the country.

The following year, he attempted to emigrate to Australia but that most racist of countries invoked the 1901 Immigration Restoration Act, which insisted on a language qualification. In that Kisch spoke several languages fluently, that should have presented no problem but he was eventually caught out on his grasp of Scottish Gaelic and refused entry! A High Court decision over-ruled this blatant anti-Semitism and Kisch lectured the Australians on the evils of Nazism. By 1937, he was in Spain, reporting for the Republicans. Returning to Czechoslovakia or Austria was clearly not an option for him and Kisch found himself turned down, on racial grounds again, for entry to the United States. They clearly had enough 'huddled masses' for the moment and Roosevelt's government was adamant that they were not going to become a dumping ground for Europe's dispossessed. Most accounts give Egon Kisch's location as Mexico in 1940 but the List has him in Britain.

It is difficult to know where in this chapter – or, indeed, this book – to place Gerald Hamilton (H23). There is no doubt that he worked for *The Times* as a sales rep in Germany and that he was a fixer for Willi Muntzenberg (M191), the 'notorious Communist', as SIS describe him. Like many characters on the List, Hamilton is rather larger than life. Revelling in the unlikely description of the 'wickedest man in Europe', he was born in Shanghai and educated at Rugby. He was Catholic, homosexual and had a wide circle of friends, including Winston Churchill, Christopher Isherwood and the American actress Tallulah Bankhead. He was imprisoned in the First World War because (he claimed) of his association with the Irish spy Roger Casement. In the 1920s – again, according to him – he worked as go-between for Special Branch and Sinn Fein, not to mention an association with the British military mission in Berlin. He was jailed several times before the war for fraud, theft, bankruptcy and gross indecency and was considered a threat to national security. It did not help that he once shared a flat with the 'great beast', Aleister Crowley, who made equally lurid claims about his Intelligence work at this time. Since all of Hamilton's various autobiographies contradict each other, it is doubtful that we will ever know the truth about him.

* * *

Bearing in mind how hugely important the BBC was to both sides in the Second World War, the List has very little to say on the matter. The *Gestapo Handbook* is very clear – 'The extent to which English radio broadcasting has supported anti-German agitation and propaganda is well known', and so the coverage of the topic is brief. During the war, *everybody* in Britain got hold of a wireless set. The news, read by Alvar Lidell and John Snagge, was compulsory listening. Lord Haw-Haw (William Joyce), broadcasting ever-more preposterous propaganda from the Reich, was regarded as light entertainment. Resistance movements, establishing themselves all over occupied countries in Western Europe in the weeks before the List, used BBC frequencies to transmit vital code messages. Even Berliners like Marie Vassiltchikov listened eagerly for what the enemy was up to.

That said, we might expect the List to be full of newsreaders and airwave propagandists but there is only one – J. B. Priestley. P24 was born in Bradford and attended Belle Vue Grammar School, before leaving at sixteen to work on local and London newspapers. He was badly wounded on the Western Front, serving with the Duke of Wellington's Regiment, and he resumed an academic career at Trinity Hall, Cambridge in 1919. Most of his plays and novels had a moral tone, perhaps the best known being *An Inspector Calls*. He wrote for Cyril Connolly's *Horizon* magazine, only six months old when Schellenberg compiled the List, but it was as a broadcaster that Priestley came to the fore. Graham Greene wrote that he 'became in the months after Dunkirk a leader second only in importance to Mr Churchill. And he gave us what other leaders failed to give us – an ideology.'[95] Priestley's Saturday-night *Postscript* programme was quietly socialist (as of course was much of the BBC) but it sounded so much like common sense and so superbly anti-Nazi that it was unlikely that most of his listeners noticed.

The oddest entry among the literati of the List must be P121, George Ward Price. His inclusion alone, perhaps, persuaded historian David Lampe that the Black Book is not actually a 'hit' list at all. A Cambridge graduate, he wrote for the *Daily Mail*, where he said that Hitler was 'doing an immense amount of good'. He was the only foreign journalist, the Führer claimed, who reported him fairly. A friend of Oswald Mosley, Price founded the January Club in 1934 to raise funds for the British Union of Fascists. Various fellow travellers of the Right, like Francis Yeats-Brown, H. W. Luttman-Johnson and Wing Commander Louis Grieg, were members too. There is a photograph of Price, smiling proudly at Hitler's first foreign dinner party; alongside the *Mail*'s owner, Lord Rothermere (he of the banner headline 'Hurrah for the Blackshirts!' is the Right Club's W. E. Tennant, Josef Goebbels and, of course, the Führer himself. Price's book, *I Know These Dictators*, produced for members of the Right Book Club, is full of platitudes and examples of the journalist having bought Goebbels' claptrap wholeheartedly. Shortly before war broke out, the increasingly Germanophile Price started to wear a monocle in silent homage to his favoured nation. His inclusion on the List is inexplicable.

'JUDMAS'

On 8 July 1940, while Schellenberg's team were compiling the List, Admiral Sir Barry Domvile, former commander of the Third Cruiser Squadron of the Royal Navy, ex-President of the Naval College at Greenwich and sometime Director of Naval Intelligence, was arrested and interned under Defence Regulation 18B. How a decorated naval officer could be considered a danger to the peace of the realm shines a sharp searchlight onto the topsy-turvy world of inter-war politics.

Domvile first visited Germany in 1935, the year of the Anglo-German naval agreement and was invited by Joachim Ribbentrop to witness the astonishing theatricals of the Nuremberg rally in the following year. He became a member of the Anglo-German Fellowship at the same time and two years later founded the Link, an organisation with the largest following in London, which drew anti-Semites and pacifists in equal numbers. The confusion of the times meant that those who opposed war on moral grounds, many of them socialists, were seen as Nazi supporters. The Peace Pledge Union, for instance, came under fire in this context from both the *Daily Telegraph* and the *News Chronicle*. By the year that war broke out, Domvile was openly supporting the new British People's Party, founded by the MP John Beckett. Even after the war had started, an unrepentant Domvile continued to back the German cause. In June 1940, his mistress, Olive Baker, was arrested for distributing leaflets advertising *Reichssender Hamburg*, a German shortwave radio station that was part of Goebbels' propaganda empire. The importance of Domvile to this book is that he covers hundreds of entries on the List under a phrase he coined – 'Judmas'; the Jewish-Masonic conspiracy, which was, according to the Nazis, the source of all evil in history.[96]

Domvile was one of the Fellow Travellers of the Right, a broad church that backed German National Socialism. Some of these, like Domvile, were members of the establishment, including the aristocracy and almost certainly the Duke of Windsor, whose fear of Soviet Russia bordered on paranoia. It included a group who believed that Germany had been too harshly treated at Versailles; informed men like Sir Ian Hamilton who had led the disastrous Gallipoli campaign in 1915. And it included the rough-neck Jew baiters who had put on Oswald Mosley's black shirts and stormed London's East End in the 'battle of Cable Street' in 1936.

The alleged conspiracy between the Freemasons and the Jews was based essentially on the *Protocols of the Elders of Zion*, which first saw the light of day as a pamphlet in 1864, aimed at Napoleon III, the French emperor. The Tsarist police in Romanov Russia used it in their pogroms across the empire. The book was supposed to be the minutes of an actual conference of Jews bent on a world domination of Zionism. The first *actual* Zionist conference was held at Basle, Switzerland in 1897 and had nothing to do with the *Protocols*. In 1903 and 1905, two versions of the book were published in Russia and by 1920 it was available in all European languages, as well as in Arabic, Chinese and Japanese. The racist American entrepreneur Henry Ford was only too happy to see it printed in his *Dearborn Independent* newspaper, although he was forced to withdraw it after a lawsuit. In 1921, *The Times* outed the *Protocols* as a forgery of the Okhrana, the Russian secret police, and this was ratified by a Swiss court of law in 1935.

By that time, of course, the damage had been done. A surprising number of otherwise intelligent people believed it. Alfred Rosenberg, ideologist of the Nazi Party, edited a German version and Hitler refers to it in *Mein Kampf*. In fact, the *Protocols* is an appalling book on every level. It is a libel on the Jewish people (by no means the first in history) and is also terribly dull. Its outrageous claims – that the Jews *already* control big business, international finance, education and propaganda and have destroyed both democracy and aristocracy – are supported by no evidence at all. Because of that, it is difficult to see how a reading of the *Protocols* could convert anybody to anti-Semitism. A reader has to *begin* with that mindset or the *Protocols* would achieve nothing.

'There is a straight line,' wrote the Jewish historian Raul Hilberg, 'from "You have no right to live among us as Jews" to "You have no right to live among us" to "You have no right to live".' Simply put, this is an accurate description of anti-Semitism from the Middle Ages to the twentieth century. The *Gestapo Handbook*, as we have seen, outlines the history of British Judaism from relative tolerance under Richard the Lionheart to expulsion in 1290 on the orders of Edward I and the return of Sephardic Jews under Oliver Cromwell. The end of the nineteenth century saw the arrival of thousands of Ashkenazi Jews fleeing the pogroms of Tsarist Russia and Poland. The *Handbook* breaks its Jewish section down into politics, finance, the economy and the media, listing thirty-five Jewish organisations, together with their addresses and their leading personnel, most of whom appear on the List.

In terms of politics, the *Handbook* cites Benjamin Disraeli as the 'breakthrough' politician who brought Jews to the fore. In fact, in his day (Disraeli entered parliament in 1837), MPs had to be Christian in order to take the oath of office and Disraeli had been baptised. Not until the Jewish Disabilities Act of 1857 could Jews enter the Commons. Next, historically, comes a List member (I13) Rufus Isaacs, the 2nd Marquis of Reading. A product of Rugby and Balliol, Oxford, he inherited his father's title in 1935 but had a distinguished career before that. He was a KC in 1929, Viceroy of India before that and Vice President of the Anglo-Jewish Association that had its headquarters at Woburn Place, WC1. Among its officers were three other Listees. Another Vice President was Sir Osmond D'Avigdor-Goldsmid (A86), who died in the year that the List was compiled. Yet another was the Reverend H. I. Hertz (actually Josef), who is described as *Hauptrabbiner* (Chief rabbi) and has four different addresses, no doubt representing the various organisations to which he belonged; oddly, Woburn Place is not among them. The last Vice President named is Lionel de Rothschild (R123) of Kensington Palace Gardens, one of two members on the List of the fabulously rich family of bankers and property owners.

Two Jews, the *Handbook* tells us, were included in Neville Chamberlain's government. Philip Sassoon at the Ministry of Works is not on the List but Leslie Hore-Belisha is. B91 was a graduate of St John's College, Oxford and reached the rank of major in the First World War. A flamboyant speaker, he had been an MP since 1923 and, as Transport Minister, had given his name to the flashing orange lights at pedestrian crossings. He had also rewritten the Highway Code and introduced driving tests. By 1937, he was Secretary of State for War and tried to introduce conscription as early as the next year; Chamberlain refused. Clashing with the king as well as the prime minister, Hore-Belisha resigned over army use and refused to take up another post. Some branded him a warmonger of the Churchill mode but, even so, he was not belligerent enough for others. Ronald Cartland, the MP for King's Norton, thought he should be shot. As a Jew, Hore-Belisha came in for his share of the minority but extremely vocal anti-Semitism of a section of the British people. He was dubbed 'Horeb-Belisha' and, days before war was declared, a member of the British Union of Fascists wrote into the *Hackney Gazette* – 'Look at [the army's] leader – Hore-Belisha! Whenever I see this man's physog [face] in the paper, a horrible, revolting feeling comes over my stomach.'

The *Handbook* sounds quite relieved that there were no Jews in Churchill's cabinet but it was well known that Churchill himself, along with Anthony Eden and Duff Cooper, were pro-Jewish. Cooper had extolled the virtues of Judaism in a recent tour of America and Eden, when in opposition, had been supported by the Fabian Socialists, whose leader was Israel Sieff (S59) who, with his wife Rebecca, was dominant in various Jewish and Zionist organisations. Parliament, the *Handbook* tells us, had nineteen or twenty Jewish MPs – four of them named, only one of whom (Lewis Silkin in S65) is on the List. Their importance lay in their links to big business. In 1934, the 581 MPs held 646 posts on various boards of directors.

We shall consider business in a separate chapter because

control of the economy was obviously essential in a totalitarian state. A number of Jews held key positions in the 'big five' High Street banks: Victor Schuster was at the National Provincial; Walter Samuel, Viscount Bearsted (B60 and B61) was at Lloyds; Lord Groschen ran the Midland; he, with Lord Melchett (M109) and George Schuster (S59), dominated Barclays. Much of the economy, according to the *Handbook*, was in Jewish hands. Shell Transport and Trading was riddled with them. Sir Robert Waley was chairman and director of no less than twenty-six different oil companies. The Maypole Dairy Company and the Home and Colonial chain were examples of the Jews' control of the food industry. The Rothschilds and their cronies ran the country's insurance and the gold and diamond business was entirely in Jewish hands.

It almost went without saying that the British media was, as the *Protocols of the Elders of Zion* insisted, an instruct of the Jews. The sense of outrage seeps from the *Handbook* when it quotes Lord Beaverbrook in 1930:

'The commercial and intellectual capabilities of the Jews are so abundant in Britain because they are held back by neither ban nor barrier. Here, the Jewish question is solved by their complete integration in our various activities and the nation is therefore richer and happier. The Continent will eventually discover that there is no other solution.'

But Hitler was not listening; for him the solution was the Holocaust and it would take a world war to prove Beaverbrook right.

Much of the anti-German propaganda that came out of the British cinema, the *Handbook* continued, came from the censors Ivor Montagu and S. Bernstein, neither of whom is on the List. The Ostrer brothers (Isidore is O35) owned several hundred cinemas and music halls across the country; Mark was director of twenty-six film companies and Maurice twelve more. Oscar Deutsch (D44) controlled 500 cinemas since the Gaumont and Odeon companies had merged.

The Jewish organisations have a total of 113 officers, of whom sixteen are on the List. There is no doubt, however, that, had the eagle landed, *all* of them would have been visited by the black-coated gentlemen of the Gestapo. There was, of course, overlap. Prominent Jews were chairmen and presidents of a number of committees and although their methods varied and the shades of opinion could sometimes seem quite diverse, the aims and objectives were largely the same – safety and security for a faith that had been persecuted for centuries and the creation of a new homeland; Zion.

Central to the last was the President of the Zionist Federation of Great Britain and Ireland, based at Hinksey Hill, Oxford – W53, Chaim Weizmann. He was born the son of a timber merchant in Belarus, then part of the vast Russian Empire and went to Germany to study at the universities of Darmstadt and Berlin before taking his doctorate in chemistry at Friborg. He moved to Britain in 1904 and became a lecturer at the University of Manchester. Here, as a British citizen, he was Charles Weizmann and quickly became associated with the growing Zionist movement, working with Arthur Balfour for the cause in 1905-06. He moved in exalted circles among the politicians of the day and the wealthiest Jews, like the Rothschilds. C. P. Scott of the *Manchester Guardian* said of him that he had 'an intense and burning sense of the Jew as a Jew'. When the Peel Commission was looking into the restructuring of the Middle East – Canaan's 'land of milk and honey' – as the new Jewish homeland, Weizmann reminded them that Europe had 6 million Jews 'for whom the world is divided into places where they cannot live and places where they cannot enter.'[97]

When war broke out, Weizmann became an honorary adviser to the Ministry of Supply at Shell-Mex House in the Strand. That was also the year when a conference held at St James's Palace decided that no more money was to be spent on creating a homeland for the Jews and the whole topic was effectively shelved for six years.

Weizmann forms a bridge between the two groups of Jews that feature on the List. The first is British Jews, men and women with British birth certificates. Israel Cohen (C76) appears in the politics category. Manchester born and bred, he attended the Jews School, Manchester Grammar and went on to University College, London. He ran the English department of the Zionist Central Office in Cologne and Berlin and found himself interned during the First World War in Ruhleben POW camp. Throughout the Twenties, he was an active fundraiser for the Zionists and visited Poland and Hungary, where he witnessed pogroms at first hand. He wrote articles for various Jewish publications, as well as *The Times* and when war broke out, was General Secretary of the Zionist Federation in London.

L41 is one of the few on the List who simply has *Jude* (Jew) after his name. *Hauptmann* (Captain) has been added, although E. F. Lawson was actually a Brigadier by 1940. An historian from Eton and Balliol, he played polo for Oxford and was commissioned into the Bucks Hussars yeomanry while carrying on the day job as a reporter for the *Telegraph* in Paris and New York. He was in the thick of things in the First World War, his regiment posted first to Gallipoli, then to

Gaza. He rode behind General Allenby on his triumphal entry to Jerusalem in 1917.[98] By the time he was twenty-six, Lawson was acting Lt. Colonel and had the medal ribbons of DSO and MC stitched to his tunic. By 1920, 'the Colonel' as he was known, was back at the *Telegraph* and took over the *Morning Post* in 1937. When war broke out, he was commanding the artillery of the 48th (South Midland) Division with the rank of brigadier. He won the CB for his heroic action in the retreat to Dunkirk. For all Schellenberg was adamant with the bald *Jude* reference, there is nothing overtly Jewish about Lawson at all. He was the grandson of the newspaper magnate Joseph Moses Levy, who was British-born, and none of the family seems to have espoused the cause of Zionism. Perhaps, to the Nazis, the original family name was enough.

The same can be said of S5, 'Steffan Spender'. It would have been perfectly feasible to place Stephen Spender in the literati section but his mother was half-Jewish and in the Nazi scheme of things, that would have made him a full Jew. A friend of the poets W. H. Auden and Christopher Isherwood, Spender left University College, Oxford without a degree and moved to Hamburg in 1929 as the Weimar government was rocked yet again by economic disaster. He found writing here liberating. Weimar was, in Nazi eyes at least, appallingly decadent – Spender appreciated the lack of censorship. By 1936, he had veered to the Left, joining Harry Pollitt's Communist Party and reporting on Stalin's show trials for the *Daily Worker*. He was imprisoned briefly in Spain during the Civil War but, like many others, his faith in the Left was seriously dented by the revelation of the Molotov-Ribbentrop pact. Bisexual, he had a number of affairs with men and women throughout the Thirties, asserting, 'I shall always have a boy, a railway fare or a revolution.' What more, in the 1930s, could anybody ask?

The Sieffs were a fascinating couple at the heart of the Jewish community. Israel is listed as President of the English Zionist Organisation. Rebecca's address is given as Brook House, Park Lane and each was wanted by a different Amt of the RSHA. They both hailed from Manchester and attended university there. By 1916, Israel was managing director of the company that would become Marks and Spencer (Simon Marks, M69, was a boyhood friend). That was the year in which he met Chaim Weizmann and became involved in the Zionist movement. Three years later, he was part of the Zionist Commission of Palestine at the deliberations at Versailles. Rebecca founded the Women's International Zionist Organisation at 75, Great Russell Street, WC1, sitting on the board with Weizmann's wife. Her father had fled Russia in the pogroms of 1882, so Rebecca was no stranger to anti-Semitism. From 1933, she had set up the Women's Appeal Committee of the Central British Fund to rescue refugees from Nazi Germany.

S17 was perhaps the most influential Jew in British politics, although the *Handbook* makes little of him. Herbert, First Viscount Samuel, was born in Liverpool and attended University College School in London before going up to Balliol. Despite his Jewish upbringing, he renounced his faith as a young man (which may be why the *Handbook* ignores him) but he married a Jewish woman and kept Shabbat and kosher to please her. MP for Cleveland in 1902, he became Home Secretary under Asquith and his pro-Zionist stance influenced the Balfour Declaration. In this context, he worked with Weizmann but fell foul of both sides in the tortuous politics of the Middle East in the 1920s. In the end, both the Zionists and the Arab nationalists were disappointed by his fence-sitting. The British working class despised him because his Commission into coal mining in 1926 led to the decision to reduce miners' wages and that in turn led to the General Strike. He was virtual leader of the Liberal Party until he lost his Commons seat in 1935. Samuel's fence-sitting continued into the late 1930s. Receiving the Viscountcy in 1937, he backed Chamberlain's appeasement policy, believing that Germany should be allowed to get her colonies back. The following year, however, he became an ardent supporter of the *kindertransporten* movement, which was getting Jewish children out of Nazi clutches across Europe.

Hermann Budzislawski (B250) is another Listee with *Jude* against his name. Born in Berlin, he attended Jewish schools there before going on to university and becoming a *privatdozent* by 1926. His specialism, in which he had obtained a doctorate three years earlier, was eugenics. Until 1933, he wrote for two Berlin newspapers and continued to do so under the pseudonym Hermann Fischli from the safety of Zurich. In 1934, he set up the anti-Fascist *Neue Press Korrespondent* in Prague and became chairman of the German Popular Front Committee. By the outbreak of war, he was already in Paris, having restarted *Die Neue Weltbiene*, officially banned in Germany. He was briefly interned when France fell but managed to get out with the help of the New York based Emergency Rescue Committee run by Varian Fry. His stay in Britain was short; by October 1940 he was in America.

We get the impression that E52 was on the List just because he was a famous, successful Jew and there is nothing in his career that marked him out as an enemy of the Reich. He was Jacob Epstein, *Bildhauer* (sculptor) with a London address at Hyde Park Gate. The son of Polish emigrants, he was born in New York's Lower East Side and took up art as a child because he was often ill with pleurisy. He came to Europe in 1902 and joined a crowd of Bohemian artists, moving to a studio in the

Strand in London six years later. His stark sculptures, usually nude, offended the more Puritan sections of polite society to the extent that various 'projections' of his anatomically correct statues were hacked off in the 1930s as being 'dangerous' – whether to aesthetic sensibilities or life and limb is not clear! He sculpted fellow Listee Paul Robeson's head in 1928 and some of the reviews of his work veered to the anti-Semitic.

Eva Reading (R23) deserves rather more of a fanfare than she gets on the List. She was Eva Violet Isaacs, Marchioness of Reading, the wife of the second Marquess and daughter of the 1st Baron Melchett. Her father's money had originally come from the nickel alloy business and a company which merged with ICI in 1926. Eva was a Christian, so her marriage to Gerald Isaacs (as he then was) had to be a civil one. She converted to Judaism, learning Hebrew and worshipping at the liberal synagogue in St John's Wood. Since she was involved in Zionism and child welfare, it was perhaps inevitable that she worked with the Children's Refugee Movement, smuggling Jewish youngsters out of Germany before the war.

Such was the obsession with race in Nazi Germany that there is no explanatory comment in the *Handbook* for attitudes towards Jews; nor, often, is a reason other than the obvious, for their inclusion on the List. The Nuremberg Laws of 1935 had deprived German Jews of their citizenship. The Aryan Clause two years earlier was applied to German media and to the churches. The Lublin Plan and the Madagascar Plan were abandoned ideas of the Nazi high command to move the Jews physically into those places as permanent areas of settlement. Neither of these was workable for practical reasons. The future lay with the shootings and hangings of the *Einsatzkommandos* and the ovens of Auschwitz.

The other group of Jews was the one we have met already

in an earlier chapter – the 'aliens' often rounded up in 1940 – who had fled the Nazis in 1933. Dr Elise Baumgartel became B55. The daughter of an architect, she had read Medicine at Berlin University but her natural enthusiasms led her to Egyptology. The excitement of Howard Carter's discovery of Tutankhamen's tomb in the Valley of the Kings shone a spotlight on ancient Egypt and Elise was writing learned treatises throughout the Twenties. She was almost always the only woman toiling under a hot sun with trowel and brush but it all came to an end in 1933 because Elise was a Jew. British universities fought over her and she ended up teaching at University College London. When the war broke out and conscription began to take its toll, she found herself heavily involved in the Petrie Museum of Antiquities. Apart from being Jewish and a woman in a man's world, it is difficult to see how Dr Baumgartel could have upset the Reich.

Max Katzenellenbogen, alias Max Bloch, was different. K27 was born to assimilated Jews in Frankfurt and was sent to various boarding schools to learn languages. He graduated in jurisprudence from Frankfurt University in 1920, studied art history later in the decade and obtained a doctorate in the year that the Nazis came to power. Surviving for a while as a *privatdozent* and with the support of his Swiss pianist wife, Katzenellenbogen was interned for his liberal views and 'non-Aryan' background in Dachau in 1938. Released the following year, seriously ill because of the camp's deprivations, he and his wife emigrated to Switzerland and then to Britain, where he taught at the Warburg Institute. Oddly, both his entries in the List (as Katzenellenbogen and Bloch) have him down as *chemiker* (chemist), a discipline with which he was never connected.

L89 was Hermann Liebermann from Drohodycz in Austria-

217

Hungary. He was a lawyer and socialist politician and served in the Vienna parliament for a total of eight years. In the First World War, he enlisted as a private in Pilsudski's Polish Legion and, as a lawyer, defended members of the unit who refused to swear allegiance to the Kaiser. From 1919 to 1923, he was a Socialist MP in the Sejm, the Polish parliament. It all came to grief in the *coup d'état* of 1926 and Liebermann found himself at the sharp end of police brutality and a two-and-a-half year stretch in prison. Moving to France, he supported the Republicans in the Spanish Civil War and joined Sikorski's exiled cabinet in Britain after the collapse of Poland in the September War. He was the first Jew in any Polish government.

Gustav Mayer could easily appear in this book in the writers' chapter. Nearly seventy at the time of the List, M25 was born to a middle-class family in Preszlau, north Germany and obtained his doctorate in economics from Basel in 1893. He worked as a trade and business journalist on the *Frankfurt Zeitung* before freelancing in Heidelberg and Berlin. The First World War saw him conscripted and he was attached to the German army of occupation in Belgium. By 1922, he was professor of political parties at Berlin universities and wrote a definitive biography of Friedrich Engels, who had co-written the *Communist Manifesto* with Karl Marx in 1848. By the time the second volume emerged, the Nazis were in power and the book had to be sent to be printed in the Netherlands, followed swiftly by Dr Mayer. He was in Britain by 1936 but his poor English meant that he found educational employment difficult. Eventually, he became a staff member at the International Institute of Social History (no doubt one of those organisations that the *Gestapo Handbook* believed was anti-German) and won an unpaid fellowship at the London School of Economics.

By the time of the List, the Rockefeller Foundation had come to his rescue to the tune of £300.

M95 was Israel Mattuek, one of the 'three Ms' who were well known in Jewish circles between the wars. Matteuk was born in Lithuania and his family moved to America when he was still a child. A Harvard graduate, he was ordained in the Hebrew College in 1910 and spent two years as a rabbi in the Liberal synagogue of New York before moving to London. He was instrumental in setting up the World Union for Progressive Judaism in 1926 and wrote the first Liberal Jewish prayer book in 1937. His fascinating book *What are the Jews?* appeared two years later. The other Ms – Montefiore and Montagu – are on the List too. Montagu was almost certainly in the United States by the time of the List, teaching at Rutger's University and writing on racial issues. Montefiore could be any one of the Jewish-Italian family who had made their name in academe.

★ ★ ★

But if the Jewish Listees needed no explanation, the presence of Freemasons did. The German word is *freimaurer* and it appears only once on the List, making the masons difficult to identify and adding to their mystique as a secret, sinister organisation. Even today, freemasonry divides the world. Most books and articles on them are written by masons themselves, with an inevitable bias or by those who essentially believe in the 'Judmas' theory of Barry Domvile and the *Protocols*; a sensible middle path is as difficult to find as the List's masons themselves. The *Gestapo Handbook* has over six pages on the subject, beginning with the bizarre line we have recorded already – 'England is the country of Freemasonry'. According to most accounts, the first acolyte to join the Order was Sir Robert Moray in Newcastle-upon-Tyne in 1641. He was also a founder of the Royal Society (1661), as was fellow mason Elias Ashmole. The origins of Freemasonry are lost in legend but the links with Judaism are there from the beginning. The original masons were the architects and builders of the temple of Solomon in Jerusalem, which has given novelists and film-makers a vast source of pseudo-history and claptrap on which to weave their stories.

According to the *Handbook*, the lodges of Britain (a list is available in the Special Search List's index) form an alliance between Jew and Christian, king and commoner, ruler and ruled, all in the name of equality, liberalism and humanitarian welfare. This, the *Handbook* contends, is a front and the real purpose of the masons is to govern and to extend the ideals of British imperialism to the Empire, especially India and Africa. There were lodges composed of men of similar occupations, lodges of public schools and universities, and lodges of the armed forces and political parties. 'What concerns us,' said the *Handbook*, 'is that in its ideological orientation and its political effectiveness – as long as it lasts – it is a dangerous weapon in the hands of Britain's plutocrats against National Socialist Germany.'[99]

In the absence of reliable information from the various lodges in wartime Britain, I am able to identify very few masons from the List. The first, alphabetically, is D38, Lord Derby. The Stanley family had held lands in the Midlands and the North since the Middle Ages and had been prominent in national politics for five hundred years. *This* Lord Derby had been responsible for the scheme bearing his name in the First World War, whereby a man promised (attested) to join the colours if called upon in the days before conscription (brought in in 1916). He himself had been commissioned in the Grenadier Guards in 1885 and served on Lord Robert's staff in the Boer War, mentioned in dispatches, not only for his 'thorough knowledge of men and affairs' but for his 'tact and discretion'. In peacetime, he held various cabinet posts under Lord Salisbury, Arthur Balfour and H. H. Asquith. He was Lord Lieutenant for Lancashire and Grand Master of the Masonic Order, his own lodge in the same county.

Henry George Charles Lascelles, the 6th Earl of Harewood, was a mason too, Grand Master of the United Grand Lodge, but he was not elevated to that status until 1942. H34 on the List, he attended the Royal Military College at Sandhurst and was commissioned in the Grenadier Guards, commanding the Third Battalion in the First World War. He married May, the daughter of George V in 1922, this fulfilling one of the tenets of the *Gestapo Handbook* – the masonic link with the royal family. Only his London address – the rather humble-sounding 32, Green Street – is given in the List.

William, Viscount Leverhulme (L80), more properly belongs to the next chapter, since he was co-founder of the huge Lever Brothers business empire in 1930. Eton was followed by Trinity College, Cambridge and he caused something of a stir in masonic circles when he created the new Mersey Lodge (No. 5434) in 1934. The company, and Leverhulme himself, had a less than caring attitude to the natives of the Belgian Congo, where the company had a base from 1911. He demanded 'more troops, more police and more brutality'[100] to keep the locals in check.

The Judeo-Masonic conspiracy is one of the great myths of history. It has no basis in fact and can be interpreted as an example of the politics of envy. Europe was full of desperately poor Jews, whom the Nazis categorised as human vermin. But there were also rich Jews – the plutocrats that the *Handbook* talks about. The Freemasons, for all their talk of equality and liberalism, were elitist, their Grand Masters all the scions of noble houses. Rich, successful cliques that were not dedicated to National Socialism were precisely something the Nazis did not need.

And in case any British Jews had missed the point. As early as 1930, before there was a Nazi state, Josef Goebbels had put his racial case in block capitals in his propaganda leaflets:

'We are enemies of the Jews because we are fighters for the freedom of the German people. The Jew is the cause and the beneficiary of our misery... He is the real cause for our loss in the Great War... He has corrupted our race, fouled our morals, undermined our customs and broken our power... The Jew is the plastic demon of the decline of mankind .... The Jew is uncreative. He produces nothing... It is not true that we eat a Jew every morning at breakfast[101]... It is true, however, that he slowly but surely robs us of everything we own. That will stop, as surely as we are Germans.'[102]

And, according to the plan for British Jews and their allies, the Freemasons, it was going to stop in the summer of 1940.

CHAPTER TWELVE

BUSINESS AS USUAL

Adolf Hitler often admitted that he had next to no interest in economics. Having abandoned the socialist view of the Nazi Party's original twenty-five points, he embarked in the later Twenties on a campaign to woo Germany's big business, realising that, in a capitalist state, even one dependent on American money, as Weimar was, these fat cats called the shots. They, in turn, were as suspicious and scornful of the Bohemian corporal as the army generals were but, once the Party following began to rise, they changed their minds, especially when they themselves took at least some of the hits of the Wall Street crash in October 1929.

For most German industry, there were two elements of National Socialism that appealed. The first was Hitler's drive for *lebensraum*, which promised ever larger markets. Whatever the downside of wartime conditions, in theory, German companies were selling to Austria, Czechoslovakia, Poland, the Netherlands, Belgium and France by the summer of 1940; Britain would be next. The low wages fixed by the Reich, amounting to little more than slave labour in some cases, automatically increased profits. The other plus from the plutocrats' point of view was the discipline created by the Nazis – the irritating delaying tactics of the Trade Unions, with their Leftist, anti-capitalist attitudes, was swept away after 1933 by Robert Ley's Labour Front. As 1939 loomed, the drive became one directed towards armaments – guns, not butter, in Goering's phrase – but that, too, created jobs and *huge* profits for the armaments industry, which in itself quadrupled in size once the war was underway. Various cynics have pointed out that war, while hell, is also profitable; it was the outbreak of the Second World War that jolted Britain out of the economic disaster of the hungry Thirties.

Hitler wooed the fat cats himself and sent Goering and Hess to swarm around men whose factories had bankrolled earlier Reichs. The Krupp family had been building weapons of war since the fifteenth century and Gustav Krupp von Bohlen, running the vast armaments complex in Essen, Kiel and Magdeburg, became an overnight convert to Nazism three weeks after Hindenburg appointed Hitler chancellor. Von Bohlen was made chairman of the *Adolf Hitler Spende*, a fund actually administered by the party hack Martin Bormann, to which all businessmen were expected to contribute. During the war, the Krupp company had a factory inside the huge death camp complex at Auschwitz-Birkenau, where men were literally worked to death.

Emil Kirdorf was another industrial lion tamed by Hitler. He was a coal baron from the Rhineland and, unlike Krupp von Bohlen, supported the Nazis from the early days. A ruthless employer, his workers hated him and he even found the sabre-rattling of Kaiser Wilhelm too limp. He died in July 1938 but his company continued its ardent support of the Nazis as the saviours of Germanism until the end of the war.

Another early backer of the Party was Hugo Stinnes, a mining engineer, whose family money enabled him to sink 50,000 DM into a company of his own in 1892. Expanding into iron, steel and shipping, his firm supplied most of the towns of Germany with electricity and gas. He bought newspapers that backed Right-wing views and closed down those that did not. His death in 1925, before the Nazi Party really got off the ground, slowed the company down but it continued to back Hitler and was key to the Nazi military machine during the war.

I. G. Farben, the huge chemical and pharmaceutical company, was formed in 1925, the same year that Hitler instituted the SS as his personal bodyguard. It was the result of similar mergers that were happening all over the world at the time and, by the time of the Anschluss (1938), had 218,000 employees. The company worked hand in glove with Hitler in the takeover of both Czechoslovakia and Poland and, like Krupp, had a huge factory at Morowitz, part of the Auschwitz complex. It also manufactured the cyanide pellets called Zyklon B used in the gas chambers both there and elsewhere.

Perhaps the only major industrialist who saw the light and realised what a monster National Socialism had unleashed was Fritz Thyssen. His Ruhr business, iron and steel, was badly hit by the French army's occupation of the area in 1923-24 and he threw his lot in with the Fascists, contributing over a million marks to Hitler by the time he became chancellor. Thyssen had joined the Nazi Parry two years earlier. He became a leading economist under the Führer but, by 1935, he was cooling towards his leader. He disliked the fast-growing anti-Semitism of the Reich and called Robert Ley 'a stammering drunkard'.

He left Germany towards the end of 1939 for Switzerland and wrote a letter to Hitler – 'Stop the useless bloodshed,' he demanded, 'and Germany will obtain peace with honour and will thus preserve her unity.'[103]

Hitler never replied but Thyssen's property was seized and he was declared a non-citizen. He spent three years in a concentration camp before liberation in 1945.

There was a great deal of gobbledegook about economic measures and motives from the Reich Chancellery. Country must come before profits but competitors must be eliminated. Hjalmar Schacht was Hitler's financial expert, as President of the Reichsbank since 1923. He was very able but resented having to hang on to the coat-tails of the Americans twice in the 1920s in the Dawes Plan and the Young Plan. For three years, he was Reich Minister of Economics, desperately trying to balance the inflationary books as the cost of re-armament rocketed. The Night of the Long Knives and the rising Jewish persecution rattled him and he had the nerve to resign his post in 1937. He was still necessary, however, so was retained as Minister without Portfolio and was still bank president. Slowly, as the war progressed, he veered towards the growing opposition to Hitler, clashing frequently with Goering, who had been given responsibility for the radical four-year economic plan. Two months after *Fall Weiss*, Schacht was removed from the bank presidency and replaced by Walther Funk, who had been the Führer's personal finance guru since 1931. He served under Goebbels as a journalist with the Ministry of Enlightenment and effectively chaired the Reich Broadcasting Company. Schlact described him as a 'harmless homosexual and alcoholic' and Funk remained utterly loyal to Hitler to the end.

With German big business and finance in the pocket of the

Nazis, what does the *Gestapo Handbook* have to say about the British economy? It recognised that the country could never be self-sufficient in terms of food production, so all the Ministry of Information's exhortation to 'Dig For Victory' and tighten belts was all rather a waste of time. Britain, essentially, could not survive without raw materials (only coal was plentiful) and this would be bound to have a detrimental effect in the long run.

The *Handbook* describes the importance of Trusts, the large companies like Imperial Chemicals but stresses the importance – crucial to the List – of individuals of huge influence who sat on the boards of dozens of those Trusts at the same time. The Lever brothers' giant, Unilever, is highlighted, as well as Van den Bergh and Jurgens, producers of margarine. Such was the nature of international co-operation and competition before the war, of course, that these companies also held shares in similar German firms. The *Handbook* is scathing about the Jewish element in various companies – ICI was founded by 'the Jew' Sir Alfred Mond in 1926 as a result of a merger of several smaller firms. It had £95 million worth of capital by 1939 and employed 65,000 workers.

As Lord Melchett (M109), Mond appears to be on the List. Born in Widnes, Lancashire, he was the son of a chemist who had emigrated from Germany. It may well have been an embarrassment to his father that Mond failed the Natural Sciences tripos at St John's College, Cambridge. Undeterred, he studied law at Edinburgh and was called to the Bar in 1894. Business was his forte, however, and he joined his father's Nickel Company before going on to directorship of Westminster Bank and the Industrial Finance Investment Corporation.

As a politician, Mond sat as Liberal MP for Chester and

Swansea before joining the coalition government of David Lloyd George in the later stages of the First World War. He was Minister of Health in the Twenties but he veered to Conservatism after falling out with the Welsh wizard over his proposed nationalisation of farming land. He was created Baron Melchett in 1928 and, as a Jew, supported Chaim Weizmann's Zionist cause, accompanying him to Palestine in 1921. Since Mond died in 1930, the Listee 'Baron Melchett' is likely to refer to his son, Henry Ludwig, who was director of ICI throughout the war. This branch of the family had little to do with politics but it may be that Schellenberg was unaware of that.

In terms of transport, four companies ran the railway network: the Great Western; the London and North Eastern; the London, Midland and Scottish; and the Southern. The huge merchant navy fleet could not cope, the *Handbook* says smugly, with the outbreak of war but it does not mention the U-boat menace specifically. Air traffic all over the world was dominated by British concerns, working hand in glove with the oil industry. The famed British shipyards were also failing, according to the *Handbook*, to keep pace with the loss of ships. Passenger lines get a mention too, probably because the 1930s was *the* decade of cruise lines. White Star is there, as are Cunard and P&O. Many of these ships would see service as rather exotic troop-carriers during the war.

The motor industry is described and the Germans were aware that many car manufacturers were now making tanks and aircraft for the war effort. Germany and Italy, the *Handbook* contends, had surpassed Britain pre-1939 in car manufacturing and the Americans were challenging fast. In fact, there seems to be no business area where the German 'economic miracle' has not succeeded in toppling Britain from its once pre-eminence as 'workshop of the world'. Coal, iron and steel, and even textiles (the preserve of the Courtauld family), are all examples of British silver medals as opposed to Germany's gold.

Cropping up constantly on the List are the *täterkreis* of Ignatz-Petschek; the headquarters of Anglo-Iranian Oil; Brittanic House; Unilever House; Shell Mex House (Royal Dutch Shell); various banking concerns and the ever-mysterious 'Merton'. While the other multi-nationals are listed as companies, Merton stands alone, either with or without inverted commas. There are twenty-two men and two women '*mitarbeit*' (connected with) Merton, and Merton himself is M120 (Israel Richard Merton), born in Frankfurt in 1881. His is one of the twenty-eight photographs with the original List. He is described as '*Emigrant, Jude*' and has links with the British Metal Corporation. He was a deputy of the German People's Party under Weimar but lost his business position in 1936 because of his Jewish ancestry. His assets were confiscated and two years later he was interned in Buchenwald. Although the camp was later to achieve a grim reputation as a death camp, that was not the case at the time and Merton was released. He and his wife, Princess Elizabeth of Sayn-Wittgenstein-Berleberg, fled to Britain, presumably with most of the twenty-four associates on the List, the bulk of whom were Jewish.

Most of the Merton group are obscure today but one who stands out is L149, Captain Oliver Lyttleton. As the son of the 4th Baronet, he was one of those men noted in the *Gestapo Handbook* as having a finger in a vast number of pies. A product of Eton and Trinity, Cambridge, he won the DSO and MC in the First World War (when he met and was friendly with Churchill). After the war, he became, among other business ventures, managing director of the British Metal Corporation when it was a major shareholder in the German Metallgesellschaft A.G., which supported the Nazi Party. The year of the List was a busy one for him. He became Conservative MP for Aldershot in 1940, a member of the Privy Council (by virtue of his title) and President of the Board of Trade.

Another emigrant business group like Merton's, the Petschek Group, came under Schellenberg's microscope. Ignatz Petschek was the founder of a family business of Jewish financiers and businessmen with assets all over Germany and particularly in Moravia and Bohemia before the First World War. When Hitler came to power, the company's assets were seized. All over the Reich, companies large and small benefited from the sudden disappearance of Jewish business. Not only did premises, machinery and markets become available at a stroke but competition was reduced too. The Petschek company had been big in the coal business since 1857 but the mines became the property of the Reich in 1940. The headquarters of the group in London, which would become a target for the Luftwaffe in the late summer, was Shell Mex House, used by other industrial concerns, that stood between the Strand and the Thames. This building, an art deco monolith which housed 'Big Benzene', the largest clock in the capital, had become the home of the Ministry of Supply at the outbreak of war and would take a direct hit once the Blitz began.

Another landmark building mentioned several times in the List is Unilever House in Blackfriars, built in 1929-33 on the site of the original Bridewell Palace of Henry VIII, which, in its turn, had become one of the grimmest of London's prisons. Its Ionic columns and stark sculpture (Controlled Energy probably the most iconic) fronted a huge building that housed not only the London headquarters of the Lever Brothers Corporation but the Dutch Margarine Company. The merger of those two made Lever Bros. the world's first genuine multi-national business empire. A number of Listees are linked with this organisation. M. G. Baat (B2) was secretary to the Board of Directors in 1940. Horatio Ballantyre (B20) boasted an impressive CV – he was FIC, KCMG, MVO and FCS. He was also a Unilever chemist who wrote several books on patent law. F. D'Arcy Cooper (C89), of Westbridge, Reigate was a company director who doubled as a baronet. It was not that the Lever Corporation was particularly involved in the war effort, although the production of margarine must have gladdened the collective hearts of the Ministry of Food, but the sheer size and scale of the concern made it a natural target for the Reich. Its German assets had been seized on the outbreak of war.

At the heart of much of the world's foreign policy, then, as now, was oil. The Anglo-Iranian Oil Company (AIOC) was originally the Anglo-Persian Company, founded in 1908. It would become British Petroleum (BP) in 1954. Its headquarters was at Britannic House (mentioned frequently on the List), a Lutyens building in Finsbury Circus. Sir Eric Alfred Berthoud (B127) became a director of the group at its Paris headquarters in 1926 and, three years later, as Weimar fell apart under the weight of the Wall Street crash, in Berlin. He was back in Paris in the late 1930s and the outbreak of war saw him advising the Ministry of Fuel and Power. Frank Tiarks (T32) was another director and another of those universal men the *Handbook* seems to have despised. He was educated on board HMS *Britannia* and ultimately became a partner in his father's business and Director of the Bank of England. His links with Germany were tangible – he was Civil High Commissioner in the Rhineland and married a German woman. The *Gestapo Handbook* was convinced that AIOC was the major contributor to SIS.

Royal Dutch Shell is listed in the *Handbook* and features

often on the List itself. The company came into existence in 1897 as a result of mergers and by the 1920s was the leading oil company, supplying eleven per cent of the global output. Recession in the 1930s had led to cutbacks, including its huge tanker fleet, but progress in the use of chemicals and a brilliant advertising campaign restored confidence. Across the world, even before the war, its service stations for the rapidly expanding car industry exuded confidence. Months before the Netherlands fell in May 1940, the company's headquarters had moved to Curacao, far beyond the range of the Luftwaffe's bombers. The company's head of operations from 1936 was J. F. de Kok (K110), last heard of by Schellenberg's team in Gravenhage (The Hague). The gloriously named Jan Carel Panthaleon von Eck obtained his doctorate in Law at the University of Utrecht and went originally into banking. By 1928, he was secretary to the President of Shell Oil in The Hague and was based in London a year later. Although he travelled all over the world after 1937, his base by 1940 was St Helen's Court, EC5 and he had become Schellenberg's E4. Shell, too, was bankrolling the British Secret Service. Major Stevens, who was so helpful to Schellenberg, told him, 'whatever is known to Shell is also known to the SIS'.[104]

Imperial Chemical Industries were in direct competition with the German giant I. G. Farben before the war. The company made chemicals, fertiliser, insecticides, dyestuffs, paint and non-ferrous metals. Dulux Paint appeared in 1932 and polyethylene five years later. More relevantly to the war effort, ICI made explosives and played a key role in the production of Perspex – vital, for instance, to the RAF – and, although Schellenberg was not aware of this, was, by 1940, advising the government on the nuclear weapons experimentation known as Tube Alloys. The company headquarters was at Millbank.

BUSINESS AS USUAL

Geoffrey Heyworth (H136) had a foot in two commercial camps; he was Chairman of both Unilever and ICI by the time of the List.

Inevitably, especially at a time when Goering's Luftwaffe was supposedly paving the way for the invasion of Britain, the aircraft industry came under scrutiny. Large numbers of engineering and metalwork companies found themselves doing their bit for the war effort, working round the clock particularly in the building of aircraft. Since the same thing was happening in Germany, the Nazis could not have been unaware of this. Their target on the List, however, is limited to the air companies per se and not so much the subsidiaries. One exception is actually on the List as a person – 'Everett, *Motoreningenieur*' of Britannic House (E62). This was actually Everett and Company, on the Air Ministry's list as suppliers of aluminium powder. Its parent company was based in Canada.

Likewise, the British Aluminium Corporation, of King William Street, supplied the RAF. Its managing director (F110) was Freeman-Horn. M20, Edward Henri Macuarie, ran Imperial Airways, which had merged with the British Overseas Aircraft Company in the year that war broke out. This, of course, was a civilian airline but it needed to be tackled because it had a supply of experienced pilots (of which the RAF was desperately short in 1940) and it maintained links with the Empire and the rest of the world. A truly isolated Britain, without those links, would be easier to defeat. In March 1939, Imperial Airways aircraft took a mere ten days to fly from Southampton to Australia, with nine overnight stops! The crew were all male and the total number of passengers was twenty. M77, Hans Martin, was managing director of another airline, KLM (Royal Dutch) which flew regularly between Amsterdam and Croydon, then Britain's largest airport. The company flew de Havillands, Fokkers and Douglases and in May 1940, when the Germans invaded the Netherlands, a number of these aircraft were actually in the air. Four of them were safely rerouted to Croydon.

The oil companies and the banks, the *Handbook* believed, were linked with shipping, the various lines totalling 18 million tonnes on the outbreak of war. As we have noted, the White Star Line, Cunard and P&O are singled out as paramount in the movement of people but an altogether smaller outfit features on the List, its managing director (F136) the Dutchman Reeltje Fries. His Royal Mail Steam Packet Company was founded in 1839 when steam-driven ships were revolutionary. By 1932, it had become a cruise line, many of its vessels lent to the war effort as troop carriers. E. T. Oliver (O19) appears on the List in connection with the Merseyside shipyards of Coubro and Scruton. The company had links in Rotterdam; by 1940, of course, under German occupation.

In this context, John Reeves Ellerman (E31) may have been the richest man in Britain between the wars. His family owned the Ellerman Line, almost forgotten today, a business he inherited in the year that Hitler came to power. Educated at Malvern and the Inner Temple in London, his estates were valued at the time at a staggering £36 million, three times the nearest record. It was not his wealth that made him a Nazi target, however; it was that he was helping Jews escape from North Germany. Over the radio, Lord Haw-Haw sneered that Ellerman was Jewish himself. This was not true; his grandfather was German.

The *Handbook* says little about Britain's banks, other than to note the leading five High Street businesses and the fact that Jewish financiers are often senior shareholders and board members. Their numbers are few on the List. Dr Robert Blank

(B153) was director of the Credit Suisse bank, with addresses in London and Folkestone. D39 was Willi Derkow, born in Charlottenberg, Berlin, and a banker there in the Weimar period. He became a political activist, writing for the press department of the SPD. In 1933, he fled to the Netherlands and then to Britain in May 1940. By August, after a brief period of internment, he became editor of the *Zeitschrift IGB Bulletin*. Given this political dimension, his credentials as a banker were probably by the way. Alfred Falter (F8) seems to have continued his financial work, at least by way of advice. He was the managing director of a Polish mining company until 1939 and sat on the board of the Polish National Bank. From 1940 onwards, he served as Treasury Minister in Sikorski's exiled government.

Almost unnoticed in the List's early pages is John Astor and his wife, of 18, Carlton House Terrace, SW1. This was John Jacob Astor V, a scion of the Anglo-American house, whose wealth was legendary. Born in Manhattan – a large portion of which the family owned – Astor spent much of his life in Britain from the age of five and attended Eton and New College, Oxford. In 1916, as a captain in the Life Guards, he married A77a, formerly Violet Elliott-Murray-Kynynmond, the daughter of Lord Minto. Her first husband had been killed in the opening weeks of the First World War and more grief was to follow when John Jacob lost a leg at Cambrai three months before the war ended. He had won a gold medal in racquets at the 1908 Olympics and retained his military role as Honorary Colonel of the Kent and Sussex Royal Artillery after the war.

Astor was one of those who held umpteen positions on the directorial boards of companies, including the Great Western Railway, Barclays Bank and the Phoenix Assurance Company.

He also owned *The Times* on the death of Lord Northcliffe in 1922 and, by the time of the List, commanded a London Home Guard unit made up entirely of his own newspaper employees. The Astors were associated with the Cliveden set, the friends who often descended on their country house near Ascot. Rather tellingly, for those who would claim later that this was a centre of Nazi sympathisers, Lady Astor is described in the List as *'deutschfeindlisch'* (anti-German).

But the Astors were not the only Americans linked with big business. B44, Bernard Baruche, was born in Camden, South Carolina, the son of a doctor. The family moved to New York, where young Bernard enrolled in City College on his way to making a fortune in sugar. Dubbed 'the lone wolf of Wall Street' because of his refusal to join any financial house, he became an adviser on peace and defence to President Woodrow Wilson, heading up the powerful War Industries Board before accompanying Wilson to Versailles in 1919. He did not approve of the crippling reparations foisted on Germany by the Allies and was very much a League of Nations man.

Throughout the inter-war period, Baruche continued as a key presidential adviser, believing, like Churchill, that Nazi Germany posed a threat to stability. He backed Roosevelt in his New Deal and National Recovery programmes and made enemies as a result. He was investigated for war profiteering. His trademark method of operation was to chat to 'Joe Public' in local parks, gauging the economic mood of the nation. It would be fun to imagine him doing the same in St James's Park in London but, if he was ever in Britain, it could only have been for fleeting visits.

The departments involved with the big business group were Amt III and IVE2. The first was the Deutsche Lebensgebeite: Sicherheitsdienst (SD Inland), dealing with economic issues and commerce. It was run by Willy Siebert. The second, run by Schellenberg himself, dealt with economic counter espionage.

The *Handbook* was well aware of Britain's economic shortcomings – 'almost all raw materials have to be imported… Food and wood are particularly short and there is no source of oil.' Napoleon's regime in the early nineteenth century had discovered that it was not possible to starve Britain out in the event of a blockade. Invasion, however, was a different matter. The fortress that was Britain was, after all, surrounded by sea and, if that sea could be controlled by the *Kriegsmarine*, Churchill's people would eventually run out of everything that gave them their freedom.

CHAPTER THIRTEEN

THE TRAITORS

No doubt the SS would have regarded anyone who ran from the Reich as a traitor, especially the German nationals. Although the diaspora of Jewish academics, deprived first of their livelihood and then of their citizenship, is perfectly understandable – and a matter of survival – these people were still, technically, Germans. Once war broke out, they could be categorised as traitors.

The *Gestapo Handbook* divides the émigré organisations in Britain into three areas: a general group (largely Jewish); a German group; and a Czech group. According to John Anderson, the Home Secretary in February 1940, there were 62,244 Germans from the 'old Reich' (Weimar and earlier) along with 11,989 Austrians. This was small by comparison with the estimated 3.5-4 million foreigners living in Britain at the outbreak of war. It was important, on a small island, to monitor the rate of immigration in peacetime, and the outbreak of war made that imperative. Throughout the twentieth century, there had always been Germans in the country. In 1914, several of these were waiters in the country's tourist business and most of them went home in August of that year, before the First World War took its inevitable toll and they faced internment in British prisons.

The *Handbook* rather sneeringly makes the comment that immigration was all about 'Christian compassion'. In July 1934, Anthony Eden told the Commons that the government was prepared to allow permanent resettlement of refugees as far as was economically viable, but that it retained the right to refuse entry to individuals. The early 1930s saw a catastrophic rise in unemployment in Germany (on which the Nazi Party capitalised) and the figure was nearly as grim in Britain.

Anti-Nazi immigration groups before the war tended to revolve around the various Jewish organisations, the pacifist, liberal and religious groups, and the Labour Party and trades unions. The *Handbook* specifies the ringleaders of the Jewish group. Dr Gustav Warburg (W18) had been the editor of the SPD's newspaper the *Hamburger Echo*. He lived at 1, Woodside, Ersken Hill, NW11. David Yaskill (Y2) had links with Willi Munzenberg (M191) and was chairman of the British International Jewish Agency. He could be found at 25, Southampton Street, Fitzroy Square and could be contacted on MUSeum 0446. Likewise, Dr Hans Priess (P114) ran a bookshop at 41a Museum Street, one of the known centres of Jewish intellectualism in London.

While the pacifist and liberal organisations had not reached the degree of influence they held in France, they nevertheless bore watching. Dr Rudolf Olden (O14), the ex-editor of the *Berliner Tagblatt*, was, according to the *Handbook*, 'especially notable'. So were Prince Lowenstein and Otto Lehmann-Russbueldt, although neither of them made the

List. A hot-bed of anti-Germanism was the London home of William, Earl of Listowel (L104), whose Hungarian-born wife held court at 36, Onslow Gardens, SW7. The man was well known for leading protests outside the German Embassy and had links with the Vatican.[105]

Few individuals are singled out in the religious organisations but the Quakers, with their International Friends headquarters at 1, Arundel Street, London, were prominent in promoting immigration. They were supported financially by the chocolatiers Cadbury, Rowntree and Fry, 'who are very rich'. Elizabeth Cadbury is C2 on the List. Then there were the Friends of New Europe, who were particularly anti-German. S111, Remy Smith, 'distinguished himself' in this movement. There were claims that he was in touch, in 1940, with opposition groups inside Germany but no evidence was forthcoming to that effect. They were also believed to be tied in with British Military Intelligence.

The Labour Party's opposition to Germany was spearheaded by S16, Victor Schiff, the Paris correspondent of the *Daily Herald*, at 12, Wilson Street, EC2. The Aid Committee for the Relief of the Victims of German Fascism in Litchfield Street, Charing Cross Road was busy spreading what the *Handbook* calls 'the horror stories' about concentration camps. The Labour leaders Clement Attlee and John Simon had both backed the Saar miners' leader Kurt Thomas and the renegade journalist Matz Braun (B215). Thomas had leaked scurrilous nonsense, as far as the *Handbook* was concerned, over the burning of the Reichstag in 1933, claiming that it had been a Nazi plot to discredit the Left.

The Trade-Union movement actually employed traitors who had abandoned the Reich. H160, Karl Holtermann, ex-editor of the *Reichbanner*, worked hand in glove with William Gillies,

Political Secretary of the Labour Party at Transport House, London. Dr Franz Neumann (N20), who had been legal adviser to the SPD, was a lecturer at the London School of Economics and could be contacted on HOLborn 0747. Transport House was also the business address of Walter Citrine (C55) Secretary General of the TUC, who was also secretary of the grandly-named World Non-Sectarian Anti-Nazi Organisation to Secure Human Rights. Both Citrine and Lord Marley (M71) were assumed to be receiving Communist support. The official line of the TUC, as of August 1938, was that it was the job of all democracies, the English brand in particular, 'not to let the victims of Fascism suffer'. The government's attitude, however, was different and the Labour Party was accused of grandstanding on the issue.

Fourteen general émigré organisations are listed in the *Handbook*, mostly based in London, and the names of several of their officers we have already met on the List. The banker Anthony Rothschild (R122) of Berkeley Square ran the Committee for Mass Colonisation. The Cambridge professor Ernest Barker (B25) was Treasurer of the International Student Service, operating from 49, Gordon Square. Leonard Montefiore (M166) and Otto Schiff (S15) shared the chairmanship of the Jewish Refugees Committee at Woburn House. The businessman Robert Waley-Cohen (C81) used the same building for the Jewish Resettlement organisation.

The specific organisations for German émigrés ran to ten, from the High Commission of the League of Nations for Refugees from Germany along Northumberland Avenue, WC2 to the Union for Displaced German Scholars in Clare Market, which we have met already. Osmond d'Avigdor Goldsmid was chairman of the Central British Fund for German Jewry and Viscount Samuel shared offices in the overcrowded Woburn

House. Chaim Weizmann was nearby in 77, Great Russell Street as president of the Central Bureau for the Settlement of German Jews in Palestine, pushing the Zionist envelope.

Apart from the Czech politicians who formed the government in exile around Benes and Masaryk: the Social Democrat Johann Becker (B78); state minister Dr Ladislaus Feierabend (F11); minister Jaromir Necas (N9); former Parisian envoy Stefan Osuski (O37); the finance minister Edouard Outrata (O42); Dr Hubert Ripka, editor and state secretary (R70); Dr Juraj Slavik (S100); Dr Rudolf Viest, state minister (V23) and Divisional General Sergei Ingre, ex-commander of the Czech Legion in France – the RHSA had little interest in Czech nationals. Of the thousand or so believed to be living in Britain, their return 'is not sought'. The rest had been living in the country for so long that they were probably politically indifferent and could be ignored.

The *Handbook* had something to say about those German émigrés who had flocked to the red flag of Communism. Until France fell, the German Communist Party (KPD) had been run from Paris. Naturally, its leaders fled to Britain, where it became affiliated to the Communist Party based in London. Although the British Communists can hardly be classed as traitors to the Reich, they are on the List nonetheless: John Murphy (M196), a Manchester journalist; William Gallagher (G4), a metalworker from Paisley; Harry Pollitt, who we have met before; and Albert Inkpen (I8), the newspaper proprietor, are listed among its founders. The *Handbook* dismisses the British Communist Party as of no influence. Not only was it ignored by the mainstream parties, even the Socialists, it had effectively squandered its estimated £100,000 1936 subsidy from Moscow by achieving nothing.

The message between the lines in the Communist Party

section of the *Gestapo Handbook* is the transient nature of the Molotov-Ribbentrop Pact. It was only a non-aggression agreement to partition Poland and the RSHA was under no illusions that the state of affairs was in any way permanent. Throughout, Moscow and Soviet Russia are seen as the enemy, colluding behind the scenes with German émigré groups and British Communists. Two things, the *Handbook* contends, prevented Britain from becoming a paid-up member of the Comintern. First was the innate conservatism of the establishment and its hold on society. The second was the innate common sense of the working classes, who are 'not amenable to loud and bloodthirsty propaganda' of the Left. Even so, there were a number of Communist-affiliated groups: the Rank and File Movement (250,000 strong); the National Unemployed Worker's Movement, with its hunger marches and clashes with the police; the Hands Off Russia Committee; the Society for Cultural Relations with Russia; the Friends of Soviet Russia led by Norman Angel (A51), with his chambers at King's Bench Walk in the Temple; and the Anti-Fascist League, dominated by well-known Jews like Harold Laski, Lord Marley and Bernard Baron (B31).

More easily identified as traitors were the membership of the German Freedom Party. It did not see itself as a party in the political sense and its sole aim was the overthrow of National Socialism in Germany. The Communists did not take the Party seriously, as they believed its bourgeois members lacked the nerve for explicit action. Its leader was Dr August Weber (W32), a banker from Oldenburg who had been in England since May 1939. Another leading light was Karl Spiecker, from Munchen-Gladbach, who ended up as S11 on the List. Unlike many other Listees, he had evaded Schellenberg's microscope; the *Handbook* says his current whereabouts were unknown.

THE TRAITORS

Dr Hermann Rauschning was off the radar too but he was one of the most high-profile politicians of his day and, had the List been prioritised, he would have been high indeed. R14 was born in Thorn, the son of a Prussian officer, and was two years older than Hitler. He obtained a doctorate from Berlin University and was wounded, with the rank of Lieutenant, in the First World War. He became a landowner and something of a local historian in the Danzig area, the Polish city that was made 'Free' under the terms of Versailles. By 1932, he had become leader of the Danzig Land League and joined the Nazis because he believed that the city should be German again and saw Hitler as the man to achieve that. Hitler befriended him and he became President of the State of Danzig in the year that the Nazis came to power in Germany.

While he was a staunch patriot, the excesses and anti-Semitism of the Nazis finally drove Rauschning out. In 1934, he left both the Senate and the Party and began a series of retreats from the Reich, first to Poland, then Switzerland, then France and, on the outbreak of war, to Britain. He denounced Hitler in two blistering books – *The Revolution of Nihilism* (1939) and *The Voice of Destruction* (1940). Today, the veracity of his series called *Conversations with Hitler* is doubted by historians but his leaflets were dropped by the French air force over Germany during the phoney war and there is no doubt that the Gestapo wanted him. Ever the brilliant speaker and crafty politician, he was mistrusted by exiled Germans in Britain because of his Right-wing opinions and he clashed with Spieker of the Freedom Party.

One group that caused Hitler problems at home were the old, baronial families of the Prussian *junker* class. Such men peppered the upper ranks of the Wehrmacht, leftovers as many of them were of the days of the Reichswehr and the Kaiser.

They despised the 'Bohemian corporal' as surely as he despised them. From those ranks came B81, Johann Heinrich, Graf von Bernstorff. After 1919, when the 'old' Germany gave way to democratically elected 'new', Graf became a name, not the title it had once been. Bernstorff was born in London, the son of a Prussian foreign minister who had lost favour when he clashed with Otto von Bismarck, the founder of modern Germany. Bernstorff senior was ambassador to the Court of St James and it was not until 1873 that his son went to Germany. He was commissioned into the artillery and served in the Reichstag before taking on a series of ambassadorships around the world. In London in 1902-06, he thought Wilhelm II an idiot and favoured an Anglo-German rapprochement at a time when those countries were locked in a naval arms race.

Back in Germany by the start of the First World War, his Intelligence work enabled him to ferry German Americans out of the war zone. At the same time, in a rather schizoid about-face, Bernstorff was involved in the anti-US sabotage plot at Black Tom Island in New York harbour. British Intelligence was on to him, publishing a photograph of the man 'in a swimming costume with his arms around two similarly dressed women, neither of whom was his wife'.[106] He was in hot water after the war too, his honorary degree from Bruno University revoked because he was 'guilty of conduct dishonourable alike in a gentleman and a diplomat'.[107]

Nevertheless, Bernstorff founded the German Democratic Party in 1921 and became the first president of the German Association of the League of Nations. More alarmingly as far as the Nazis were concerned, he was chairman of the Zionist pro-Palestine Committee and of the German delegation to the World Disarmament Conference. Hitler specifically cited Bernstorff as being responsible for the collapse of Germany on the world stage. The odd thing about this man who never equated Germandom with Nazism was that he died in 1933 and there is no record that he was in Britain after 1906.

Another 'big' name with his own *täterkreis* on the List is Gottfried Treviranus (T60) from Schieder/Lippe. Unlike most of the people the Gestapo were looking for, Treviranus had come close to an SS bullet once already. He was a naval officer in the First World War and represented the Nationalist Party in the Reichstag between 1924 and 1932. In 1930, he formed a new political group, the Peoples' Conservative Union, adding to the weakness of a government that was already floundering under acute economic distress. He held various posts in Chancellor Heinrich Bruning's cabinet and remained a firm opponent of Hitler's Nazis. He had already retired by 30 June 1934 when he heard the doorbell ring. He was in his shorts, ready to play tennis, and glanced out of the window. Two truckloads of SS men were about to surround the house. Treviranus jumped over his garden wall and essentially did not stop running until he got to England!

One of the trickiest customers on the List is S37, Baron Rudolf von Sebottendorf. He was actually Rudolf Glauer, born in Saxony in 1875. He studied engineering briefly at the Berlin Technical Institute but abandoned the course early and signed on as a stoker on a merchantman. By 1901, he was in Turkey, working as an engineer, and was introduced to the local Masonic Lodge. Glauer became fascinated by eastern magic and joined the mystical cult called the Sufi Order of Bektashi, an eighteenth-century blend of Islamic Shi'ism and Christianity.

He was back in Germany by 1913, managing to avoid the First World War altogether on account of his Turkish citizenship. In 1918, an avowed hater of Jews, Communists and Masons (even though he was one!), Glauer formed the Thule Society. Whole books have been written about the Nazi obsession with a mythic Aryan past and the need to establish an historical, anthropological and archaeological precedent for the supremacy of white Anglo-Saxons. The Thule Society was a study group for German antiquity, an occultist and *volkische* organisation based in Munich. Many of its members were Nazi leaders – Rudolf Hess, Alfred Rosenberg, Deitrich Eckart and Heinrich Harrer. Hitler himself was never actually a member. Glauer's money seems to have come from Baron von Sebottendorf, who adopted him in Turkey. Using the old man's title and cash, Glauer, the ultimate conman, bought the *Volkischer Beobachter* newspaper, which he sold to the Nazis in 1920. By that time, the conman was on the run, having leaked Thule membership to the press and the short-lived Bavarian Communist government keen to track them down. Back in Turkey by 1935, Glauer published *Before Hitler Came*, an account of the Thule Society in its pre-Nazi days. Hitler read it, hated it and banned it, ensuring a figurative price on Glauer's head. Although his address is given on the List, rather vaguely, as 'the Guild Hall', it seems unlikely that he was anywhere but Turkey at the time.

Otto Klepper (K79) was a lawyer from Bretterode and, even though he is on the List, the *Handbook* believed he may still have been in Basle, Switzerland and perhaps never got to Britain at all. He was a friend of Willi Munzenberg, a genuinely working-class Marxist who was the son of a publican from Erfurt. As a young man, he had joined the SPD and spoke for the Trade Unions, travelling to Zurich to meet Lenin before the Germans allowed the leader of the Bolsheviks into Russia, in Churchill's phrase, 'like a plague bacillus.' In bitter, chaotic Germany after the First World War, Munzenberg founded the KPD. A brilliant propagandist, he organised a fund to help victims of the Russian famine of the mid-Twenties and worked with the Comintern and the Russian secret police, the Cheka (which evolved into the Ogpu), until 1934. Known in Germany as the red millionaire, he drove a flash limousine and had a state-of-the-art apartment. In 1932, he set up the World Committee against War and Fascism but thought it best to leave the country when the Nazis came to power the following year; he fled to Paris.

In the mid-Thirties, Munzenberg toured America with Babette Grosse (who became his wife) and the British Socialist Nye Bevan. He also sent Egon Kisch to Australia. All of them warned of the threat of Nazi Germany, which must have seemed somebody else's problem to the Americans and the Australians. In July 1936, Munzenberg formed the Hollywood Anti-Nazi League and stars like Dorothy Parker, James Cagney and Paul Muni flocked to it with something like the enthusiasm that would condemn the Communist 'Hollywood Ten' in the McCarthy era of the Cold War.

Men like Munzenberg made enemies and he found himself expelled from his own party on trumped-up charges. By the late 1930s, he was as much anti-Stalin as he was anti-Fascist. His wife was imprisoned by the Russians and handed over to Hitler, who had her placed in Ravensbruck, the camp for women to the north of Berlin. As far as the List is concerned, the odd thing about Munzenberg's entry is that he was already dead. He had been arrested by Daladier's government in France in June 1940 and imprisoned in Chambaran camp. His body was found slumped at the foot of a tree in a nearby forest. He had been garrotted. Did the Gestapo kill him? Or was it Stalin's NKVD? Either his entry on the List is a mistake or his murderers were the Russians.

The other Communist group of traitors that annoyed the Gestapo was the RSO, the Revolutionary Socialist Party of Austria. However, Hitler chose to dress it up as a sane and welcome move, the Anschluss, the union of Germany and Austria in March 1938, was a military *coup d'état* that fell little short of invasion. The Chancellor, Kurt von Schuschnigg, unable to count on the support of Chamberlain's Britain or Daladier's France, was outmanoeuvred by Hitler and forced to resign. His successor was the card-carrying Nazi Artur Seyss-Inquart and the Anschluss became reality, adoring crowds strewing Hitler's way into Vienna with flowers. On 10 April, a plebiscite (referendum) was held asking the Austrians whether they approved of what had happened. 99.07 per cent of eligible voters did.

The overwhelming statistics masked a bitter truth – not all Austrians were Nazis. The RSO had been formed as early as February 1934 but it had evolved into a hard-line outfit by the time of the Anschluss, pledged to achieving the revolution of the proletariat by any means. Rudolf Gessner (G34) is simply listed as 'Emigrant' but the *Handbook* tells us that he was the leader of the RSO that had its headquarters at Toynbee Hall in Commercial Street, Whitechapel. Crucial to the organisation was L46, Dr Maric Lazarsfeld-Jahoda, from Vienna. She appears in a number of categories in the List, as a Jew, a journalist and a politician. Her address was 10, Regent's Park Terrace, NW11. Of her five 'collaborators' referred to in the *Handbook*, only one, Emil Sladky (S98), appears on the List as 'RSO Funktionär'.

There is no mention in the *Handbook* of the Black Front but a number of its leaders were believed to be hiding in Britain and their names are on the List. The *Schwarze Front* was the generic name of the KGRNS (*Kampfgemeinschaft Revolutionarer Nationalsozialisten*), the Combat League of National Socialism. The original Nazi Party, the German Workers' Party, was one of many such groups that emerged from the chaos following the armistice of November 1918. It was the brainchild of the Munich locksmith Anton Drexler and half of its twenty-five-point programme was socialist in nature, which has confused generations of schoolchildren ever since! Once Hitler joined and came to dominate, Drexler was cold-shouldered and the socialist elements of the programme quietly dropped. It was important, however, that socialist ideas were *seen* to be important in order to woo the voters, faced with a plethora of rival parties in the 1920s. The problem for Hitler was that some party members took socialism – or radicalism, as it came to be called – seriously. Ernst Rohm, the commander of the SA, was one. And the Strasser brothers were two more.

Gregor was the elder, winning the Iron Cross First and Second Class in the First World War (but as a lieutenant, as opposed to Hitler's corporal rank). While the future Führer was writing *Mein Kampf* in Landsberg, Strasser ran the small, technically illegal party in his absence. He founded the *Berliner Arbeiter Zeitung* (the Berlin Workers' Paper), which was edited by his brother Otto. Otto had been a Social Democrat and did not join the Nazis until 1925, the year in which the SS was established and the party experienced something of a rebirth. If anything more left wing than his brother, Otto relegated Germany's past, with its feudal obligations, to 'history's rubbish heap'. He wanted, in common with British socialists at the time and since, a complete nationalisation of the banking system, industry and agriculture. He approved of strikes and admired the successes of the Soviet Union. While Gregor saw himself as a better leader of the Nazi Party than the clearly emotional and even unstable Hitler, Hitler in turn dismissed Otto as 'a parlour Bolshevik' and the brothers' followers as 'doctrinaire fools, uprooted literati and political boy scouts.' Despite the defection of Josef Goebbels (Gregor had employed him to write *NS-Briefe*, a party newsletter) to Hitler in 1926, the feud between the Strassers and the future Führer rumbled on for another six years and in 1932, Hitler made Gregor Reich Organization Leader. This move may have been a last-ditch attempt to weld the party together but Hitler had already expelled Otto from the Nazis two years earlier. It was then that Otto formed the *Schwarze Front* as the true embodiment of National Socialism but it failed to win votes at the polls.

Gregor, in the meantime, quarrelled again with Hitler and resigned his post in December 1932. There the matter might have ended but Hitler was not the kind of man to forgive or forget. On the night of 30 June 1934, the Night of the Long Knives, Gregor was rounded up in the purge and shot through the bars of his prison cell by a jubilant SS officer who shouted, 'I have killed the swine.'

Otto fled to Prague, taking many of his Black Front people with him, and, the following year, wrote an account of his brother's murder – *The German Bartholomew's Night*[108] – published in Zurich. He was in France on the eve of the war, still spreading malicious rumours about Hitler's involvement in the murder of his own niece (and possible lover), Geli Raubal. 'She told me things,' he wrote, '[about their sexual relationship] that I only knew from my reading of Krafft-Ebing's *Psychopathia Sexualis*[109] in my college days.' There is no hard evidence that Otto Strasser was ever in Britain. He is listed (S55) as a journalist from Windsheim, Bavaria, using a number of aliases – Baumann, Berger, Loerbrocks and Boorstrom. Most accounts maintain that he fled to

Bermuda via Portugal, leaving his wife and children behind in Switzerland.

His followers, the 'political boy scouts' with their symbol of the crossed sword and hammer as a reflection of the Soviet hammer and sickle, are scattered alphabetically throughout the List but again, their *actual* living in Britain must be doubted. Hans Kohout (K109) was an editor also known as Hans Jager. According to the List, he lived at 21, Anson Road, N7 and his landlady was a Mrs Greening. Walter Lenbuscher (L76) was a technician from Marburg. Hermann Meyren (M128) was an economist from Mulheim, and so on. Aliens were being interned throughout 1939 and 1940 simply for having a German (and later, Italian) name. Most of these were released after weeks or months, although they continued to be monitored, were not allowed to travel or to own a bicycle. The problem was that the Black Front, for all they had quarrelled with Hitler, were still Nazis and it is unlikely that Churchill's government would have forgotten or forgiven that.

Today it seems odd that B138 should be included in a list of traitors but, according to the facts, Bernhard Biesterfeld was just that. That was because Prince Bernhard of the Netherlands had, not long before, been a card-carrying Nazi. Born in 1911, Bernhard was the elder son of Leopold IV of Lippe and the baby rejoiced in the usual overkill of names accorded to royalty. He was Bernhard Leopold Friedrich Eberhard Julius Kurt Karl Gott, Graf von Biesterfeld. After the First World War, the family lost its extensive German lands but the prince retained links with the country, attending gymnasia in Berlin. He obtained a Law degree from the University of Lausanne, however, and quickly established himself as something of a playboy prince. Safaris and fast cars took their toll – in 1928 he crashed at 100mph and broke his neck and two ribs.

It was while he was still at university that Bernhard joined both the Nazi Party and the SA. He also joined the Ritter (cavalry) SS in 1925 and the NSKK (the Nazi Motor Corps). In later years, the prince denied all this as the politics of the day developed in the way that it did but his membership is a matter of public record. Working for the German industrial giant I. G. Farben as one of its Paris directors, Bernhard married Princess Juliana in 1937 and became a Dutch citizen. In his role as Prince Consort, he met Hitler at this time – the Führer mentioned it in his *Table-Talk*.

As war loomed, things became uncomfortable for Bernhard. His brother was a Wehrmacht officer and both SIS and the Abwehr were watching both men closely for signs of collaboration with the other side. The outbreak of war led to a clean break with the 'Nazi' side of the family. When the Wehrmacht invaded the Netherlands in May 1940, Bernhard organised the palace guards and personally opened machine-gun fire on the raiding Luftwaffe snarling over his palace and his country. When he surrendered, he refused to speak German, using only Dutch in his formal declaration of defeat. At first, he refused to leave the Netherlands but, concerned for his wife and children, flew to the safety of London. He broadcast to his occupied nation on 25 June, denouncing Hitler and all he stood for. He sent his family to Canada in the teeth of Operation Sealion but was determined to do his best for the country that had taken him in. He volunteered for service with SIS but the man's Nazi past haunted him and they turned him down. Nothing daunted, he spent over a thousand hours flying Spitfires with No. 322 (Dutch) Squadron of the RAF, managing to wreck two planes on landing. No one could claim that the Prince of the Netherlands was careful!

But there can be no doubt that the highest-profile traitor

on the List, in the eyes of the Reich, was H30, Dr Ernst Hanfstaengel, of 28, Gunterstone Rd, Kensington. He also appears under his alias of E. F. H. Sedgwick (S38) from Munich. 'Putzi' was the son of an art publisher and had an American mother, which explains his enrolment at Harvard. A gifted pianist, he wrote songs for the university football team before graduating in 1909 and returning to run his father's Fine Arts publishing house in Bavaria. In his time in America, he met both Roosevelts – Theodore and F. D. – the tycoon William Randolph Hurst and the great star of the silent screen, Charlie Chaplin. When the First World War broke out, Hanfstaengel was in the States and wanted to return to Germany but was prevented from doing so and his property was confiscated once America joined the war in 1917.

Back in Germany, he was mesmerised by hearing Hitler speak in various beer halls. 'He was able to create a rhapsody of hysteria,' he wrote. 'What Hitler was able to do to a crowd in two and a half hours will never be repeated in 10,000 years.' Although he did not actually join the Nazi Party until 1931, he was an active Hitler supporter long before that. When the wounded leader ran from the disaster at the Feldernhalle in the putsch of 1923, it was Hanfstaengel's house he hid in, and it was Hanfstaengel's money that helped to bankroll the publication of *Mein Kampf*. He wrote marches for the SA and Hitler Youth, introduced the gauche ex-corporal to sophisticated German society and even claimed to have invented the '*Sieg Heil*' chant that so characterised the Hitler regime.

As head of the Nazi Press Bureau, Hanfstaengel met Winston Churchill at the Hotel Regina in Munich and offered to introduce him to the party leader. Churchill quizzed him on why Hitler hated the Jews so much and his general attitude (Churchill was an unpopular outsider in Britain at the time) convinced Hanfstaengel that a meeting of the two might not be in the best interests of anybody!

'Putzi' clashed with Goebbels repeatedly over press matters, especially as he had sunk a great deal of capital into the *Volkischer Beobachter*. 'The scheming dwarf', as Otto Strasser called Goebbels, dropped his usual poison into Hitler's ear and Hanfstaengel was dropped from the Führer's staff in 1933. In an extraordinary incident four years later, Putzi was taken by plane to Spain. During the flight, he came to believe, from various hints and a disturbingly terrifying atmosphere, that he would be dropped over Communist territory as the Civil War raged below. The plane developed 'engine trouble' and returned to Leipzig but the shot across the bows worked and Hanfstaengel ran to Switzerland. His card was now marked by the very man – Hitler – who had been his god and was still godfather to his son, Egon. 'Putzi' would have regarded his brief internment as an enemy alien in Britain in 1939 as a minor inconvenience. But, by the summer of 1940, Walter Schellenberg knew where he lived...

CHAPTER FOURTEEN

THE SPYING GAME

There is no category in Schellenberg's List that is more difficult to pin down than those involved in espionage – and that is how it should be. Many of the entries today are very obscure, especially given the situation that by the summer of 1940 there were not only home-grown members of the SIS in Britain but agents of Polish, Czech, Dutch, Belgian and French secret services. Many of them only have surnames in the List and some have several *decknames* (aliases), since subterfuge was their business. Some of these may be code names, rather than actual names. Since the publication of J. C. Masterman's *The Double-Cross System* in 1972, we are all familiar with double agents from Balloon to Zigzag. In the List, Vleugels (V28) and Walzer (W14) may be surnames but, equally, they could be codes – *vleugels* means 'wings' and *walzer* is a dancer. Most of the books on the espionage of the Second World War in today's bookshops focus on the code-breakers of Bletchley Park (vital, if tedious and frustrating work), the exploits of SOE (formed in the month the List was compiled) and the brilliant 'turning' work of Colonel J. C. Masterman at Latchmere House (the Double Cross Committee). All these developments post-dated the List and none of them would have happened had the Germans actually invaded in the summer of 1940.

There is an African proverb which says, 'Until the Lion learns how to write, every story will only glorify the Hunter'. History is written by the winners and the winners have been quick to belittle the German war effort in all its aspects, while 'bigging up' the brilliance and heroism of the British. This notion of hidebound, stupid Germans lasted for years – look at the ludicrous body count of the Wehrmacht in the film *Where Eagles Dare* (1968), where Richard Burton and Clint Eastwood take on a whole castle full of puppet Wehrmacht villains. So the notion persists that, somehow, the SD were inferior to their British counterparts.

Reinhard Heydrich and many members of the Nazi elite were, as we have seen, in awe of the British Secret Service, if only because there had been government agents in England since at least the time of Francis Walsingham, Elizabeth I's spymaster in the 1570s. They might have been less impressed had they known that the upper echelons of the service were largely ex-public schoolboys still playing games. As F. A. C. Kluiters wrote in the 1990s, 'British politics consists in large part of informal networks, advice proffered by old friends, school and university chums, exchanged at dinner or in bars and only very rarely recorded on a document.'

This makes research, of course, very difficult. And it is no way to run a secret service network. Interestingly, Hitler operated in a similar way, dropping oblique hints in his table-talk and expecting underlings to pick them up and orchestrate them. Both sides were flawed.

The *Gestapo Handbook* quotes a reply to a Commons question from an anonymous MP regarding SIS's budget that 'It is the nature of the Secret Service to be secret. Therefore, it cannot be talked about. Any discussion would contribute to endangering secrecy.' This is very convenient for those who do not want overspending exposed and it has bedevilled serious researchers for the last eighty years. The belated, toothless Freedom of Information Act in 2000 has made barely a dent in the tower of silence that still stands. The *Handbook* goes on, 'Indeed the secrecy begins with its official description, *which nobody seems to understand in detail*.' [my italics] It would be nice to think that Stevens and Payne Best, interrogated with surprisingly kid gloves by Schellenberg, were being deliberately vague about the organisation to which they belonged but neither of these men was very experienced and I suspect they were genuinely mystified about its structure. The Germans, said the *Handbook*, needed detail and precision; the British did not. And it has a very prescient observation to make about future generations and the need to know:

'If any details [about SIS] are ever made known... one can be sure that only those authorities and offices whose existence cannot be hidden in the long term will be highlighted. The head and hands of the entity called the Secret Service... remain secret.'

In the List itself, even the head (the senior officers) are vague; the hands (the agents themselves) were shadows.

At the head, the *Handbook* speculates on Maurice Hankey, 'a small, humble man,' a minister without portfolio. He is mentioned in parliamentary proceedings only marginally, was sixty-three and 'used to be a colonel'. From 1902 to 1906, he worked for Naval Intelligence (NID), the oldest of the forces' Intelligence units. He was secretary to Lloyd George's War Cabinet in the First World War and accompanied the Prime Minister to Versailles, where Hankey dealt personally with President Wilson and Georges Clemenceau. He was known to be keen on greater collaboration with the Americans and detested the Japanese. As if proof were needed that the compilers of the List and the *Handbook* were not *quite* one and the same, Hankey's entry is woeful – 'H31 Hankey, Sir, brit ND – Agent'. Schellenberg's own department wanted him. Years later, Roy Jenkins called Hankey 'waspish and two-faced'[110] and Schellenberg might have taken heart had he known Hankey's views on Churchill only months before the List was compiled. 'I found complete chaos this morning,' he wrote to Samuel Hoare on 12 May. 'No one was gripping the war in its crisis. The Dictator [Churchill] instead of dictating, was engaged in a sordid wrangle with the politicians of the Left about secondary offices.'[111]

Hankey was born in Biarritz and attended Rugby School. His political career, outlined above in the *Handbook*, earned him a reputation for competence and reliability. In 1939, he had officially retired from government and became a director of the Suez Canal Company. Under Churchill, he was brought back (despite Hankey's views!) as Chancellor of the Duchy of Lancaster. He was not a member of the War Cabinet and certainly not in charge of SIS.

Rupert Vansittart was another matter. Credited on the List as a leading figure *(führend)* of British Intelligence, he was Permanent Under-Secretary of State for Foreign Affairs until 1938 and chief diplomatic adviser to the Foreign Office after that. He was well known as anti-German and believed that the country should never have been allowed to re-arm after the First World War. The *Handbook* had proof that Vansittart ran his own personal secret service with a team of agents who reported only to him and were willing 'to indulge in treachery'. Harold Nicolson paints an intriguing portrait of the man – 'There he is – having reached the summit of his profession [this was 1943] loaded with stars and ribbons... married to a lovely wife, owning a beautiful Queen Anne mansion, replete with tapestry and pictures,' but he was still whingeing about Chamberlain's supposed betrayal of him and, clearly, a little thing like rationing did not bother him – he gave Nicolson trout, lamb, fruit and a bottle of Pomeroy '98.

Thanks to Stevens' candour, the *Handbook* was able to list more likely heads of Intelligence. One was Admiral Hugh Sinclair, who *may* be the '*Sinclair, Beamter inn Asw. Amt in London*' (S86). Although he had retired from active service at the Admiralty (his old address was given as '54, Broadway Buildings, near St James's Park station') he had, Stevens told Schellenberg, been made head of SIS with the code letters CSS. This was back in 1923 and 'Quex', as he was known after a character in a play by Pinero, was a natural for a spymaster at the time. He loathed the Bolsheviks and was secret almost to the point of paranoia. He was chubby and affable but his temper was legendary and few were brave enough to cross him. Sinclair died of cancer days after the Venlo incident, so if S86 *is* the same man, this is clearly a mistake.

He was succeeded, as the *Handbook* notes, by Colonel Stuart Menzies, who, oddly, is not on the List at all. Anthony Cave Brown, the only biographer to interview Menzies at length, produced the definitive book on the man in 1988 and exposed SIS in a way that would have delighted Schellenberg. The Scotsman's appointment was never officially listed, though everyone knew about it and Menzies, never Churchill's choice,[112] was now officially 'C'.[113] His ADCs, the *Handbook* contends, were Captains Howard (H188) and Russell and H17, Major Hatton-Hall, who was the military section head of Y Headquarters. From Stevens, Schellenberg learned that SIS was subdivided into various departments; army, navy and air force, each with its section head and even on which floor of the Broadway buildings their private offices could be found. Men who never made the List, presumably because they were mere cogs in a machine, were Wing Commander Winterbottom, Gambier Perry ('calls himself Colonel but this seems to be untrue') and Major Vivien, who 'is also a police officer.'

'Vee vee' Vivian *is* on the List (V27) in the last capacity, *'offizier d. ind. Politzei'*. He was yet another spy who sported a monocle. Cave Brown describes him as 'tall, willowy, languid, erudite, well-tailored'[114] but he was never a policeman. The confusion arose either because of the overlapping units of the RSHA, where the police and security services were indistinguishable, or perhaps resulting from confusion with Scotland Yard's Special Branch. One of the agents reporting to Vivian indirectly was the List's H102, Henry Hendricks, with the call sign 101B in Antwerp. The Gestapo knew where to find him when the time came; he lived at 7, Rolands Gardens, SW7.

At the Head of Section D of SIS was Laurence Grand, a thin, tall chain-smoker who habitually wore a carnation in his buttonhole. Like many of the spymasters, he was a Cambridge graduate but the List, ironically, has him down as (G101) Grant, fingered, as ever, by the obliging Stevens and Payne Best. He is described as *'Leiter der Sabot. Abtlg, der S.I.S'*. The description was not far out – D did indeed stand for Destruction and, in this context, Grand attended a meeting ten days after the Anschluss, with Halifax, Menzies and Cadogan. His brief was to take 'a few active preparatory steps... in deadly secrecy... to counter Nazi predominance in small countries Germany had just conquered or was physically threatening.'[115]

Operating out of St Ermyn's Hotel, Colonel Grand was constantly on the lookout for brilliant mavericks to help him in this enterprise. Unfortunately, one of those was Guy Burgess, the homosexual and Communist who came highly recommended both by MI5 and the BBC. Grand himself, rather like Stevens and Payne Best, was something of a laughing stock. One of his more stupid ideas was to pay Slovenians to put sand in the axle-boxes of trains bound for the Reich. Since both the gangs and the money sent to them disappeared without trace, it is unlikely that a single grain was put into the service of the 'Destruction' unit. Gladwyn Jebb of the Foreign Office wrote to Cadogan demanding Grand's removal, 'to pit such a man against the German General Staff and the German Military Intelligence Service is like arranging to attack a Panzer division by an actor mounted on a donkey'.[116]

F27, David Footman, of 25, Collingham Place, London, came from the same stable. Guy Burgess, whose lover he became, first met him at the BBC. 'He's an intelligent, quiet man of the English type, but quick, smart and elegant.'[117] Footman had been vice-consul in Egypt and Belgrade before joining the boards of various Balkan companies. Back in the civil service again by 1937, he worked with the Passport Control Office, that wide-open sieve of British Intelligence which Schellenberg so effectively destroyed at Venlo.

Educated at Marlborough and New College, Oxford, Footman is described by Anthony Cave-Brown as 'intellectually tough but morally weak'.[118] Ironically, because of his links with Burgess, Footman ended up on another list of undesirables later in the war. By 1943, there was more concern over

Communists than Nazis and Stewart Menzies had his doubts about Footman. He wrote to a colleague, 'And don't forget to see to it that Footman's name is on the list.'[119]

Richard Tinsley (T38) is, curiously, not categorised as an agent on the List but, as MI6 head in Rotterdam before the war, it is certain that Schellenberg had come across the name and may even have known him personally. His cover in Holland was as a director of Cunard but an incident years earlier had alerted him to the Kaiser's Intelligence service. In 1911, as managing director of the Uranium Steamship Company, he had tried to secure visas for fifty Finnish/Russian emigrants seeking a new start in life. The Dutch were furious and Tinsley himself was branded an 'unwanted alien'. It was only the highly unusual intercession of Queen Wilhelmina that allowed him to stay.

During the First World War, using the rather unimaginative code name 'T', he became the most successful station chief in the business. His inclusion on the List may have been mostly historic, however. He retired in 1923 and seems to have played little, if any, part in the Second World War.

The Communication Section, the Political Section, the Cipher Section, the Financial Section, the Press Section and the Industrial Section are all listed in the *Handbook*, together with their principal purposes. According to Schellenberg, the other department, purporting to be concerned with propaganda, was actually co-ordinating sabotage. Interestingly, it was this Section, headed by Colonel Monty Chidson (C43), who had been in charge of the Passport Office at The Hague since 1936, that would be subsumed by SOE. SO1 handled propaganda after July 1940, most of it black, and SO2 carried out sabotage by dropping agents behind enemy lines, usually liaising with various Resistance groups.

Inevitably, the Passport Control Office (PCO) in the

Netherlands was of interest to Schellenberg. As a result of Venlo, he had forced Menzies to find other methods to liaise with allied secret services and to monitor events. This was where Claude Dansey came in, whose career and reputation we looked at in Chapter Seven. Schellenberg knew that 'Z' operated out of Bush House in the Aldwych and that his seconds were Kenneth Cohan, Keith Crane and Robert Craig. Those surnames are so similar that we might, in fact, be looking for one man, not three; none of them made the List.

The *Handbook* is confused about the actual role of MI5. Its compilers knew that it concerned counter-intelligence but were unsure how far Scotland Yard was involved – there are two Yard men on the List. MI5's headquarters were at Thames House, Millbank and its seventy-five-strong team occupied the top floor. These men watched Communists and Fascists with an even-handed diligence which probably appalled Schellenberg. In this context, the List's C87a, Colonel Hinchley-Cook confused the RSHA. They knew he wore glasses, had a ruddy complexion and spoke fluent German with a Saxony-Hamburg dialect. What they did not know was whether 'Cookie', as he was known in Whitehall, was SIS or the police. Unlike Germany, of course, there was no such thing as a secret police in Britain; even Special Branch fell short of that definition. Hinchley-Cook was born in Dresden, with a German mother and a British father, and read Science at Leipzig University. At the outbreak of the First World War, he was expelled as an alien and was recommended to Vernon Kell, Head of MI5 in the 1920s by Arthur Duff, the British Resident in Saxony – 'He is entirely British in sentiment and the fact that he speaks English with a foreign accent must not be allowed to militate against him.' Several months later, Kell was still having to write with exasperation on various papers relating to Hinchley-

Cook, 'He is an Englishman!' He deciphered codes, using the schoolboy ploy of invisible ink and even went undercover in prisoner of war camps, where his English 'sentiments' were missed entirely. He had been involved in a number of high-profile spy trials in the 1930s, arresting Norman Baillie Stewart, a British officer selling secrets to the Germans, and of Dr Herman Goertz. He famously turned the agent Arthur Owens, known to SIS as Snow and to the Germans as Johnny.

Captain M. King (K59) had his offices at 308 Dolphin Square, using the name Coplestone as an MI5 cover. He lived in Whitehall Mansions. If Schellenberg could have cast his net in that particular part of London, he would have caught a great many of the fish he was after.

Female spies have always held a fascination, not just for the public but, I suspect, for the men who employ them. If most of the real agents in the Thirties and during the war were the real-life equivalents of John Le Carré's fictional George Smiley, Martha McKenna (M104) was James Bond! She also appears as C67, Martha Cnockaert, and the Gestapo were on to her. Born in 1892 in West Flanders, the little Belgian girl went to medical school in Ghent but her training was interrupted by the First World War. She ended up working as a casualty nurse in German field hospitals and was awarded the Iron Cross for her steadfast heroism under ghastly conditions. Her heart lay elsewhere however and in 1915 she was recruited by a friend into working for Anglo-Belgian Intelligence.

Using the code name Laura and working with an old Belgian spy known as 'Canteen Ma', Martha picked up military gossip in the wards and in her parents' café, where she worked part-time as a waitress. Some information she passed on through whispered conversations during church services. More detailed stuff was dropped by Number 63, as she was also known, in a post box addressed to British HQ. She worked as a double agent for a time but felt such pangs of guilt that she had her German handler murdered.

Sabotage may have been a step too far, however, and she was caught in the autumn of 1916 with sticks of dynamite. She was sentenced to death but her possession of the Iron Cross made the military authorities relent and she spent only two years in prison before the war ended and she was liberated. Now a celebrity, given the Legion d'Honneur and mentioned in despatches by Field Marshal Haig, she went into print with her British officer husband with *I Was A Spy*, published in the year before Hitler came to power. This led to a string of highly successful espionage novels written by the McKennas, which the *Independent* has recently described as 'a breathless mix of Celia Johnson crossed with Enid Blyton'. Hollywood filmed her romanticised life story in 1933 with Madeline Carroll as 'Laura'. There is no evidence that Martha was still active as an agent in 1940 but the Germans had been duped by her before and were presumably taking no chances.

The various branches of the Secret Service, the *Handbook* contends, obtained information, especially with an economic bias from what it calls 'social espionage' – 'Talkativeness, intimacy instead of distance and reserve and a false need to be candid with others, have done a lot of damage.' Newspapers were particularly pernicious in this respect, hence the focus on them in Chapter Eleven in this book. Reuters in particular was up to its neck in the spying game, the RSHA believed and it was no accident that most of its British journalists were ex-military men. With astonishing paranoia, the *Handbook* asserts, 'every British expatriate is an agent for his country and each expatriate German a traitor by negligence'. The British admired their secret service whereas the Germans despised theirs, believing it to be 'a dirty business for gamblers, gangsters and desperadoes'. All sorts of people, the *Handbook* believed, from humble clerks to globe-trotting adventurers, fed negative information about Germany to the Royal Institute of International Affairs at Chatham House, whose purpose – and library – were clearly sinister.

That said, the *Handbook* found that SIS were particularly penny-pinching, not using paid informers and not paying regular agents enough.[120] The *Handbook*'s Espionage section ends with the question mark on just how effective the SIS is. The British were hidebound and yoked to tradition. Yet the British can – and will – respond to emergencies like the threat of invasion with speed and determination. Schellenberg had no intention of underestimating them.

★ ★ ★

Of course, it was not merely the British Secret Service that interested the RSHA. A number of people on the List known to be spies are Poles, Czechs, Belgians and Dutchmen, even a few French. One or two are women, although the rise of the female spy belongs to the months and years after the List was compiled. Of all the exiled Intelligence services based in London by 1940, the most efficient and important was Section II of the Polish organisation. Until the late Thirties , Russia was seen by Warsaw as the most likely enemy and all major Russian cities had Polish embassies, which had Intelligence units built into them. Information gathering on Nazi Germany had not been neglected entirely but the speed of the September War and the sheer numbers of the Wehrmacht involved in *Fall Weiss* meant that the Secret Service had no time to organise. The whole thing was over in four weeks.

Traditionally, national espionage outfits did not share

information with other nations, for obvious reasons, but the war changed that. In fact, even before *Fall Weiss*, on 26 July 1939, a group of Polish agents met their British counterparts in the Kabaty Woods, south of Warsaw and handed over their decryption methods of the German enigma machines, which they had cracked since 1932. It does not detract from the brilliance of the work carried out by Alan Turing and his team at Bletchley Park to say that, without Polish help, the code-breakers would have had to have gone back to basics. Most of the boffins at Kabaty, along with other agents, got to France via Romania and then to Britain by the spring of 1940. At General Sikorski's insistence, the Poles kept their own ciphers throughout the war but an estimated 43 per cent of all Intelligence gathered between 1940 and 1945 came from Polish sources, according to a report published in 2005.

Who ended up on the List by July 1940? There was A41, written as 'd'Alton', of the Rotterdam Intelligence Service. Lieutenant Ernest Dalton had got into debt over gambling and had been helping himself from PCO funds to cover it. He shot himself in the head on 4 September 1936 and his removal led to the appointments of Stevens and Payne Best. All in all, it was not an auspicious beginning. As we might expect, there were others from the Dutch PCO network. V45 was Adrianus de Vries, who also appears four places later as Adrianus Vrinten. He used a number of aliases and hailed from Loon op Zand. He managed to get out of Holland as the Dutch capitulated and worked with Bill Hooper recruiting Dutch agents working under the auspices of SOE after July 1940.

Hooper was H173 with the alias Konrad. Part of the Stevens/ Best *täterkreis*, he was a Dutch-born citizen working in what F. A. C. Kluiters calls 'the wilderness of mirrors' that was British European-based espionage. F60 Reginald Fletcher was there too, in charge of The Hague Passport Control Office in the 1920s; effectively Hooper's boss. With the advent of Hitler as Chancellor in 1933, all agents were ordered to switch their observation from Communism to Fascism. Frank Taylor (T7), a native of Burton-on-Trent, was at The Hague too but he was fired by Sinclair after Dalton's suicide in part of a general clear-out of dead wood. One of the new men who replaced him was D37, Rodney Dennys, Section V officer. After Venlo, he was transferred to Brussels but continued to liaise with The Hague by visiting the offices there twice a week. This explains why he was on a list (compiled by Whitehall this time) to be evacuated from Holland in the event of invasion. The last name connected with the Venlo disaster was Payne Best's business and Intelligence partner, W86, Piet van der Willik. The pair's cover was a pharmaceutical company called Pharmisan, one of several apparently above board institutions that masked an altogether different purpose.

H16 was an old-school spy, Sir Reginald 'Blinker' Hall, a larger than life type whose eyes 'flashed like a Navy signal lamp', and who had been Director of Naval Intelligence in the First World War. He was seventy in 1940 but was still a formidable code-breaker and had held numerous naval commands before turning to Intelligence. A religious man and an innovator, as commander of the battle cruiser *Queen Mary* he had been the first in the Royal Navy to introduce a chapel, a library and a cinema for the ratings. His spirit of co-operation in Intelligence-sharing with MI5, MI6 and Special Branch set a standard that continued throughout the war. Throughout the Thirties, he travelled widely in the States, promoting the British cause against Nazism.

His name appears as one of the *täterkreis* of Captain Franz Dagobert von Rintelen (who himself appears as R67, 68 and

69). As a real-life agent with a bewildering range of personae, the List obviously did not know quite how to categorise him. The 'Corvette captain', as the List calls him, was a German naval Intelligence officer and could easily have appeared in the 'Traitors' chapter in this book. While he was still loyal to Germany, in the First World War, he had carried out sabotage on American shipping anchored at Black Tom Island in New York harbour. The RSHA clearly did not know that Rintelen spent the whole of the war interned by the American government.

Someone else the List did not know how to place was D32, Denis Sefton Delmer, known to his colleagues as Tom. Since he wrote for the *Daily Express*, it is natural that we find him among the literati, but Delmer was far more than a hack. Born in Berlin, he was registered as a British citizen at the consulate there, although his parents were Australian. His father was professor of English Literature at Berlin University and the author of a standard language textbook used in most German schools. After he was interned in the First World War, the family moved to London and young Tom attended St Paul's School and Lincoln College, Oxford. Since he had spoken nothing but German until he was five, he was a natural as a newspaper German correspondent and in this context wrote freelance for the *Express* as the Nazis came to power. He befriended Ernst Röhm, commander of the SA and got the first British interview with the new Chancellor as a result. It was a first, too, for a journalist to interview a politician on a plane – Hitler took to the air on the campaign trail in 1932 and 1933, and Delmer was at the Chancellor's elbow when he inspected the burned-out shell of the Reichstag on the morning of 28 February 1933. So convincing was Delmer as a Nazi acolyte that elements in Britain thought he had been recruited by the

Abwehr. The Abwehr, on the other hand, were convinced that he was working for MI6!

Delmer seemed to be everywhere, covering the Spanish Civil War and the grim days of *Fall Weiss*. He even wrote his observations for the *Express* as Guderian's tanks rolled west through the forests of the Ardennes in the spring of 1940.

But if anyone doubted Sefton Delmer's loyalties, such doubts were dispelled when he replied to Hitler's peace offer in the Reichstag speech on 19 July 1940, which the Führer called a last appeal to reason. In an extraordinary act of bravado, which could (should?) have cost him his job, Delmer rejected it single-handedly in a BBC broadcast, referring to Hitler's 'lying, stinking teeth', which sounded more Australian than the cultured tones of a distinguished foreign correspondent. Goebbels believed that the message came direct from Whitehall and, three days later, the government backed Delmer without, it seems, a reprimand. By the time of the List, Delmer was in Lisbon, almost certainly working for MI6 since that city was a hotbed of rumour and espionage. By September, he had been recruited as a black propagandist for the Political Warfare Executive, hatching all kinds of dubious plots for SO1.

His colleague there, Leonard Ingrams, the 'flying banker', has all but disappeared from the record. Research on the Internet brings up his son and grandson but the black propagandist of wartime has vanished – perhaps he wanted it that way. He is I6, in the *täterkreis* of Julius Petschek, as befits his banking and financial credentials. Sefton Delmer described him a year after the List was compiled –'he looked the part of the mysterious Mr X to perfection. He was tall and athletic... his eyes and mouth had just the right expression of drawling, sardonic pity for the world around him.'[121] Born in 1900, Ingrams had been educated at Shrewsbury and Pembroke College, Oxford. He held a commission in the Coldstream Guards. From 1924, he was the European representative of the Chemical Bank and Trust Company of New York and earned his nickname from his fascination with the Puss Moth biplane he flew. He was a member of the famous Boodles gentlemen's club, had a fierce temper and was surprisingly pro-German in the 1930s. He may have shared the upper class Englishman's mistrust of Jews and may have been a member of the Anglo-German Fellowship.

Frank Foley (F69), on the other hand, has earned a reputation of being the 'English Schindler'.[122] Unlike most of the British agents on the List, with their public school and university backgrounds, Foley was the son of a railway worker and only attended the Jesuit school at Stoneyhurst because he won a scholarship. Originally considering the Catholic church as a career, he changed his mind and attended Sandhurst before gaining a commission in the Hertfordshire Regiment in 1917. There, he gravitated towards Intelligence work and retired from the army in 1920. Throughout the next two decades, he was an MI6 head of station in Berlin, recruiting agents and gathering military information. He had no diplomatic immunity but consistently bent the rules to provide passports for Jews, to get them to Britain or Palestine. He visited internment camps and even hid Jewish refugees in his own home. For his liaison work with the Norwegians in the campaign of 1940, he was awarded the Order of St Olaf.

An altogether flashier agent, in the true James Bond style, was the splendidly named Conrad Fulke Thomond O'Brien-ffrench, the Marquis de Castelthomond. With such an array of monikers, it is not surprising that he appears four times on the List! He was privately taught in Italy and attended various Prep schools in Britain before enrolling in an agricultural college in the Forest of Dean. A brilliant horseman, he joined the prestigious Ledbury Hunt and, at the age of seventeen, moved to Canada, where he joined the Royal Canadian Mounted Police in Saskatchewan.

Back home shortly before the First World War, he developed a passion for motor racing and drove frequently at Brooklands, then the country's only motor-racing track. Joining, rather unconventionally, the Royal Irish Regiment, he was wounded at Mons and taken prisoner. The escape-proof Augustabad prison did not hold him for long but while he was there, he sent home letters (laced with coded Intelligence) to his sweetheart, Cathleen Mann, who was Stuart Menzies' secretary. At the end of the war, he was recruited by Menzies into MI6. Having learned Russian in jail, his brief, in the British Legion in Stockholm, was to keep an eye on the Bolsheviks. In 1920, he accompanied David Lloyd George on the first British diplomatic visit to the new Communist government of Vladimir Lenin.

The early Twenties saw him commissioned in the 16th Lancers (Oswald Mosley's old regiment) and he became an expert mountaineer, joining the Alpine Club in London and conquering various peaks around the world. In India, he was ADC to the governor at a time of growing national unrest and met both Gandhi and Nehru in this context. It was mountaineering that was his cover as Z3, based at Kitzbuhel in Austria. He met the Fleming brothers, Ian and Peter, of Naval Intelligence and it may be that it was O'Brien-ffrench that Ian had in mind for the future 007. Immediately after the abdication crisis in 1936, O'Brien-ffrench attended the Duke and Duchess of Windsor and provided Menzies with Intelligence on the peculiar fascination that the Nazi leadership had for the occult.[123] O'Brien-ffrench's spying activities effectively came to an end on 11 March 1938 when, in order to report by telephone on German troop movements at the Austrian border, he was forced to blow his cover. Interestingly, he belongs to the Stevens/Best *täterkreis*.

★ ★ ★

The majority of European agents are very shadowy figures. Louis Allettrino (A37) was a journalist who was also a member of the Dutch Resistance. He would be murdered on 29 August 1942 in the concentration camp at Mauthausen. Stanislaus Demikowski (D34) was a university professor who has the distinction of being on the Polish Secret Search List too. Brijnen van Houten is not on the List in his own right but he is the centre of a *täterkreis*. The secretary of an anti-Nazi group of Dutch intellectuals, he had a private army of agents who collected information for him. General von Oorschot (O27) was head of GSIII and sent his agent Dirk Klop to liaise with Stevens and Payne Best before Venlo. A probable appeaser and ambivalent towards the Germans, he was recalled in November 1938.

George (Jerzy) Sosnowski is well known and his story is a salutary reminder of just how dangerous – and depressing – the work of a spy was. S138 was born in Lvov (Lemberg) in 1896, the scion of a rich family in the days of the Austro-Hungarian Empire. The date of his death, however, is very problematic. He joined the Polish 1st Legion at the outbreak of the First World War and gravitated first to the cavalry academy at Holitz, then to an aviation course at the Theresian Military Academy. With Poland an independent nation after the war, Sosnowski led a cavalry squadron in the 8th Regiment and competed in various international horse shows in the Twenties. He was drafted into the Second Department GHQ as an Intelligence officer and became head of the famous 3 in 1 office. Posing as Baron Ritter von Nalecz, pro-German and a rabid anti-Communist, he was a well-known figure in any number of European capitals. He was suave and handsome, with a string of women in tow, but one of them, the exotic nightclub dancer Lea Niako, shopped him to German counter-intelligence and he was deported.

He appeared to learn nothing from his dalliance with Niako and was soon extracting classified secrets from the German General Staff via Baroness Benita von Falkenheyn. He also had Gunther Rudloff of the Abwehr in his pocket. Occasionally calling himself Graves and posing as a British journalist, he had, by the late 1920s, four aristocratic women working for him as informants.

The arrival of the Nazis made life more difficult for Sosnowski. Actress Maria Kersek reported him and the Gestapo arrested him at a party. Rudloff and Falkenheyn were rounded up too and Sosnowski behaved in a very un-James Bond-like way in co-operating with the authorities. Rudloff would shoot himself in 1941 but Falkenheyn and another confidante, Renate von Katzmer, were executed at Plotzensee in February 1935. 'I am haunted,' Sosnowski wrote the following year:

> 'by the deaths of those two women... the tragic deaths of... my former associates... haunt me day and night and I can only attempt to gain peace through prayer for their souls.'[124]

Sosnowski was put on trial by his own government for fraud and treason in March 1938 and sentenced to fifteen years. He was still appealing the sentence when war broke out. Why he is on the List is something of a mystery, since it is unlikely that he was ever in Britain. One account of his death says he was shot by prison guards near Brzesc on 11 or 17 September 1939. Another version has him murdered by the Russian NKVD in the Lubyanka several weeks later. Yet a third has him becoming an NKVD agent and dying in 1944. The spying game is labyrinthine.

And no more so than in the case of R38, Sidney Reilly, the 'ace of spies'. He was actually Zigmund Rozenblum, a Jew from Odessa, Russia. There are so many stories about every aspect of his life (most of them dreamed up by Rozenblum himself) that it is now not possible to find the truth. After various espionage adventures, he turned up in London in 1896, where his cover was the Ozone Preparation Company, selling patent medicine. As a multi-linguist, his skills were sought by Special Branch under William Melville and by 1909 he had joined the Secret Service. When he had married Margaret Thomas in 1898, he changed his name to Reilly. He many have been involved behind the scenes in the Russo-Japanese War of 1904-05 but his claim that he was behind German lines for much of the First World War has been disproven. In Russia, soon after the Bolshevik revolution, he may (or may not) have been in a plot, along with fellow Listee Robin Bruce-Lockhart, to assassinate Lenin. By 1919, he was working for SIS in liaison with the White Russians, who were trying to wrest power from Lenin's Bolsheviks. One man who knew him then was a Russian agent, Alexander Yakushev –'The first impression [of Reilly],' he wrote, 'is unpleasant. His dark eyes expressed something biting and cruel.'

Just as Sosnowski's entry on the List is surprising, Reilly's is incomprehensible. There were strong rumours at the time – since confirmed by Intelligence documents released in 2000 – that the 'ace of spies' was shot in a forest near Moscow on 5 November 1925. There had been speculation that Reilly had survived and turned traitor, working for Soviet Intelligence. Did this rumour account for the List entry or did Walter Schellenberg know something that we do not?

Another blast of espionage from a bygone era was D133, Oberst. (Colonel) Paul Dyks, using the alias Pavel Pawlowitsch. His real name was Paul Dukes and Pawlowitsch is merely one of over thirty aliases he is known to have used. The son of a congregational minister from Bridgewater in Somerset, Dukes was educated at Caterham School and studied music at the St Petersburg Conservatoire. He taught languages in Riga, Latvia and was recruited into British Intelligence by the original 'C', Sir Mansfield Smith-Cumming. In the frenetic and highly dangerous world of the Bolshevik Revolution and its aftermath, Dukes was busy spiriting White Russians, Pimpernel-style, from Soviet prisons. The 'man of a hundred faces' was able, because of his language skills and acting ability, to infiltrate the Comintern, the Cheka and even the Politburo. In 1920, he was knighted by George V as 'the greatest of all soldiers'. To this day, he remains the only person to be ennobled purely for the rather dubious trade of spying. At the time of the List, he put his head briefly over the parapet again with his book *An Epic of the Gestapo*.

In the 'Ukrainians in England' section of the *Gestapo Handbook* is an odd entry:

'Ukrainian Bureau, London. The owner is the American citizen Makohin, a very dark personage who apparently serves American espionage. There are documents about the Bureau and Makohin at IIIB15.'

If Paul Dukes was the 'man of a hundred faces', Makohin held a similar number of aliases. For the Gestapo to have referred to him as 'a very dark personage', he must have rattled them. In July 1941, with America still not in the war, *Time* magazine had a pop at Makohin, using his real name. He was Prince Leon Bogun Mazappa-Razumowski and he was descended from the hetmen of the Ukraine in Catherine the Great's reign in the eighteenth century. *Time* sneered that he had not fought in the First World War as he had claimed, that he had become an antique dealer (as though this were some sort of crime) and that he had 'made a good living pushing his [aristocratic] claims'. In December, the Prince hit back, demanding a retraction. He was not 'one of Hitler's stooges, quislings or puppets':

'My opinion of Hitler and all he represents may or may not differ in no important detail from that of President Roosevelt or Rabbi Wise, or, for that matter, the editors of *Time*. My considered opinion... is that Hitler and all the forces behind him, will not be defeated by oratorical flag-waving or wishful thinking... I not only was once a member of the US Marine Corps, but I still am.'

He appears four times in the List, M7 being merely the first entry, with various spellings of his name and alias. Recent research has uncovered the fact that he was born in Russia in 1880 and, after an attempt on his life in 1907, left his troubled homeland. In the States, from that year, he used the name Jacob Makohin, after the man who had saved his life, and he lived in Massachusetts. He joined the Marine Corps as an enlisted man and returned from a six-month tour of duty, presumably in Europe, in August 1918. He was promoted to 2nd Lieutenant and was serving in South Carolina a year after the First World War ended. It is not clear why *Time* magazine should have attacked him, nor why its editors doubted his pedigree. One thing is certain – the 'dark personage' is not on the List because he was a Marine, an antique dealer or even the leader of the Ukrainian Bureau in London. As with so many of the spies on the List, there has to be more to it.

The last word in this chapter belongs to G126, H. E. Gruner, apparently a British agent, born in 1916 and wanted by Amt IVE4. A cryptic entry online, citing National Archives HS 9/629/3 – SOE's personnel files – says that information on him will remain closed until 2031. So much for the Freedom of Information Act! How many more secrets are still buried in Whitehall, Paris, Berlin, Prague, Amsterdam, Brussels, Lisbon and any other headquarters of the spying game in 1940? It was, after all, nearly eighty years ago. What can be left to hide?

CHAPTER FIFTEEN

THE OTHERS

Beyond the categories we have looked at so far, the List contains several hundred names that do not lend themselves to a full chapter. There are some that are now so anonymous that we might never know why they were included in the first place.

One clear group is that of officers, from Lieutenant to General and from the armies, navies and air forces of every country that the Reich had overrun by the summer of 1940. Most of these, at least in the British List, are not fighting soldiers. There is no Wavell, Auchinlech, Montgomery or the dozen other senior commanders who were going to make things difficult for Germany in the months and years ahead. They are often 'political', ADC appointments to statesmen and governments in exile, like the Czechs whose headquarters was at 53, Lexham Gardens, London. In a handful of cases, they are naval officers who had already retired from the service but were brought back in 1939 to command armed merchantmen that kept the vital convoy system going.

C31 was Victor Cazalet, a friend of Churchill who had been commissioned in the West Kent Yeomanry and had won the Military Cross in 1917. A sportsman and traveller, he was anything but a conventional English gentleman. His sister, Thelma, was a noted feminist and he was a member of the Ninth Church of Christ Scientist in London. He supported Franco in the Spanish Civil War but opposed the Nazis and was contemptuous of Chamberlain's appeasement. He lived in the grounds of Cranbrook School in Kent and set up, typically of the amateur spirit at the start of the war, the 83rd Light Aircraft Battery of the Royal Artillery in Sevenoaks. He would be killed along with Sikorski in a still-unexplained plane crash on 4 July 1943.

Just as unconventional, in a different way, was C48, Archibald Church. He had served in the Royal Garrison Artillery in the First World War, winning the MC. He added DSO to his list of credentials in action with the White Russians during the Civil War, which ended in 1921. Eight years later, he was Labour MP for Wandsworth and three years after that brought in a Eugenics Bill which pushed for the eventual compulsory sterilisation of 'the unfit'. This was some time before the National Co-ordinating Agency for Therapeutic and Medical Establishments was set up at Tiergarten-strasse 4 in Berlin. That in itself was a euphemism; T4 was a euthanasia programme designed to rid the Reich of its physical and mental 'undesirables'. Unsurprisingly, Church's Bill failed and after the collapse of Ramsay MacDonald's National Government in 1931, he did not stand for parliament again. Why he should be on the List is a little obscure.

Frank Mason-MacFarlane (M88) had served with the

Artillery in the First World War, in France and Mesopotamia and he too had won the MC. It was while he was military attaché in Berlin in the Thirties that an altogether darker side of his character emerged. He offered to shoot Hitler but his superiors turned him down. Six years later, Geoffrey Household wrote his thriller *Rogue Male*, in which a somewhat disturbed survivalist officer makes exactly the same offer. Household never claimed that Mason-MacFarlane was his role model (it is very unlikely that he knew of the situation) but it does seem an odd coincidence. By the outbreak of war, Mason-MacFarlane was Director of Military Intelligence with the British Expeditionary Force in France, his 'MacForce' doing sterling work in covering the right flank's retreat to Dunkirk. By the time of the List, he was second-in-command of the forces defending Gibraltar.

The highest profile British officer on the List is T55, Lord Trenchard, with a house – Dancer's Hill – in Barnet. Trenchard was one of those men who achieved fame and rank for no good reason. His family claimed descent from William the Conqueror, which, at one time, meant *everything*. He failed twice to get into the 'Shop', the Artillery's academy at Woolwich and twice to get into the Militia, whose standards were appreciably lower. He eventually scraped a commission in the Royal Scots Fusiliers and was badly wounded in the chest during the Boer War. In 1912, he joined the Central Flying School with only weeks to go before his fortieth birthday, which would have made him too old to fly. He commanded the military wing of the Royal Flying Corps at the outbreak of the First World War and became Chief of the Air Staff three years later. Having clashed with Lord Rothermere, then Minister for Air, Trenchard resigned but was given the post again in 1919 and held it until 1930.

Throughout his career, there is a sense that Trenchard's superiors regretted appointing him and, in 1931, he was made Commissioner of the Metropolitan Police. Crime historians are divided over his usefulness here; personally, I believe he almost destroyed the Met with his high-handed decisions, proving for all time that putting a military man in charge of a police service is not the answer. Even then, he was not able to let military matters go, bombarding the War Office and the Committee of Imperial Defence with suggestions of all kinds. He visited Germany in 1937 and had dinner with Goering, who assured the ex-Air Chief that 'one day Germany's might will make the whole world tremble'. Stuck for a more erudite answer, Trenchard told the Reichsmarschal that he must be 'off his head'.

From the outbreak of war, he was offered half a dozen posts by Chamberlain and Churchill and he turned them all down. Schellenberg probably assumed that the man had more influence than he actually did, hence his inclusion on the List.

Someone else whose inclusion is difficult to explain is Hauptmann Hugo Bouvard (B194). The man was an artist from Austria and he had been conscripted in 1914. By the following year, he was an official war artist but the Anschluss was too much for him and he moved to Britain. Why is he on the List? Because he was an Austrian artist who could actually paint and was a graduate of the same Vienna Academy of Fine Arts that had turned down the future Führer (twice!) in 1913.

General Josef Snijdarek (S120) was wanted by the Prague police. The son of a miller, he had joined a cadet school and fought in the Austro-Hungarian army in the First World War. Bored by civilian life afterwards, he enlisted in the French Foreign Legion before joining the newly created Czech Legion in France. He led them to victories in the Twenties against

Poland and Hungary and fought dozens of duels on the way – the last of the *beaux sabreurs*! He had retired by 1939 in exile in France and got out to North Africa as the panzers moved west. There is no record of his ever having been in Britain and his inclusion is probably guesswork on the part of the RSHA.

S156 Jerzy Swirski was certainly in London, however. He came from a military academy in Kalisz (then in Russian Poland) and joined first the Russian army, then the Marine Corps. By 1902, he was rapidly rising through the ranks of the navy and commanded the Black Sea fleet in the First World War, ending up with the rank of Rear Admiral. After the war, he became increasingly Polish in politics and took the same rank with the Polish navy by the outbreak of war. On 5 September 1939, as the September War was destroying Polish independence on land, Swirski arranged for three destroyers, two submarines and two training ships, complete with 800 experienced sailors, to make for France, where the Admiral joined Sikorski in Paris. He signed an accord with the British two weeks later and, with the fall of France, the whole outfit crossed the Channel.

★ ★ ★

There is no category in the List that deals with performers but there is a handful of them who incurred the wrath of the Reich for other reasons. Some of these, like the music teacher Myra Dolivo (D84) and the composer Karl Deichmuller (D31), last heard of in Southampton, are very obscure or forgotten today. Others have stood the test of time.

R32 was the actor Bernhard Reichenbach from Berlin. He was born in Hamburg but his acting credentials pale against his political involvement. He was a member of the Executive Committee of the Communist International and of the KPD in

Germany. A Conscientious Objector in the First World War, he nevertheless served with the Medical Corps at Verdun. After the war, he travelled to Russia and met Lenin. When Hitler came to power, Reichenbach thought it prudent to move first to Holland, then to Britain. He joined the Labour Party in 1935 and became a member of the Left-wing writers' group, Club 43, in London. Briefly interned in 1940 in the Isle of Man, he spent the rest of the war working on anti-Nazi publications for the Foreign Office.

Bertholdt Viertel (V22) is merely described as 'emigrant' in the List. He was something of a universal man, with a CV that included playwright, journalist, and film and theatre director. Oddly, bearing in mind the international quality of his work, nearly all books on Viertel today are in his native German. He was born in Vienna and worked in the burgeoning Berlin film industry from 1922. Six years later, he was working for Fox in California, before moving first to Paramount, then to Warner Brothers. He disliked, as many European directors did, the strait-jacket of the studio system and became the centre of a group of intellectual ex-pats at his home in Santa Monica. They called themselves the *Exilliteratur*, writing and reading anti-Nazi books by authors driven out by the increasing occupations taking place from 1935. That was the year that Viertel directed the iconic *Passing of the Third Floor Back*, to be followed the next year by *Rhodes of Africa*, starring Walter Huston.

Sybil Thorndike was a 'home grown' star. T25 was the daughter of a canon of Rochester cathedral and trained at the Guildhall as a classical pianist. Recurring cramps put an end to this glittering career, however, and she turned to acting, training at the Central School of Speech and Drama housed at the Albert Hall. At twenty-one, she was touring the United States playing a galaxy of Shakespearean ladies and she met her future husband, Lewis Casson and George Bernard Shaw (one of the List's notable absentees), who wrote his *St Joan* especially for her in 1924.

Sybil was an active Labour Party supporter, backing the General Strike even when it affected the *St Joan* run. She became a Dame Commander of the British Empire in 1931 but it was her role in the Peace Pledge Union that brought her to the attention of the Gestapo.

An equally colourful character was Vic Oliver, the Jewish all-round entertainer born Victor von Samek in Vienna. O21 had planned to be a doctor but the First World War intervened and he found himself fighting in an Austrian cavalry unit. Demobbed, he joined the Vienna Conservatoire and became assistant conductor at the Graz Opera House. It may be that he found all this too high-brow because by 1926 he was touring the United States playing the piano in honky-tonk bars and cinemas. He became a comedian by accident, specialising in playing the violin (badly) to get laughs. In Britain, by 1931, he performed at the London Palladium, *the* yardstick of success in those days. Audiences loved him but one who did not was Winston Churchill, whose daughter, Sarah, Oliver married in 1936. 'An Austrian citizen,' Churchill described him almost contemptuously, 'a resident in the US and here on licence and an American passport; twice divorced [this was untrue], 36 or so he says [he was 38] ... and common as dirt.'

It may be that this Churchill link is why Oliver is on the List, unless he told some anti-Nazi jokes that the Reich found unamusing. In January 1942, he became the first celebrity to be interviewed on the BBC's new show *Desert Island Discs* and had a regular radio slot called *Hi, Gang!*

Karel Stepanek ('Paul' – S27) on the List is described as an emigrant film actor. He was actually Czech, although the

German cinema between the wars was where the money was and, ironically, his most frequent role after his arrival in Britain was as a Nazi. In *Sink the Bismarck* (1960), he played Admiral Lutjens as a rabid Nazi because that was what the script demanded. In reality, in common with most of the *Kriegsmarine* high command, Lutjens disliked and distrusted Hitler. It was Lindemann, the *Bismarck's* captain, who was the real zealot.

It was politics, not the piano, that brought Ignacy Paderewski, '*musiker*', to become P3 on the List. He was born in Russia to Polish parents and his father managed a large estate. He was also actively involved in nationalist politics and when he was arrested by the authorities in the January Uprising of 1863, the boy was farmed out to relatives for his own safety. At the age of twelve, clearly a prodigy, Paderewski was enrolled in the Warsaw Conservatoire. After the deaths of his wife and child, he immersed himself in music, touring France, Britain and the States in 1899. Remarried by 1913, he became involved in various philanthropic causes and moved to California.

With the ending of the First World War, Paderewski became the spokesman for the new Polish state set up by Versailles. He tried to encourage investment by American Jews in the new country but the scheme failed. Nevertheless, he was appointed Prime Minister by General Pilsudski and held the post (doubling as Foreign Minister) for a year. Feeling himself a failure, he resigned and became ambassador to the League of Nations before returning to Switzerland and music. The outbreak of war brought him back to politics, however, and, at the age of eighty, he was head of the National Council of Poland based in London, administering the Polish relief fund.

If Paderewski remained fiercely Polish all his life, Sandor Laylo Kellner (K119) switched national identities more easily.

THE OTHERS

Today, as Alexander Korda, he is usually referred to as being more British than the British! One of three film-making brothers from Pusztaturpaszto in Hungary, he directed his first effort in 1914 and, on its success, built the largest film studio in the Empire. As a Jew, he was arrested during the White Terror, which put down an incipient Communist state by 1921. Despite a chequered career – not many of his films made much money – Korda worked all over Europe before reaching Hollywood in 1940. He disliked the rigidity of the American studio system and preferred the freedom of Britain. His London Films, with its studios at Denham in Buckinghamshire, produced iconic pictures – *the Private Life of Henry VIII*, *The Four Feathers*, *The Drum* and (in the year of the List) *The Thief of Baghdad*. It is true that Korda regularly employed the renegade German actor Conrad Veidt as leading man and it is equally true that Veidt, who became a British citizen in 1938, gave a fortune to the anti-Nazi cause. The reason that Korda is on the List however (Veidt is not), is that not only was the Hungarian chummy with Winston Churchill but it is now believed that London Films was an undercover espionage unit, taking clandestine photographs all over the Reich on the pretext of establishing location shots.

Paul Robeson ('*Negersänger*' R80) was another star whose card was marked because of his politics. If Robeson had chosen deliberately to annoy the Reich, he could not have done it better. A successful, intellectual, Communist black man was far too much for the RSHA to swallow. A vicar's son from New Jersey, Robeson was only one of four black students to be enrolled at the prestigious Rutgers University and he went on to read Law at Columbia. His sporting prowess and his impressive baritone voice made him highly popular at a time when African Americans were making a stand against

'Jim Crow' laws of various states. Equally at home in musicals and Shakespeare, Robeson and his wife bought a house in Hampstead during the hugely successful London run of *Showboat* and were widely feted in London society. Two years earlier, the great Russian film director Sergei Eisenstein had invited Robeson to the USSR and the singer-actor became a convinced Communist, a stand underlined by the events in Spain. His latest film, released three months before the List was written, was *The Proud Valley*, made on location in the Rhondda in South Wales. Robeson had an affinity with the working men who put their lives on the line daily for the war effort and he remained a hero in Wales for the rest of his life.

The great baritone was no stranger to subversive lists. As a result of his anti-appeasement speeches and above all, his pro-Soviet statements, he found himself on a P-R blacklist compiled by Beaverbrook for the *Express*; it is rather ironic that both men should feature in Schellenberg's List two years later.

Perhaps the highest-profile star from Britain to appear on the List is C96, Noël Coward. There is no explanation alongside the name on the original document, although, inevitably, various commentators have highlighted his presence. There is the suggestion that Coward worked for British Intelligence, if only obliquely by 'selling' beleaguered Britain's plight in America before Pearl Harbor. People either loved Noël Coward or hated him. Harold Nicolson fell into the former camp – 'So patriotic he was, so light-hearted and so comfortable and well-served. He is a nice, nice man.' Still in Paris when war broke out, Coward had this to say on the propaganda leaflets being scattered by the RAF during the phoney war – 'If the policy of His Majesty's Govt is to bore the Germans to death, I don't think we have the time.'

★ ★ ★

THE OTHERS

The original readers of the *Gestapo Handbook*, the Gestapo and *Einsatzkommando* officers responsible for implementing the List would have known far more about the religious history of Britain than most Englishmen. The relevant section deals with the Reformation and the creation of high, low and broad churches, which is slightly artificial. Arcane subjects such as funding of the Anglican church and the mysteries of communion are dealt with, with additional sub-sections on Catholicism, Methodism, the Salvation Army and the Young Men's Christian Association, which was 'entirely in the hands of the Freemasons'. Numbers of devotees of each denomination and sect are quoted from 1930. The RSHA found something sinister in the Oxford Group – not to be confused with the nineteenth-century Oxford Movement – which appeared in 1928. What probably struck Schellenberg was the number of high-profile politicians associated with the group. Of thirteen leading members, only two – Lord Halifax and Viscount Trenchard – are on the List but ten of the others were members of the Lords and the Earl of Athlone was ADC to the king.

Twenty-eight associations are listed in a religious context, from the secretariat of the Archbishop of Canterbury at Lambeth Palace to the Oxford Group itself, 'exploited by the Intelligence Service' based at Brown's Hotel in Dover Street, W1. Particularly suspect was the Religious Division of the Ministry of Information, especially anti-German in its secretariats. 'Taking possession of this department's material would be absolutely necessary.' Likewise, the Archbishop's Commission on Relations of Church and State spearheaded by Viscount Cecil of Chelwood 'has made propaganda very efficiently against Germany'. The Church of England Council on Foreign Relations would also have its material grabbed, as would the Missionary Film Committee, led by the Reverend Dr Scott Lidgett; the celluloid was vital to the RSHA. Schellenberg was under no illusions of the hypocrisy of these institutions. The Student Christian Movement pretended to work for the worldwide spread of Christianity, whereas it was actually criticising Germany and its leadership was highly political.

All that said, the number of wanted theologians on the List is very small, most of them already on the run from the Reich. No doubt had Britain been invaded, the country would have thrown up its own Martin Niemollers and Father Kolbes to make a stand and carry out acts of heroism but that moment never arrived.

W19 *is* there. He was the Reverend W. L. Wardle, President of the Methodist Conference based in Manchester, the movement generally supporting the Freemasons' idea of a world council of Christian churches. Most of the others were associated with the Hildebrandt-Boeckheler-Raeger-Freudenberg *täterkreis* and Amte II B3 and VI H3 wanted to know all about them.

Franz Hildebrandt (H140) was the son of an art professor and read Theology at Marburg, Tubingen and Berlin by 1930. It was here that he met Dietrich Bonhoeffer, one of the most famous victims of Nazi Germany. Hildebrandt became a Lutheran pastor but resigned in protest at the Aryan Paragraph, which forbade Jews to hold official positions. He moved to the tolerance of Britain, where he joined Bonhoeffer's German church at Sydenham, south London. Three months later, he was back in Germany at the request of Martin Niemoller, helping to organise the Covenant of Pastors *(pfarrernotbund)*, which opposed Nazism. This group became the Confessing Church in the following year and those who supported it – like R61, Dr Julius Raeger – were classified as members of the *Benkennisfront* as a result. Hildebrandt was still in Germany when the war began and was held for four days by the Gestapo. Astonishingly, friends managed to get him out and he made for Britain, this time for good. Interned briefly at Huyton and the Isle of Man, he set up his German church in Cambridge before drifting to Methodism.

Dr Henry Leiper (L63) was already a Methodist. An American, born in New Jersey, he studied in Knoxville, Tennessee and graduated from Blair College in 1917. With his wife and two children, he carried out missionary work in China, Japan and Russia and was back in the United States by 1922. Wherever he went, he spoke publicly against the Nazis, even before they assumed power in Germany, often risking his own safety as a result. In 1936, he tried to persuade Roosevelt to pull the American team out of the Olympics in protest. His papers contain hundreds of news articles on Nazi attacks on churches and priests and he personally wrote to Hitler at one point, asking him to release Martin Niemöller from internment. But this was the age that Leiper called 'the new paganism' and the Führer was not listening.

★ ★ ★

A sizable number of names has no explanation in the original List and no clue as to their origins or occupation. Many of these were rescued under the auspices of the British Committee for Refugees from Czechoslovakia, which became the Czech Refugee Trust Fund later. The names of 13,400 individuals, together with their dates of birth, can be found in the HO294/612 and 613 files in the Public Record Office at Kew. The Gestapo were well aware that Czech émigrés had moved to Britain after the collapse of France and there is a separate section in the *Handbook* devoted to their organisation.

Taken at random, P35 and P36 were clearly members of the

same family – Anton and Karl Pecher, born four years apart, from Neudeck. R119, Rudolf Rossmeisl was forty years old, from Rothau. V38 was Max Vollerth, born in 1903, but his birthplace may have been Hamburg. In all cases, the Amt looking for them was IVA, concerned with opponents of the Nazi regime, which may have included acts of sabotage and emigrants generally. The Germans had, of course, swallowed Czechoslovakia in two bites – the Sudetenland in 1938 and the rest of the country a year later. By the time of the List, Czech refugees had been on the road for months.

★ ★ ★

Two of the many mysteries of the List are the inclusions of draft dodgers and policemen. There are twenty or so *dienstpflichtertiger* (literally, one who flies from service) but why they should be singled out for the List and why its compilers should assume they were hiding in Britain is unknown. Paul Berlin (B122) was from Petersdorf and was living at 29, The Barbican, EC1. The List says that Amt VD 2f was interested in him but no such department existed and this may be a typographical error. G134, Friedrich Gerhard from Graudenz, fits this category too, so the error theory that various commentators have pointed out does not make sense. Amt VD, under the command of *Oberführer* Arthur Nebe, was specifically concerned with identification and search and 2f must have been a sub-division of that. None of this explains why these names alone have surfaced on the List. There must have been untold others, as there were in any country, including Britain. A panicky government, then still under Chamberlain, had announced in April 1939 that conscription was inevitable, at a time when the country was still at peace. When war broke out, the National Service (Armed Forces) Act stipulated that all men between the ages of eighteen and forty-one were eligible to receive the brown envelope falling on their doormats. This was not fully realised until June 1941 and even then, there were exceptions for the reserved occupations, such as mining, munitions and farming. Even so, despite the arrival of thousands of patriots who volunteered, the flag-waving hysteria of 1914 was not repeated and there were men who spent the entire six years of war hiding out from the authorities.

In Germany, the situation was rather different. In defiance of the Versailles treaty, Hitler had reintroduced rearmament and conscription in March 1935. The 100,000 limit stipulated by the Allies at Versailles stood but an additional 100,000 were added each year. In practical terms, that meant a four year head start over Britain. Voluntary enlistment continued at the same time and, given the huge impact of Nazi propaganda, the newly named Wehrmacht – until May 1935, the German armed forces had been called Reichswehr – attracted young men keen to do their bit for the Fatherland and to avoid the colossal unemployment of the Weimar years. Clearly, draft dodgers were not impressed by these blandishments but there is no clear explanation why a handful of individuals should have found their way onto Schellenberg's List.

F48 is not a draft dodger but Sergeant Fisher of Scotland Yard. Amt IV E4, the SS department concerned with defence and the armed forces, wanted to talk to him; why is unknown. The *Gestapo Handbook* gives over twelve pages to a description of the British police system, probably because it was so different from the Nazi structure. It was 'inexplicable', according to the compilers. For obvious reasons, the Met's Special Branch was of greatest interest to the Gestapo. Its officers outranked, according to the *Handbook*, local chief constables, spoke at least one foreign language and were working hand in glove with SIS. Of the senior policemen, only Lord Trenchard (T55) is on the List, although Assistant Commissioner Norman Kendall and his number two, Chief Constable J. E. Horwell are specified in the *Handbook*. What the humble Sergeant Fisher had done to merit inclusion is anybody's guess.

The entry of Ronald Graham (G99) who is listed as a private detective, makes even less sense than that of Fisher. We have no idea, after nearly eighty years, why such a man should be here. If his sleuthing skills had been appropriated by the government and he worked as an agent, the significance is obvious. But the List does not refer to him in this way.

Officers, media people, religious leaders, refugees and draft dodgers; they came from a broad spectrum of society and a score of nationalities but their sheer diversity was not going to let any of them off the hook.

CHAPTER SIXTEEN

NAZIS THROUGH THE LOOKING GLASS

G ary Sheffield, Professor of War Studies at Wolverhampton University, has this to say about those on Walter Schellenberg's List:

> 'At the very least they would have been arrested and interrogated. Very possibly, for many of them, it could have been far worse.'

To see what would *actually* have happened to the 2,694 men and women in the RSHA's spotlight, let us look at the treatment of such people in other occupied countries. The general principles of the occupation followed a similar pattern for all the territories involved but there were important differences. All of them were run for the good of the Reich, providing raw materials and finished goods which found their way into German cities, towns and villages. Wages for workers were fixed at a low level and in some cases prices were controlled.

There was very little movement of labour. The Reich racial policy was carried out everywhere in an escalation of anti-Semitism, which ended in the Holocaust. Countries with a large Aryan/Nordic population, like Norway, Denmark and the Netherlands, were allowed an often considerable right of self-government; areas with Slavic or Jewish populations were not. Censorship operated everywhere, newspapers and radios checked regularly. 'Bad' war news for the Reich was banned. In most countries, the Nazi salute for SS and senior Nazis was mandatory. Anyone opposing the Reich, by active or passive means, was likely to be transported to one of the growing numbers of concentration camps or shot.

There is little doubt that Poland suffered more than most. The plan, part of *Generalplan Ost*, was to Germanise the country to the extent that it no longer existed. In the long term, only primary school education would be available for Polish children. The aim, Himmler ordered:

> '... should be to teach the pupil solely: how to count up to a maximum of 500; how to write his name; that it is God's command that he should be obedient to Germans, honourable, industrious and brave. I regard reading as unnecessary.'[125]

It was not only unnecessary, it was dangerous. The group in any country that would cause most trouble for an army of occupation were the intellectuals, the thinkers who had the imagination to dream and the brainpower to organise resistance and outwit opponents. The Reich's first task was to eliminate this intelligentsia by whatever means. The rest of the population were mere cannon fodder and could easily be cowed into submission.

Ever since 1937, Reinhard Heydrich had been busy in this respect. His Unit II P (Poland) of the Gestapo spent two years doing for Poland what Walter Schellenberg did in a single month for Britain; they drew up the Special Search List, also translated as the Special Prosecution List, which contained the names of more than 61,000 intellectuals who were likely to be trouble when *Fall Weiss* became a reality. Unlike the British version, the Polish List has no addresses or other details and no numbering system. It was compiled largely by members of the 20,000 strong German minority living in Poland, many of whom formed the dreaded *Selbstschutz* militia, once the invasion was underway.

The Polish List was part of the first phase of *Grandplan Ost*, called Operation Tannenberg, and was linked with the Gestapo-NKVD conferences held between Germany and Russia in their co-ordinated destruction of Poland. The first of these was held at Brzesc on 27 September 1939, only five days after a joint Reich-Soviet victory parade had signalled the end of the September War. In fact, some Polish units were still fighting but the end was inevitable and the government was looking to Paris for its safety and its new start in exile. Other meetings were held at Lvov, Przemysi, Krakow and Zakopane and out of them undoubtedly came Stalin's decision to slaughter 22,000 Polish officers at Katyn, a war crime which Russia only partially acknowledged for the first time in 2010.

In the Germanisation process, a sizeable chunk of Polish territory was called the *Generalgouvernement*, run by its gauleiter, Hitler's Party lawyer, Hans Frank. 'Poland shall be treated like a colony,' he wrote, 'the Poles will become the slaves of the Greater German Empire.' The Operation *Intelligenzaktion* had top priority under his authority but it was carried out by the SS, the Selbstschutz and even (although its generals denied it) units of the Wehrmacht.

Inevitably, the 61,000 on the Polish 'hit' list grew to over 100,000, sometimes including children, who were eliminated in the phases of the Operation. Academics, priests, publishers, teachers, youth leaders and politicians, both national and local, formed the hard core of the victims, along with the leaders of organisations that the Reich believed to be harmful. In one well-documented case, on 6 November 1939, all the lecturers at the Jagiellon University in Krakow were ordered to attend a lecture given by SS chief Bruno Muller on the future of Polish education. 138 of them turned up, no doubt hoping that some kind of civility would emerge. In the event, once trapped in Room 56 of the Collegium Novum buildings, Muller harangued them with the usual racial tirades of the SS. Any who protested were slapped and hit with rifle butts before they were all herded off to temporary prisons on their way to Sachsenhausen and Dachau. Astonishingly, interventions by the Pope and even Mussolini secured the release of some of them by February 1940 but by then many had died from disease and ill-treatment, standing in thin prison rags for pointless roll-calls in the prison courtyards which could last for hours.

Warsaw, as the capital, was seen as the focus of potential unrest by the Reich and here, between October and March, thousands were arrested and interned, many of them at the notorious Pawiak prison. The exact numbers killed here will never be known. Similar arrests took place at Lodz, Lublin and Krakow. The capital surrendered on 28 September and three days later *Einsatzgruppe* IV, under SS *Brigadeführer* Lothar Beutel, barged their way into studies, offices and private houses. On 8 October, 354 teachers and priests, 'full,' according to Beutel, 'of Polish chauvinism,' were rounded up and thrown into prison. There were so many of them that the surplus had to be wedged into the basement of the Gestapo HQ at 25, Szucha Avenue. Five years later, graffiti scrawled on the walls here by the desperate inmates recorded their last thoughts. One wrote:

'It is easy to speak about Poland. It is harder to work for her. Even harder to die for her. And the hardest to suffer for her.'

Political prisoners were taken out to the Sejm gardens, behind the parliament building along Wiejska Street, and shot with a bullet to the back of the head. Torture and execution were the orders of the day, interrogations revealing the names of other hapless souls who may not have been on the original List. Today, the Museum of Struggle and Martyrdom stands on the Szucha Avenue site. According to its official findings, over 12,000lb of human ashes were found in the building's perimeter.

Phase two began in the spring, as Winston Churchill took over at Number Ten and blitzkrieg flashed west. This was called ABAktion, which lasted until the summer. It is estimated that in the previous September and October, about 20,000 people were murdered in 760 mass executions. The best known is the slaughter that took place on 20-21 June 1940, near the village of Palmiry in the Kampiros Forest, north west of Warsaw. Mass executions in city centres attracted too much attention. Gunshots were loud and bodies had to be burned or transported elsewhere by truck. Death in a desolate forest was another matter.

The executions at Palmiry were carried out by squads of

the Ordo, Sipo, the SS *Reiterei* (cavalry) and even SD officers led by the Warsaw commandant SS *Standartenführer* Josef Meisinger. Mass graves, 98 feet long and between eight and ten feet deep, had already been dug by Radmen (the Labour Force) or the Hitler Youth. This was the 'glade of death', which grew ever larger as trees were felled to cope with the numbers. On the days of execution, the regular forestry workers were given compulsory days off. The victims were taken by truck, largely from Pawiak, on the pretext of moving them to other prisons. They were allowed to bring one small suitcase and even a day's rations for the journey. At the site, the cases were left on the vehicles ready for the return journey. We know from exhumations made in the 1960s that Jews were allowed to retain the yellow stars stitched to their clothing and the prison's infirmary staff the red crosses on their sleeves. They were blindfolded and marched to the edge of the pits. Here, some were given wooden poles to hold so that when they fell, they would form level layers for those who would follow.

Then, uncomprehending, underweight and no doubt fearing the worst, the machine guns opened up and they toppled forward, gravity taking them onto the bodies of those already there. The exhumations prove that not all of them were dead when the earth and moss was shovelled over them.

The families of the dead were told that their loved ones had died of natural causes before such missives stopped altogether with the *Nicht-und Nebel Erlass*, the Night and Fog decree on 7 December 1941 by the Führer, to ensure that enemies of the Reich simply disappeared without trace.

The liquidation of intellectuals continued throughout the war. A second edition of the Polish Special Search List was published in Krakow in the autumn of 1940[126] and others at regular intervals afterwards. In November 1944, when the huge Allied advance was pushing the Wehrmacht back towards the Reich, HMSO in London published an extraordinary book. It was written in Polish, in February 1942, 'by several authors of necessity temporarily anonymous' and the London editors assumed that, by the time the English edition appeared, those authors would be dead. It was called *The Nazi Kultur in Poland* and dealt specifically with the destruction of Poland's intellectual elite, using chapter headings that sound very like those in the *Gestapo Handbook*.

An understandably bitter John Masefield, the poet, supplied an introduction to it:

> 'Let the readers reflect, that the gathering of these materials [the book's contents] has brought men and women to torture and death, those being the only gifts to man now put into the world by the German brain.'[127]

The Nazi state, Masefield went on,

> 'has plundered and then suppressed colleges and schools; it has murdered, imprisoned, disallowed or starved the learned, the enlightened, the devout... It has sacked and burned the libraries, the newspapers, the printing presses, closed the concert rooms, broken up the orchestras, ruined or dispersed the musicians... and always, the aim has been to kill intelligence... so that in future that land shall have no kindling mind, shall have instead the slave mind, unable to resist.'

The Warsaw authors concluded that some men could 'out Satan Satan'. It took them a year, by February 1942, to compile the sorry list of slaughter and destruction. Electricity was in short supply, so much of the typing had to be done by candlelight in coalless rooms where the temperature never rose above seven degrees. The authors sat huddled in overcoats, with frost-bitten fingers. They could check nothing in libraries, newspaper offices, nor the radio. Every page had to be carefully hidden. The post could not be used, nor the telephone, 'for who can tell the hour of the Gestapo?' Small miracles sometimes happened. Private libraries had been destroyed along with public ones but somebody, somehow, managed to get a copy of Rebecca West's article 'If Worst Comes to Worst', not dreaming that she was on the RSHA List for Britain. The original editor died in a concentration camp in December 1942. His number two was shot, along with his wife, in June 1943 – those details had been smuggled out to the London editors in the July before publication.

They wrote:

'These pages are more than enough to show the mean, cruel mind and the muddled, dark, sly method. They indict Nazi Germany... as the arch-enemy in our century of light, truth, candour and intelligence. Yet, nightmarish, almost incredible as the conditions described here seem, when read in the free air of Britain, where a man may worship, bring up his children or follow a profession as he chooses, where we have had music and the theatre to help us through the long years of war, where we have not been hungry nor yet too bitterly cold, remember while you read, that things have changed only for the worse since February 1942...'

The Warsaw authors highlighted the lies and hypocrisy of their Nazi overlords. On 26 October 1939, Gauleiter Frank had assured them that the Führer's intention was that 'you will be permitted to preserve your national Polish individuality in all the activities of public life.' On 7 November, he was holding forth again:

> We come into this country not in any wild fury of conquest, but as guarantors of work, ordered and conducted in the German fashion.'

He prayed that God would end the hatred that had for centuries emanated from the castle of Krakow towards their German neighbours.

A year later, the mood had changed. Gauleiter Arthur Greisser wrote:

> 'If there is a Lord and if there is any justice – then he has elected Adolf Hitler that he may sweep away this scum.'

He was talking about the people of Poland – 'jabbering Jews and insolent Poles.' 'Do not soften,' Greisser exhorted the SS early in 1941, 'be hard and become harder still!'

The reign of terror which began in September 1939 continued, directed at the churches – 'enemies of things German.' Monasteries were closed, so were convents, their people scattered to the camps. There is a grim list of individual priests forced to carry out pointless drill exercises at gunpoint and clean lavatories with their bare hands. One of them, the Reverend Scigala, was beaten with spades, thrown into icy water and 'washed' with brooms. Unsurprisingly, he died from his injuries. Bibles were burned, statues of saints torn down.

Presses were allowed to continue, as long as they printed only propaganda. The *Kurier Czestochowski*, in January 1941, carried a banner headline, 150 MILLION CATHOLICS AGAINST ENGLAND, as if the Poles could not wait to cross the Channel in support of Hitler.

A month later, a pamphlet published in Krakow gloated that 'German energy, German organising skills, German expert knowledge and German diligence' had built up a superb educational system from the ashes of centuries of Polish neglect. 'Pole' must be written in the German way, with no capital letter. Teachers and pupils alike were monitored by the *Volksdeutsche*, the German quislings who reported anything untoward to the gauleiter. History, civics and even geography disappeared from the school curriculum. Even Christmas was banned.

The University of Warsaw was gutted by fire, with 80 per cent of its property destroyed. Thirty-two faculties disappeared as a result. History was rewritten to prove that, historically, the Poles had invaded German territory along the Vistula centuries earlier. As we have seen, the staff of these colleges were among the first to be sent to the forests. Before they got there, all sorts and sizes of mild-mannered professors were beaten and tortured in various prisons and camps. Such was the screen of secrecy surrounding these developments that academies at other universities wrote to Polish colleagues wondering why a particular paper or piece of research was not forthcoming. Bizarrely, some of these queries even came from Germany itself.

Books vanished. The huge Sejm and Senate library in Warsaw, containing some 50,000 volumes, with periodicals running to a further 50,000, were removed in trucks on 16 November 1939. 5,000 back numbers of Polish newspapers likewise disappeared, wiping the country's immediate past. Everything from the State Museum of Archaeology went and the National Library closed on 1 February 1940. The staff from all three institutions had to find what work they could. Paintings disappeared from art galleries before the buildings themselves were requisitioned by the Reich. An untold number found their way into Goering's hands, anxious to acquire 'non-degenerate' art as he was. Private collections ceased to exist. The only gallery to survive intact was the Tatra Museum at Zakopane, probably because it featured art of the mountaineers, whom Himmler was convinced were actually lost Aryans!

There is a *huge* list of destroyed buildings, not just synagogues and churches but palaces, theatres, cinemas and nightclubs. Count Patrochi's impressive country house at Krzeszowice became Gauleiter Frank's residence. Warsaw Castle's sumptuous ballroom, with its exquisite eighteenth century wall paintings, became a building site. The Chopin monument in Warsaw was destroyed.

By 1941, there were only a handful of Polish bookshops left. All the others stocked only German texts and random searches were carried out by the SS to check that booksellers were obeying the law. As time went on, a paper shortage meant that books written in any language were in very short supply. Bearing in mind Himmler's views on the role of reading, various books were banned very early on, among them those of the British List's Aldous Huxley. The Polish astronomer, Copernicus, vanished from bookshelves; so, after 1941, did any Communist literature. Listee Baden-Powell's works were not suitable; neither were any titles linking the words 'Poland' with 'independence' or 'rebirth'. The Warsaw authors record one case of this censorship backfiring. One reader of history was unable to obtain books written by Frederick the

Great because the former king of Prussia, the iconic German hero with whom Hitler often compared himself, wrote only in French!

The press was smothered by the cloying atmosphere of Josef Goebbels' propaganda machine. Offices were raided, reporters beaten up and deported. Sad letters asking for news of vanished loved ones quickly became a thing of the past. The main newspaper in the *Generalgouvernement* was the *Nowy Kurier Werszawski* and it was entirely in German hands by the middle of October 1939. Its journalese was dreadful and it had three aims. The first was to ridicule 'old' Poland – the creation of the 'governing clique' of the intelligentsia who had been patronising the people for generations. The second was to dash all hopes of some kind of rescue, especially from Britain. The third was to display the superiority and power of German culture. The first page of the first number of *NKW* was an article by George Bernard Shaw, the Irish playwright, socialist and guru of the avant-garde. He was popular in Poland and the article talked about making peace with Hitler and ridiculing 'Churchillism'. The idea that the Führer had designs on Belgium and Holland, Shaw believed, was nonsense. This may, of course, explain why GBS is not on Schellenberg's List; the darling of the Left was a secret fellow traveller of the Right!

Throughout the autumn of 1939, the paper kept up a tirade against Britain. The country had published a Blue Book that was a 'crushing indictment of England'. Not a single Briton had died on the German-French front. Every day of the war was costing her £4000 and Beaverbrook's *Sunday Express* 'will have none of Churchill'; Ireland was on 'its hind legs', ready to revolt, and so was India. Ships could get nowhere near the British coast because of the *Kriegsmarine's* 'death zone'; it all became ever more hysterical and exaggerated.

In a more wistful tone, an editorial of the *NKW* spoke of harmony between nations. This would be possible:

> 'after the destruction of Britain's political system; Britain constantly irritates and excites nation against nation because her hegemony and power are based on their discord.'

Not for nothing did the majority of Poles refer to the *NKW* as 'the rag'.

Other papers joined in, however. The *Krakauer Zeitung*, as well as lauding German victories wherever the Wehrmacht went, had several pops at Britain: London had no gas or water because of bombing raids. The king was wisely buying a house in America. London, by 7 September 1940, was already 'a second Warsaw'. Six million Britons had not slept for weeks and even 8,500 dead Londoners were not enough for Churchill. The railway network had broken down entirely around London. The few remaining Americans had pulled out as the royal family packed their bags. The average working Englishman lived a miserable existence. The Welsh were on the point of mutiny. The Empire was being liquidated and the Rothschilds' money was behind the whole thing. The British were beastly to the Arabs and of course the SIS was guilty of 'Murder, Arson, Espionage'. Duff Cooper (the List's C88) at the head of the Ministry of Information was the biggest liar of the lot!

In terms of the airwaves, Polskie Radio was taken over by the *Reichsrundfunk*. Its staff were dismissed and all programmes were bombarded with Goebbels' style propaganda. What was slightly odd here is that the opinions of ordinary Poles *were* listened to by their conquerors. 'They employ a brutal terrorism, shoot Poles by the hundred, imprison them by the thousand, deport by tens of thousands,' but they were concerned that the people really *believe* in the rightness of German occupation and German victory. Not for nothing did the authors of *The Nazi Kultur* liken Nazi government to *Alice's Adventures in Wonderland*.

The cinema, too, was fully controlled by censorship. When one of the authors sat in a Warsaw picture house watching yet another documentary extolling the virtues of Germandom and the narration said, '... nearly all the peoples of the European continent have taken up arms against the Soviets – Germans, Italians, Romanians, Hungarians, Finns, Slovaks, Spaniards, Swedes, Danes, Dutchmen, Belgians and Frenchmen... where are the Poles?' A voice from the shadows muttered, 'In the concentration camp at Oswiecim.'

Oswiecim, by 1941, was Auschwitz-Birkenau, growing rapidly to become the most appalling killing centre of the Reich. The authors of the *Nazi Kultur* were concerned to show how their intellectual life had been destroyed. They mention the Jews and the ordinary people but these are not their primary concerns. Remember Sam Pivnik, the little boy who celebrated his thirteenth birthday on the day that the Luftwaffe roared over his town, signalling the end of a way of life? By the time that Walter Schellenberg compiled the List, the synagogue in Bedzin had long gone, the inhabitants who lived next door burned to death in the same *Einsatzgruppe* fire that destroyed it. Sam had not gone to school for nearly a year because there was no school and there were no teachers. There were curfews on the streets, armed Germans everywhere. Food was scarce and people queued for hours to get it. Before the wearing of yellow stars became compulsory, Polish children would run along those lines pointing out the Jews to prowling officials – 'Jude! Jude!' – and they would be sent to the back of the queue to start again. Sam's father was badly beaten in the street by the police.

What followed was extraordinary. First came the deportations – lists appearing on the Judenrat building's noticeboards of people to be taken away to work. Sam's big brother, Nathan, was among them. Then came the ghetto, rather later than the better-known ones in Warsaw, Lodz and Krakow. For Sam's family, their new home was an indescribable shanty town in a quarry called the Kamionka near the town. Then, shortly before his sixteenth birthday, Sam was shepherded with the rest of the Pivniks to the railway station. Their destination was Auschwitz, accompanied by jack-booted SS, vicious, barking dogs and screaming. For hours, the only word that Sam heard was '*Schiessjude*'. Shit Jew.

Suddenly, he was in another queue, shuffling off the *rampe* with the others. Ahead of him was a handsome man in an immaculate SS uniform. He was holding expensive doeskin gloves in his hand and he was flicking them to left or right. He was Dr Josef Mengele, the 'angel of death', who is today one of the worst icons of Nazi Germany. To the right was life. To the left was death. Sam's mother pushed her boy into the other queue, in that desperate second saving his life. All the other Pivniks died in Auschwitz over the next hours. When Sam, uncomprehending, asked what had happened to them, he was told that they had 'already gone to the chimneys', gassed with Zyklon B manufactured by I. G. Farben and incinerated in the ovens that glowed around the clock.

Over a million people had died at Auschwitz by 1945 and Poland's Jewish population, which had once stood at three million, was reduced to a few thousand.

★ ★ ★

If Poland stands at one end of the spectrum of the mad kaleidoscope that was Nazi rule, Denmark must stand at the other. Under Operation Weserberg, the Wehrmacht crossed the eleventh-century Danewerk fortifications on 9 April 1940. Faced with overwhelming odds and the threat of the total destruction of Copenhagen, the king and his government surrendered after a single day's fighting. Fewer than 3,000 Danes died in total and Denmark became what the Nazis called a 'model protectorate'. The *Rigsdag*, the Danish parliament, continued its business much as before and the king, Christian X, made a point of riding on horseback around his capital with no guard or escort, in full dress uniform, chatting to his people, rather as Churchill was to do in the rubble-strewn streets of the London Blitz. The courts continued to function and businesses operated smoothly. The fact was that Germany needed the dairy produce of Denmark's agriculture and the area came to be known as *sannefront* (the cream front) as a result. There was censorship of radio and press but this was carried out by Danes themselves under the auspices of the country's Nazi Party, which had been set up in 1930. Even here, there was a 'Danishness' about things – the hooked cross that was the party badge had curved ends so that it resembled a Viking rune, rather than a swastika.

It was an uneasy relationship, certainly, a free, democratic people with a monarch living cheek by jowl with one of the most vicious dictatorships in history but, until 1943, it largely worked. Under Obergruppenführer Werner Best, there was an atmosphere of tolerance. In many ways, his was the acceptable face of Nazism. He may even had tipped off the small Danish Resistance movement over the resettlement of Danish Jews in the East, giving them time to smuggle over 80 per cent of them to neutral Sweden. Anti-Semitism erupted in 1941 when the great synagogue in Copenhagen was burned. The government cracked down hard but the tensions remained high. Two years later, the HIPO Corps and the Schulenberg Corps were paramilitary organisations pledged to move against the Jews if Best did not. He was summoned to the Reich Chancellery in December 1943 and ordered by the Führer in person to tighten his grip. For every victim of the Resistance, five Danes must die, Hitler told him. By 1944, the military governor Hermann von Hanneken and the SD took matters into their own hands and that year became one of the bloodiest in Denmark's history.

One of the myths of the Second World War is that everyone in Denmark, from the king down, wore the star of David on their clothes, to show their solidarity with the Jews. This was a piece of propaganda almost certainly originating in the National Denmark America Association in the United States.

★ ★ ★

Somewhere between the extremes of Poland and Denmark came France. Blitzkrieg had hit the frontier north of the Maginot Line on 10 May 1940 and, by the time the armistice was signed on 22 June, the Wehrmacht's front line extended from Bordeaux in the west to Lake Geneva in the east. In the meantime, of course, the BEF had been ferried out of Dunkirk with its tail between its legs. France was the old enemy for Germany and the memories of 1914-18 were still raw and bitter twenty years later. The French had called that war *la der des ders*, the last of the last, but it was wishful thinking. By 1940, France was not only unprepared for war but unprepared for the consequences of defeat.

The prime minister, Paul Reynaud, warned his cabinet on 12 June:

'You take Hitler for another Wilhelm I, the old gentleman who seized Alsace-Lorraine from us . . . But Hitler is Genghis Khan.'[128]

By the end of the fighting later that month, nearly two million men, five per cent of the population, had been taken prisoner; 90,000 were dead. The rift with Britain was enormous. The British took de Gaulle's Free French officers on sufferance but their 'help' at Dunkirk was pitiful. 'In May 1918,' Marshal Petain, soon to head the collaboratist Vichy government, said in a radio broadcast, 'we had eighty-five British divisions; in May 1940, there were only ten.'[129]

The first weeks of the German occupation were chaotic. Refugees were everywhere, most people travelling south, away from the Wehrmacht. Caged birds released into the streets flapped about; dogs abandoned by their owners roamed the gutters, scavenging for food. Inmates of lunatic asylums, released by the invaders, made life even more difficult. Most of them had no idea what was happening or had any means of fending for themselves. The rumour machine went into overdrive. Little girls were being raped in the streets; little boys had their hands cut off so that they would never be able to fight for France in the future. The bestiality of 'the Boche', so redolent of 1914-18, re-emerged in those weeks.

But invasion did not make the French pull together. The country was riven by political differences before the war, Right and Left, gentile and Jew. Collaboration became the order of the day for thousands who would live to regret it after the liberation of 1944. Jean-Paul Sartre was impressed by the behaviour of the invaders. They gave up their seats to old ladies on the Paris Metro. They patted children on the cheek and gave them sweets. No doubt this was ordered behaviour but it boded well for the future in the minds of the more hopeful Frenchman. It helped that the military commander of the Occupied Zone (essentially the northern half of the country) from October 1940 was General Otto von Stulpnagel, an old-fashioned *junker* and something of a puritan. He frowned on fraternisation with the local girls, the *collabos horizontales* whose heads would be shaved in rituals of public humiliation by a vengeful population in 1944-45. Overall, there was a respect and a sense of honour which was totally lacking from German behaviour in Poland or Czechoslovakia for that matter.

In Paris, as in other cities, the night life that had stopped during the invasion was revived. Theatres and cinemas reopened, clubs were serving drinks again and the café society continued almost as if there were no war. Perhaps, Frenchmen mused that summer and autumn, occupation would not be so bad after all. Later, it would come to be known as *le temps des autruches*, the time of the ostriches.

The military terms settled on Vichy, created under Petain and covering the south of the country, were as harsh as Versailles, and deliberately so. The army was reduced to 100,000 men – exactly the same as that imposed on Germany in 1919. The navy had all but disappeared, some ships sunk by the British on Churchill's orders, as we have seen. But Petain's government retained a skeleton armed force, its control of Vichy itself and its overseas territories, still extensive, that had been the French Empire. This was an illusion, since the Reich in practice blocked a great deal of what Vichy tried to do and the *zone libre* was not as *libre* as all that. With the Allied invasion of North Africa in 1942, Vichy was absorbed into the *zone occupé* and even the illusion of freedom had gone.

Increasingly, censorship prevailed. As elsewhere, newspapers and radio were in the hands of the Nazis. Suspect organisations were banned, their buildings commandeered for the Reich. *Liberté, egalité, fraternité* became the more practical *travail, famille, patrie*. Work, family and fatherland were more modern than the lofty ideals of the revolution of 1789; they also smacked of the Reich.

In an interesting echo of the British List, denunciations took place across France. Socialists were reported to the authorities in the spirit of collaboration; so were freemasons, teachers, jazz musicians and, of course, Jews. France had been split in the 1890s over *'l'affaire'*, the case of the army staff officer Alfred Dreyfus, accused of selling secrets to France's enemies. He was innocent but he was Jewish and, in the eyes of many Frenchmen, that alone was enough to condemn him. That anti-Semitism had not vanished fifty years later, when 14,000 Freemasons were dismissed from their posts; 60,000 of them were investigated, their loyalty to the Reich tested. On 3 October, the first of many *statut des Juifs* (Jewish laws) was passed in Vichy. By March 1941, there was a special department for Jewish affairs and Jews were imprisoned or placed in what were, in effect, ghettoes under police supervision.

In 1941, all men and women had to join the *Arbeitdirect* (the Labour service) and the following year all boys had to wear the uniform of the Hitler Youth. The speaking of French was banned in schools in Alsace-Lorraine, which had been the bone of contention in the Franco-Prussian War of 1870. The beret, as typically French as the *lederhosen* of the Bavarians was German, was outlawed. Even the clocks were changed – French time became German time, an hour fast. French theatres and French cinema flourished, minus the stars who had already got out. Maurice Chevalier still found work, as did Simone Signoret, Edith Piaf and the young Yves Montand. They were not remotely Nazis but were determined to get on with their lives as best they could. No one could offer 'succour to the enemy' or listen to foreign radio broadcasts. Public meetings were a thing of the past. There were to be no parades and no flags, other than the scarlet and black banners of the Reich. As in other countries, everyone queued (was not the word itself French?); everyone carried identity cards. As the war bit the economy more deeply, ration coupons were essential. In one of the curious ironies of wartime, the French called these 'tickets', the English word. The British 'coupon' was actually French.

Food was allocated depending on the occupation of the consumer. Farmhands, manual workers and small children got more than others. Schoolchildren were given pink vitamin tablets. Nobody over seventy was allowed milk. By 1943, the average daily intake for an adult was 1,200-1,500 calories, in some cases half what it had been before the war.

Petrol was rationed and the use of cars restricted to those with permits. These were largely medical staff, firemen and night workers but, as with any system administered by underlings, permits could be bought by the less than scrupulous anxious to cosy up to the invaders. Many people took to bicycles instead. Prices generally rose, whereas wages remained at the 1940 level. Barter replaced the straight handling of cash in many instances. As in Britain, millions of French men and women availed themselves of the black market. It was a victimless crime and played into the hands of those who always knew how to handle a bad situation and make something out of it.

Except for the most ardent collaborators, however, like the *Milice*, the Fascist paramilitary, the majority of Frenchmen put up with the occupation, rather than embraced it. Teenagers (the word had yet to be invented) listened illicitly to the BBC and the jazz of Django Reinhardt, dressed outrageously and called themselves '*zazzous*'. The older generation ignored the occupiers, laughed at their Prussian correctness behind their backs and constantly referred to them as *ils*; they. Whatever type of policeman was patrolling the streets, the French called them all Gestapo and pretended not to notice the daily march-past under the Arc de Triomphe of a Wehrmacht band playing German music.

The Jewish population of France was probably less than 350,000 at the start of the war, fewer than in Britain but only half the RSHA's estimate. Foreign-born Jews were '*Juifs*'; home-grown were 'Israelites'; the SS made no distinction. As in other occupied countries, they were banned from public life. Museums, shops, markets, sporting events, restaurants, theatres and cinemas were closed to them. Radios were confiscated. They had to ride in segregated coaches on the Paris Metro. They were not even, unlike the Pivniks in Poland, allowed to queue, so they would always be the last to get whatever was going. They wore the obligatory yellow star after June 1942.

Camps were set up for Jews, both in Vichy and the Occupied Zone. By the end of 1941 there were 7,000 inmates in the three nearest to Paris. They slept fifty to a room, on bare boards. Starvation and disease haunted them all. On 27 March 1942, the dreaded resettlement in the East began. 1,112 Jews rattled out of Drancy and Pithiviers that day bound ultimately for Auschwitz. By 17 August 1944, with the Allies on their way, an estimated 76,000 had taken that journey. Less than three per cent of these survived.

★ ★ ★

The only portion of British soil invaded by the Reich was the Channel Islands. There were frantic talks in London, the lights of Whitehall burning far into the night. Could the islands be defended? Geographically, they were nearer to France than to Britain and the answer was no. Could they be evacuated? The task would be vast, hampered, no doubt, by the prowling U-boats of the *Kriegsmarine*. So, again, a resounding no. On the positive side, the bailiwicks of Jersey and Guernsey (the largest, most populated islands) were not expected to fight in the event of an invasion. That was not much consolation and there must have been many Channel Islanders who felt as bitter towards Chamberlain and Churchill as the French did. In the first four days of July 1940, as Walter Schellenberg was beginning to draw up the List, the Islands surrendered.

In the occupation that followed, each of the Reich's armed forces had its own courts and tribunals. So did the Occupation Todt,[130] a foreign workforce brought in to improve the Islands' defences against British attack. In the case of an Islander accused of a crime, he could, in theory, appear before any or all three courts, depending on the nature of the offence. Weapons were routinely handed over to the conquerors, including cutlasses, pikes and starting pistols. Food, which had previously been imported from Britain, now had to come from mainland Europe; in practice, France. The authorities took careful data of the Islands' agricultural potential – their industrial capacity was very small – including the number of cows and horses and the yellowness of the corn. Fishing, a vital Island occupation, was limited, for obvious reasons, to three miles off the coast of each island and then only under *Kriegsmarine* escort. Motor vehicles were limited (Sark, famously, had none anyway!) and even bicycles were reduced in number. Drivers now drove on the right, not the left, a small but psychologically important reminder that Islanders were no longer masters of their fate. The English and French place names that been used for centuries were replaced with German versions – *Bec du Nez* was now *Nasenfelsen*, *Pleinmont* became *Westburg*, and so on. All adults were, in theory, put to work for the Reich but many refused with endless arguments about what, under the terms of The Hague Convention, constituted war work.

As in France, the invaders were immaculately behaved. Some historians have posited a 'golden bridge' mentality here – that Hitler was being deliberately 'nice' to the occupied so that some kind of rapprochement with Churchill and Britain would have been more likely. There is no evidence for this and the reality was that young soldiers, far from home and feeling themselves to be aliens, found the rigid Nazism of Berlin and the Berghof to be unworkable. The invaders needed the Islanders as much as the Islanders needed them. It was hardly an ideal symbiosis but it worked. There were friendly girls who no doubt became '*callabos horizontales*', as they did in France; the Islanders called them Jerrybags. And there were official brothels for the first time in the Islands' history. On the other hand, there were crusty old colonels who refused the Reich any assistance at all.

Inevitably, supplies of all kinds ran low. There were two meatless days a week in Jersey by September 1940. Eggs dwindled because farmers could not feed their chickens. Flour, cheese, eggs and onions came from France; potatoes and tomatoes went in the opposite direction. A diarist in Guernsey noted in August that she could only have two baths a week and that in two inches of water! Jersey's Medical Officer of Health reported that between 1940 and 1943, the height and weight of children was declining to the tune of several pounds and up to two inches.

Two black markets operated – one home grown, the other French. Prosecutions took place in relation to this and to tampering with price control and the illegal slaughtering of animals. These crimes carried stiff fines and even prison sentences.

In terms of education, the only change was the introduction of compulsory German into its schools, which, in itself, was problematical enough. Who wanted to learn today the language of a man who might shoot you tomorrow? British films were shown, largely harmless comedies, but as they ran out, German versions replaced them. Audiences in 1941 were give permission to applaud heroes – assuming that they were Aryan supermen, of course! Photography was banned. So, at first, were dances. Careless talk cost lives on both sides of the war and casual fraternisation was frowned upon. Himmler made no impact on Islanders' reading habits, although English-language books were not replaced as they became worn out. Anything subversive was of course removed.

After much wrangling, the deportation of British-born subjects began in September 1942, many of them ending up at the concentration camp at Biberach, which, by Reich standards, was surprisingly humane.

In the final stages of preparation for this book, an article appeared in the *Daily Mail* of 8 May 2017, written by former army officers Richard Kemp and John Weigold, alleging that a full-scale concentration camp system operated on Alderney, devoid of civilian inhabitants. The inmates were largely Russian soldiers imported under the Occupation Todt scheme who were worked to death as slave labour and routinely tortured and murdered. Evidence comes from a scattering of Russians who survived and is in accordance with similar tales of atrocities supposedly committed on the defeated

Wehrmacht by American troops along the Rhine in 1944. A report was submitted by Captain 'Bunny' Pantcheff, who went on to write a book on the accepted benign behaviour of the Germans in the Channel Islands. The veracity – and even the existence – of this report must be queried.

Kemp and Weigold estimate a 'ball park figure' of 40,000 deaths on Alderney and suggest that it may be as high as 70,000. Where are the bodies? Thrown into the sea, the writers of the article suggest.

The Channel Islands were not strategically important. They *could*, with a great deal of new military infrastructure, become part of the Reich's Atlantic wall against a possible British invasion. But that was hardly necessary. If there were to be an assault on Fortress Europe, it would have to be launched against the mainland, not a scattering of exposed islands. Not until August 1942 was this attempted, in the disastrous raid on Dieppe. Once it had failed, with the loss of 3,600 men, 106 aircraft, a destroyer, 30 tanks and 33 landing craft, the Allied command claimed that this was valuable experience in measuring the effectiveness of German defences. Rather as Dunkirk gave the BEF the experience of getting off beaches, leaving most of their equipment behind. It fooled no one, least of all the families of Canadian and Free French troops who died there.

★ ★ ★

As the war went on, resistance movements grew up in all occupied countries. Some of it was passive, as in the Channel Islands, Denmark and Norway. Some of it was active – the Maquis in France perhaps being the most impressive. Reprisals against sabotage and other acts against the Reich were swift and merciless. Torture, hangings, shootings, deportations to the camps; these became the stock reactions by the conquerors to the conquered in the war years. Such activity undoubtedly increased as the war went on. Because Britain was still free, and because America had joined the Allies in December 1941, it all had a purpose. The Maquis, for instance, frequently worked hand in glove with the daredevils of SOE who parachuted into darkened fields 'somewhere in France' to help sow discord and chaos.

But what if America had not come in? What if Britain was not free, after all?

CHAPTER SEVENTEEN

IF THE EAGLE HAD LANDED

'As soon as we beat England,' said Reichsminister Richard Darré in the summer of 1940:

'We shall make an end of your Englishmen once and for all. Able-bodied men and women between the ages of 16 and 45 will be exported as slaves to the Continent. The old and weak will be exterminated. All men remaining in Britain as slaves will be sterilized; a million or two of the young women of the Nordic type will be segregated in a number of stud farms where, with the assistance of picked German sires, during a period of 10 or 12 years, they will produce annually a series of Nordic infants to be brought up in every way as Germans. Those infants will be partially educated in Germany and only those who fully satisfy the Nazi requirements will be allowed to return to Britain and take up permanent residence. The rest will be sterilized and sent to join slave gangs in

Germany. Thus, in a generation or two, the British will disappear.'

This extract purports to be a genuine speech delivered by Darré, Hitler's Argentinian-born agriculture expert, who became the Reich's Agricultural Leader and Food Minister. It only exists, however, in quoted form in *Time* magazine and is likely to be a rather clumsy attempt at black propaganda. It reads very much like the reality of Poland but has none of the hallmarks of the German occupation of more western territories. Darré himself was a known Anglophile and had lived in Britain as an exchange student, attending King's College School in Wimbledon. All in all, the pronouncement cannot be taken as a blueprint of what would have happened in Britain if the eagle had landed.

Some years ago, counterfactual history – the 'what ifs' of the past – was highly popular and gave rise to a whole library of books examining what *might* have happened had events gone down the 'other trouser-leg of time'.

One of the most persuasive of these was Norman Longmate's *If Britain Had Fallen*, written in 2003. Like most books of this kind, the jacket design has a grim-faced Wehrmacht soldier in *stalhelm* and field grey, with a swastika behind him hanging as a banner from the tower of Big Ben. It is a startling (if over-used) image and something like it would, no doubt, have happened if the summer of 1940 had gone another way.

Let us assume then that some sort of miracle happened in August and September of that year, that Goering's Luftwaffe had so crippled the RAF that the British lost command of the air. Let us suppose that Raeder's *Kriegsmarine* could have kept the marauding Royal Navy at bay in the Channel for long enough for the Wehrmacht to establish its bridgeheads along the south-east coast. After all, 1940 was the year of miracles. How else could people explain the success of blitzkrieg in the west – five nations brought to their knees in the space of four months? How else could people explain how so many British soldiers came back from Dunkirk, allowing Churchill to change a defeat into a 'victory'? The invasion of Britain *could* have happened. It nearly did.

We are not concerned with the generalities of what could have happened later. Norman Longmate paints a realistic picture of the land campaign in which the Wehrmacht makes short work of the British army. He has Winston Churchill, living up to his oft-delivered speeches in the House and on the radio, going down in a hail of bullets in Whitehall. I think this is most unlikely. We have seen already that the national instinct of virtually every threatened or toppled European government was to run, to find sanctuary ever further west as the Nazis advanced. Churchill was no physical coward – he had charged with the 21st Lancers at Omdurman as a young man in 1898 and served as colonel of his regiment in the trenches of the Western Front in 1916. But Churchill was, above all, a survivor. And his arrogance would have made him believe he could achieve far more by leading a government in exile than by dying a martyr's death in the shadow of Nelson's column.

The most likely bolt hole for Churchill's government would have been Canada. Longmate rejects this, believing that the Bahamas would be better suited. Exchanging one island for another has its romantic merits but it would have left the exiled 'Free British' marooned, distanced from the one element of the Empire – the Canadians – who had the will and ability to fight. The West Indian contribution to Britain's war effort was negligible.

And, once the British army on the British mainland had surrendered, what then? We can assume that all the exiled governments – Sikorski's Poles, Benes' Czechs, de Gaulle's Free French – would have gone west too. Doubtless, de Gaulle would have made Quebec City rather than Montreal or Ottawa his capital, trying to rally the Quebecois of the Maritime against the Nazi tyrant 3,000 miles away.

A great deal has been written recently on 'Churchill's secret army', guerrilla troops usually called Auxiliaries, operating out of observation bases, tiny hideouts scattered all over the country. There were 300 of these by the end of 1940 and we still have only sketchy details of them. The personnel were offshoots of the Home Guard, only younger, better trained and equipped and prepared to use the underhand killing methods of the Commandos. The Long Range Desert Group in the North African theatre, which morphed into the Special Air Services under David Stirling, used the same tactics in the months ahead. Peter Fleming, who was involved in their set-up, believed that the Auxiliaries could have maintained themselves, by survivalist techniques of hunting wildlife and theft, for about seven weeks. At best, they could not have made a serious dent in the armour of the Wehrmacht if, as most conjecturers argue, the bulk of the young male population was taken away, as happened in France, to become a vast slave labour force in the east. Retaliation against *any* kind of resistance would have been met, as it was in other occupied states, by savage reprisals from the *Einsatzengruppen* and the SD.

Norman Longmate uses the example of the Channel Islands to posit what would have happened to the rest of Britain but the comparison does not really work. The Islands were too small to make such a comparison at all. Jersey and Guernsey, for example, had no synagogues and each island had about ten

Jews. The *Gestapo Handbook* guessed 300,000 Jews in Britain but believed the figure to be higher; it was – nearly 450,000. The Jews of the Channel Islands barely constituted a 'problem' but the solution would have been the same. They would all have gone to the camps. The only question, which Longmate does not consider, is whether a British concentration/death camp system would have been set up to negate the need for 'resettlement in the East'.

The various occupied countries of Europe behaved as they did, to an extent, because Britain was still free. And, beyond that, the vast might of the United States stood in an agony of indecision – should she come in on the British side? With Britain gone, the *raison d'etre* would have vanished too. No doubt national pride and a sense of bitter injustice would have meant that Resistance groups in the occupied territories would have fought on for as long as they could until, outnumbered and isolated, they were systematically cut down.

In his various 'offers of peace', including the one brought by Rudolf Hess as late as May 1941, Hitler hinted that Britain could keep her Empire in exchange for Germany's free hand in Europe. But the fact is that the Empire was already crumbling by 1940 and the use of the term Commonwealth was not just a matter of semantics. How could there be a common wealth if the heart of the community was stilled?

The fictional Dr Aziz in E. M. Forster's (F81) 1924 novel *A Passage to India* says:

'Until England is in difficulties we keep silent, but in the next European war – then is our time ... Clear out, you fellows, double quick, I say. We may hate one another [Muslim and Hindu] but we hate you most... '

India, which had been the jewel in the British imperial crown for so long, was all too anxious for the Raj to end. No one in the sub-continent remembered the roads, the schools, the sanitation and the rule of law that the British brought. They just remembered Brigadier Reginald Dyer machine-gunning a peaceful crowd at Amritsar in 1919, leaving 400 dead and over a thousand wounded. Although Jawarhalal Nehru, Mohammed Jinnah and Mohandas K. Gandhi were all civilised men, they were united in their condemnation of British imperialism. The war had only been over for two years when Lord Louis Mountbatten, as the last Viceroy, was obliged to hand India back to the Indians. Without London to bully them, Indian support for Britain would have dissipated very quickly in 1940.

Britain's possessions in the Middle East were scattered and in no position to help even if they had wanted to. With the collapse of Britain and the continued policy of extermination of Jews throughout Europe, it is most unlikely that the state of Israel would have come into being, and Zionism would have remained a utopian dream of American and Canadian Jews beyond the range of Goering's bombers. Given that, Arab power in the area would certainly have grown. At the third Communist International in September 1920, one of the attendees said:

'May the Holy War of the Peoples of the East and the toilers of the whole world burn with unquenchable fire against Imperialist England.'

And an Arab did not need to be a Communist to endorse those sentiments.

There were similar rumblings of discontent in South-East Asia. The Prime Minister of Burma, U Saw, wrote to *The Times* in October 1941:

> 'What Burma wants to know is whether in fighting with many other countries for the freedom of the world, she is also fighting for her own freedom . . . The demand for complete self-government is a unanimous demand of the Burmese people . . .'[131]

Australia's loyalty to Britain was dubious to say the least. Anzac Day, to mark the assault on the Gallipoli peninsula in 1915, is regarded by Australians and New Zealanders as their coming of age. Heroic as it was, it was part of a military campaign completely bungled by the British government of the day (and specifically by Churchill as First Lord of the Admiralty). Sorrowing Australian and New Zealand families made the point that their sons and husbands had died in a cause that was not theirs, facing an enemy (the Turks) with whom they had no quarrel. When the Japanese came into the Second World War and there were rumours of an Oriental invasion of Australia itself, there was ominous silence from Churchill's government in response to a request for help. In fact, from 1941, the Australian Prime Minister, Robert Menzies, was constantly at loggerheads with Churchill. The camera shows all smiles and hand shaking but Menzies resented Churchill's high-handed decision on how to run the war (without material help) and there were those in Britain who would have preferred the Australian Prime Minister to be at Number Ten. Canada alone remained loyal and within *potential* striking distance of Europe. South Africa was too far away and its white minority government shared by

Afrikaaners who, only thirty-eight years earlier, had been at war with imperialist Britain.

America had not been part of the British Empire for 164 years by the time of Schellenberg's List. Yet America was everybody's hope, from Churchill down and to that end, all shapes and sizes of politicians and celebrities (some of them on the List) had been steaming back and forth across the Atlantic to make sure that America came in on the 'right side'. American historians remembered the past – the treachery of the traitor Benedict Arnold, the burning of the White House in 1812, the Alabama and the Trent incidents of the 1860s when it seemed that Britain was meddling in American affairs. The German ex-pat lobby in the States was powerful, easily balancing the Jewish diaspora. Whatever the average American's view of National Socialism was (and the general trend was to fear Stalin's Communism more), the United States did big business with Germany, Nazi or not. Above all, there was the isolationism of America. The America First Committee was a potent force in the 1930s. As Arthur Schlesinger wrote:

> 'We'd entered the First World War to make the world safe for democracy [and the result was] the rise of Fascism and the rise of Communism.'[132]

Who was to say that something similar (or worse) would not happen again?

The point was that Roosevelt had to balance the German and Jewish dilemma in his own country and keep his promise to the mothers of America that their boys would not be sent to die on some European battlefield. As Gordon Corrigan makes clear in *Blood, Sweat and Arrogance* (Wiedenfeld and Nicolson 2006), the American military were in no position to fight a war on their own in 1939-40. No military aircraft then in production could reach Britain directly from the United States. Neither could landing craft.

And without Britain to support, why would the Americans launch such an assault? D-Day happened because it was a joint Anglo-American effort, with support from the Free French, Poles and Czechs. And it was launched from the relatively safe and friendly ports of southern England. Anything longer range and more ambitious would be bound to fail.

No American help. No imperial help. Britain would have disappeared into the Third Reich and Englishmen, then abed, would have cause, in their sleepless nights, to regret not striking a deal with Hitler after all. Had there been any portraits of Churchill left, they would surely have been destroyed by his own people by Christmas 1940. Whether Beaverbrook would have gone with Churchill we cannot know, but there was a great irony in the gallows-humour comment that the press baron made to the Jewish Frederick Leindemann, later Lord Cherrell: 'They'll kill *me*, but they'll torture you, Prof.'[133] The irony is that Lindemann is not on the List; Beaverbrook is.

★ ★ ★

The man who would have become Britain's gauleiter was SS *Oberführer* Dr Franz Six, Party number 245670, SS number 107480. Had the eagle landed, the lives of millions of men, women and children would have depended on him. Six was only thirty-one at the time of the List but he was already losing his hair and the photographs of him taken at Nuremberg six years later show him peering short-sightedly from behind very thick glasses. He looks what he was: an unassuming academic who hardly seems suited to running a country that, half a century earlier, had been the most powerful in the world.

Six had left school in 1930 as the effects of the Wall Street crash hit Germany, sending unemployment and inflation rocketing. He read Sociology and Politics at the University of Heidelberg but he had to keep dropping out to earn money to pay for his continuing education. By 1936, he emerged with a PhD Habil[134] and was teaching at the University of Konigsberg when Hitler marched into the Rhineland. By the outbreak of war, Six was Professor of Foreign Political Science at the University of Berlin.

His political career began in 1930 when he joined the Nazi Party. Two years later, he was wearing the brown shirt of the SA under Ernst Rohm as a student organiser and, three years later, was spotted by Reinhard Heydrich as a natural to run Amt VII of the SD. This office, fully fledged by 1940, was concerned with written documentation, archive work and anti-Semitic ideology. It also monitored the impact of Nazism on German and other populations in an odd combination of Britain's Ministry of Information and the Mass Observation Unit.

It was probably this aspect that gave Heydrich the notion that Six would be suited for the British job. The Führer concurred and, on 17 September, the future *Brigadeführer* was given overlordship of six *Einsatzgruppen*, to be based in London, Manchester, Birmingham, Bristol, Liverpool and either Edinburgh or Glasgow. This is why the known addresses of the Listees are there in the first place – they were a starting point for the men whose task it was to find and kill them.

As in Denmark, there would probably have been an uneasy co-operation between Six and 'native' officials at all levels, who would be given the task of making German Britain work. I do not believe there would have been a geographical area which would have been the equivalent of Vichy, but there would have been collaborators queuing up to offer their talents and support for the Reich. Not for nothing were hundreds of Air Raid wardens and other minor officials called 'little Hitlers'; they enjoyed power and their six years of fame.

The defiance of Churchill, echoed by thousands of lesser mortals across the country, would have diminished as time went on. The experience of other occupied countries is that most people did nothing. A few collaborated gleefully, through fear or a genuine commitment to National Socialism. A few resisted actively, for ideological reasons, pride or even in a spirit of adventure. But the general response was to keep one's head down and get on. There would have been a black market. There would have been a sense of 'us' and 'them' but the overall result would have been, in terms of much later television sit-coms, more *'Allo! 'Allo!* than *Dad's Army*. It was all about survival.

The only difference – and it is a crucial one – is that the war would be over and the full terror of the Blitz would never have been known.

Two things, I believe, would have happened anyway. The Reich would still have gone to war with Soviet Russia as planned but rather later for practical reasons; Britain would have to be consolidated first. Hitler's dream of *lebensraum* had always lain in the East; the West was of secondary importance, pleasant though it was to humiliate France and pleasant though it would be to humiliate Britain. With no Western Front to worry about and no American involvement (had Japan still attacked Pearl Harbor, that would have resulted in a purely American–Japanese conflict, fought entirely in the Pacific), the outcome on the dreaded Eastern Front would have been very different. Stalin was always prepared to hurl thousands of his people into the German line of fire, rather as the Tsar had in the First World War. The extraordinary thing about the 'Patriotic War', as the Russians called it, is that they held on so determinedly. Would they have done so, however, without the British and, later, the Americans taking the pressure off them in other Fronts and supplying them with materiel? I doubt it. Hitler would have had his Eastern Empire after all.

The other constant of German occupation was the Holocaust. Again, the timing might have been different but the end would have been the same. Hitler had spelled it out clearly in a speech to the Reichstag on 30 January 1939:

> 'If international finance Jewry inside and outside Europe should succeed in plunging the nations once more into a world war, the result will be not the Bolshevisation of the earth, and thereby the victory of Jewry, but the annihilation of the Jewish race in Europe!'[135]

Six million Jews were exterminated on the orders of the Reich up to 1945. Had Britain fallen, that figure would have been higher, not merely because of the half a million British Jews who would have gone 'to the chimneys' but also because of those in Russia who would have been rounded up as a result of the likely military collapse of the Soviet Union.

We cannot know what sort of compromise government would have been set up under Gauleiter Six. The experience of Vichy and the Danish system was that the populace was generally quieter when their own nationals at least *appeared* to be at the helm. Norman Longmate discusses the possible implications of this in the context of the 'White List'. There was no such document but a variety of papers do exist, including newspaper articles and books written by the Right Book Club, which the RSHA could have drawn on. Longmate is contemptuous of these people. Oswald Mosley's name is not there. Instead, we have thirty-nine names, together with addresses, of people 'friendly towards Germany'; seventeen of these were women. The list was forwarded to the RSHA offices in Munich on 9 September 1940 and the make-up of the list is extremely banal. Some of them had visited Germany before the war; some had attended, however briefly, a German university. They were exclusively middle class and unimportant. The SD in Luneberg drew up a similar list of *Critics of Conditions in England*, hoping that there would be collaborators among them. Archibald Ramsay, the Scots MP who was a traveller of the Right and had been imprisoned under Regulation 18B, was among them. The problem was that there was a huge leap of logic, if not faith, between someone who grumbled about Churchill and the effects of war and those who would actively support Hitler. As the poet G. K. Chesterton wrote:

'I knew no harm of Bonaparte and plenty of the Squire,
And for to fight the Frenchman I did not much desire;
But I did bash their baggonets because they came arrayed
To straighten out the crooked road an English drunkard
made...'[136]

It was the very *foreignness* of the Germans that would have made a collaborative government difficult to form.

But it would have been possible. There would have been no party structure other than National Socialism. The second chamber, intended as a check and balance for any possible lunacy from the first, would have disappeared. But the English were, despite democracy and a world war (with another in progress), a 'lord-loving' country and tradition died hard. If

Hitler had the imagination, he would have brought the exiled Duke of Windsor from the Bahamas to become King Edward VIII again, as some believed he should be. There would be no problem with Mrs Simpson this time. The rest of his family would have gone with Churchill to Canada and it is a fact that the Duke was estranged from them for the rest of his life. The Danish experience had shown the psychological importance of the king moving about among his people; 'Eddie Windsor' could have done the same.

There were senior politicians whose arms could have been gently twisted to form a puppet administration. Oswald Mosley would have been a front-runner. Lords Lothian, Brockett and Tavistock, all fellow travellers, would have been interested, as would lesser fry interned under Regulation 18B, like Ramsay and Barry Domvile. The Gauleiter Ernst Bohle, though a German, had been born in Bradford and still carried a British passport. There was William Joyce (Lord Haw-Haw) to carry on working with Goebbels, as he did already. The Fascist John Amery, son of MP Leo, would surely find a niche in a puppet government. Commentators have rubbished a selection such as this. These men did not have the status of Churchill's cabinet, they argue, and could not have coped with the job. That line ignores two realities. First, memory has gilded the image of that cabinet because they won the war. As Charles de Gaulle said, leading his tanks at Montcornet in May 1940, 'If you succeed, you're a hero; if you fail, you're a *couillon* [arsehole].' Taken man by man, no one in the inner sanctum was overly impressive. Second, the Reich would not have asked the new boys to govern; merely to *look* as though they were; the job would not have been difficult.

* * *

What of the 2,694 people of the List, Schellenberg's 'target for tonight'? We must remember that none of them knew of its existence and would not necessarily have believed themselves to be targets any more than the rest of the population. Some must have left the country already, even as Schellenberg was drawing the names, sailing west in the same panic that saw the exodus of Americans when the war began. Some were dead – Sigmund Freud, George Lansbury and almost certainly the spy Sidney Reilly are among the famous names that spring to mind. Still others might not have been found at the addresses that Schellenberg gave. With the collapse of Britain, how quickly would the Rockefeller Foundation's money for displaced scholars have lasted? Universities could not afford to keep these people on their books and the scholars themselves would have had to find employment somehow or leave.

Based on what we know of what happened in Poland, I have no doubt that the majority, when found, would have been murdered. As Richard Heydrich had said to General Stulpnagel in September 1939, 'We'll spare the little men, but the aristocrats, priests and Jews must be killed.'[137] He was talking about Poland but the same would have been true of Britain a year later. Gary Sheffield's suggestion of interrogations by the Gestapo would undoubtedly have taken place but they would have been followed by imprisonment or death.

The Jews, most obviously, would have been rounded up and shipped, for want of a British death camp, to any of the killing zones earmarked for extermination in Europe. British Jews were well integrated into the community but the 'battle of Cable Street' four years earlier had proved that not everybody tolerated them. The *very* wealthy, like the Rothschilds, would presumably have been able to get out before the jack boots arrived. Others would not have had that luxury. Recent emigrants were another matter. How long would it have been before somebody reported someone to the Nazi authorities? The children pointing out the Jews queuing for food in Bedzin would have found their British counterparts and adults would have joined in too. That Mr van den Bergh in Flat 54 at Number 20, Grosvenor Square – he was a Jew, wasn't he? What about Mr Blaikie, living at 32, Fleet Lane – Jewish, surely? And as for A. S. Diamond, with his chambers at 1, Temple Gardens, he was *definitely* a Jew. It would be nice to think that no one would shop their neighbours, long-term residents or new arrivals but that flies in the face of human nature.

The scholars would have been easy targets. The experience of the Lvov professors would have been repeated in Britain. The Senate House, so recently the home of Duff Cooper's Ministry of Information, was the headquarters of London University. We can imagine hundreds of academics invited there to discuss the future of British education. We can imagine a rude awakening for them. Perhaps Edward Conze (C87) spoke out and perhaps he was hit in the mouth with a rifle butt. Perhaps Dr Eugen Glickauf (G62) did too, to be slapped to the floor and kicked. These men – and women – would have been unceremoniously bundled into trucks and sent off to whichever London prison – Wandsworth, Holloway, the Scrubs – the SS had earmarked for them. If Mussolini and the Pope had intervened on their behalf, as had happened with the academics' Polish counterparts, it was unlikely that the Reich would have listened this time. The lecturers at Oxford and Cambridge would have been easier to corral – in both towns, 'gown' was obvious and the ancient staircases would have thundered to the thud of jack boots.

There may have been a situation where the members of the fourth estate would have been given a straight choice – write propaganda for us under the auspices of Dr Goebbels or be taken to a pre-dug pit in a forest somewhere nearby. It was not far from Fleet Street to Epping Forest or Hampstead Heath or Hounslow; any of the lonely, isolated places where slaughter could take place.

It all sounds surreal; impossible. It could never have happened. That is what the Poles said to each other in 1939. The new governor, Hans Frank, said in a police conference in Krakow soon after taking office:

'The Führer told me that the leading groups in Polish society already in our hands are to be liquidated and whoever appears to replace them is to be detained and after an appropriate interval exterminated... Gentlemen, we are not murderers. But, as National Socialists, these times lay upon us all the duty to ensure that no further resistance emerges from the Polish people.'[138]

If we substitute the word 'British' for 'Polish', this could well have been *Oberführer* Dr Six talking to policemen in this country. They would have found Harold Nicolson and his wife, Vita Sackville-West, lying dead at their home in Sissinghurst Castle, the 'bare bodkin' cyanide capsules clamped between their teeth. They would have found Cyril Joad hiding out in the mountains of Snowdonia, as he did to avoid the draft in the First World War. And all the rest, from A1, ('Aalten, J') to Z32, ('Zychon, Jan Henryk') would, barring the accident of miraculous survival, have become nothing more than names on a list.

★ ★ ★

It did not happen. Schellenberg, the SS and the *Einsatzgruppen* never set foot on mainland Britain to start implementing the List. That they did not is down to the dogged heroism of Fighter Command, RAF in the Spitfire summer of 1940, and to twenty-one miles of the English Channel, which has kept Britain safe for centuries.

Could such a situation recur – and such a List be rewritten? Do not doubt it for one moment.

SELECT
BIBLIOGRAPHY

AILSBY, Christopher, *SS: Roll of Infamy*, Brown Books, 1997

BLOCH, Michael, *Operation Willi*, Weidenfeld and Nicolson, 1984

BULLOCK, Alan, *Hitler: A Study in Tyranny*, Pelican, 1952

CALDER, Angus, *The People's War*, Pimlico, 2000

CAVE BROWN, Anthony, *Bodyguard of Lies*, Star Books (WH Allen), 1979

CAVE BROWN, Anthony, *The Secret Servant*, Sphere Books, 1988

CHURCHILL, Winston, *The Second World War (abridged)*, Grange Books, 2003

CORNISH, Kimberley, *The Jew of Linz*, Century, 1998

CORRIGAN, Gordon, *Blood, Sweat and Arrogance*, Weidenfeld and Nicolson, 2006

CRUIKSHANK, Charles, *The German Occupation of the Channel Islands*, Alan Sutton, 1993

DAY, David, *Menzies and Churchill at War*, OUP, 1993

DUFF COOPER, Alfred, *The Duff Cooper Diaries*, Weidenfeld and Nicolson, 2005

FLEMING, Peter, *Invasion 1940*, Rupert Hart-Davis, 1957

GOEBBELS, Josef, *The Goebbels Diaries*, Hamish Hamilton, 1948

GOODALL, Felicity, *Voices from the Home Front*, David and Charles, 2006

HASTINGS, Max, *The Secret War*, Harper Collins, 2015

HAYWARD, James, *Myths and Legends of the Second World War*, Sutton, 2006

HMSO, *Front Line 1940-41*, 1942

HMSO, *The Nazi* Kultur *in Poland*, 1944

HÖHNE, Heinz, *The Order of the Death's Head*, Penguin, 2000

JENKINS, Roy, *Churchill*, Pan Books, 2001

JORGENSEN, Christopher, *Hitler's Espionage Machine*, Spellmount, 2000

KEE, Robert, *The Picture Post Album*, Barrie and Jenkins, 1989

KERSHAW, Ian, *Hitler: Nemesis 1936-45*, Penguin, 2002

LAMPE, David, *The Last Ditch*, Cassell & Co, 1969

LONGFORD, Elizabeth, *Winston Churchill*, Sidgwick and Jackson, 1974

LONGMATE, Norman, *If Britain Had Fallen*, Greenhill Books, 2004

LOWNIE, Andrew, *Stalin's Englishman*, Hodder and Stoughton, 2015

LUDECKE, Kurt, *I Knew Hitler*, Jarrolds, 1988

MASTERMAN, J.C., *The Double-Cross System*, York University Press, 1972

MATANLE, Ivor, *History of World War II*, Tiger Books, 1994

NICOLSON, Harold, ed NICOLSON, Nigel, *Diaries and Letters 1930-39*, Collins, 1966

BIBLIOGRAPHY

NICOLSON, Harold, ed NICOLSON, Nigel, *Diaries and Letters 1939-45*, Collins, 1967

OUSBY, Ian, *Occupation: the Ordeal of France*, John Murray, 1997

PIVNIK, Sam, *Survivor*, Hodder and Stoughton, 2012

PONTING, Clive, *1940: Myth and Reality*, Cardinal, 1990

QUARRIE, Bruce, *Hitler: the Victory That Nearly Was*, David and Charles, 1988

RANKIN, Nicholas, *Churchill's Wizards*, Faber and Faber, 2008

REES, Laurence, *The Dark Charisma of Adolf Hitler*, Ebury, 2013

REES, Laurence, *The Nazis: A Warning From History*, BBC Books, 2005

ROBERTS, Andrew, *Hitler and Churchill*, Phoenix, 2003

SCHELLENBERG, Walter, *Invasion 1940*, St Erwins Press, 2000

SCHELLENBERG, Walter, *The Memories of Hitler's Spymaster*, André Deutsch, 2006

SNYDER, Louis L, *Encyclopedia of the Third Reich*, Wordsworth, 1998

SOMMERVILLE, Donald, *World War II: Day by Day*, Bison Books, 1989

TAYLOR, Telford, *The Anatomy of the Nuremberg Trials*, Bloomsbury, 1993

UNKNOWN, *German Invasion Plans for the British Isles 1940*, Bodleian Reprint, 2007

VASSILTCHIKOV, Marie, *The Berlin Diaries*, Pimlico, 1999

WHEATLEY, Dennis, *Stranger Than Fiction*, Hutchinson, 1959

WINDER, Robert, *Bloody Foreigners*, Abacus, 2004

ZIEGLER, Philip, *London at War*, Pimlico, 2002

ENDNOTES

Introduction

1 Coward, Noel, *Future Indefinite,* Heinemann, London, 1954.

2 Sefton Delmer, *Black Boomerang,* Secker and Warburg, London, 1962. The broadcast to which Delmer refers is his off-the-cuff rejection of Hitler's peace proposals in July 1940. He was not authorised to deliver this.

3 Quoted in *Invasion 1940: the Nazi Invasion Plan for Britain* by *Walter Schellenberg,* St Ermin's Press, London, 2000.

4 Shirer, William, *The Rise and Fall of the Third Reich*, Secker and Warburg, London, 1961.

Chapter One

5 Pivnik, Sam, *Survivor*, Hodder and Stoughton, London, 2012, p. 28.

6 Pivnik, op.cit. p. 34.

7   Churchill, Winston, *The Second World War (abridged)*, Grange Books, London, 2003, p. 43.

8   The word and the idea were not new. They had been applied by the Prussian staff officer von Clausewitz to Napoleon's strategic and tactical genius in the early nineteenth century. In the early 1930s, it was the aerial aspect that was so revolutionary.

9   Unnamed reporter, quoted in *Chronicle of the 20th Century*, Longman, London, 1988.

10 This and all subsequent quotations from Harold Nicolson can be found in: Nicolson, Harold, *Diaries and Letters 1930-39* (1966) and *1939-45* (1967), ed. Nicolson, Nigel, Collins, London.

11 Goering, Hermann, quoted in Snyder, Louis L. *Encyclopedia of the Third Reich*, Wordsworth Editions, Herts, 1998.

12 All quotes from Marie Vassiltchikov are taken from *The Berlin Diaires*, Pimlico, London, 1999.

13 Quoted in Ponting, Clive, *1940: Myth and Reality*, Cardinal (Sphere Books), London, 1990.

14 Churchill, W., House of Commons Debates Vol. 361, Col, 796, 4 June 1940.

15 Corunna was the port used by the British navy to evacuate troops in the Peninsula War against Napoleon. The brilliant Sir John Moore was killed there.

16 It was, perhaps, a little disconcerting that a prominent member of the Ministry of Information believed that only a *few* of our troops would need to be evacuated.

ENDNOTES

17 Priestley, J. B., quoted in Smith, Godfrey (ed), *How it Was in the War*, Pavilion Books, London, 1989, p. 71.

18 Churchill, W., House of Commons Debates Vol. 362, Col, 60, 18 June 1940.

19 Churchill, op.cit. p. 73.

Chapter Two

20 Goebbels, Josef, quoted in Snyder, Louis L., *Encyclopaedia of the Third Reich*, Wordsworth, London, 1998, p. 295.

21 Keitel, Wilhelm quoted in Snyder, Louis L., *Encyclopaedia of the Third Reich*, Wordsworth, London, 1998, p. 193.

22 Admiral Earl St Vincent, 1801, quoted in Cohen and Major, *History in Quotations*, Cassell, London, 2004, p. 533.

23 *The Secret Diary of Harold L. Ickes* (Vol III, NY 1955), quoted in Fleming, Peter, *Invasion 1940*, Rupert Hart-Davis, London, 1957, pp. 91-92.

24 In 1798, the United Irishmen, under Wolfe Tone, had tried to link up with the Revolutionary French government to overthrow England. The whole thing was woefully mistimed and half-hearted, and the French famously ran away at the arrival of Pembrokeshire fishwives!

25 Allingham, Margery, *The Oaken Heart*, Michael Joseph, London, 1941.

26 Fleming, Peter, *Invasion 1940*, Rupert Hart-Davis, London, 1957, p. 80-81.

Chapter Three

27 The Blenheims, then used as night fighters, did not impress.

28 Richards, Denis, *The Royal Air Force 1939-45* Vol 1, quoted in Fleming, op.cit. p. 283.

29 Calder, Angus, *The People's War*, Pimlico, London, 1969, p. 164.

30 All quotations here are from *If the Invader Comes*, published by the Ministry of Information, June 1940.

31 Fleming, op.cit. p. 85.

32 Wheatley, Dennis, *Stranger Than Fiction*, Hutchinson, London, 1959.

33 As I write, an unexploded Second World War torpedo has been found in Portsmouth Harbour and safely detonated. So Wheatley's idea nearly worked!

34 Wheatley, op.cit. p. 53.

Chapter Four

35 The peace-makers who had stabbed the German army in the back by agreeing to an armistice in November 1918.

36 Quoted in Cave Brown, Anthony, *The Secret Service*, Sphere Books, London, 1987, p. 219.

37 Quoted in Schellenberg, Walter, *The Memoirs of Hitler's Spymaster*, Andre Deutsch, London, 2006, p. 94.

38 Colville, John, *The Fringes of Power*, Norton, New York, 1985, p. 40.

ENDNOTES

39 That particular Kommando must have been particularly myopic; the two men are not remotely alike.

40 The socialistic elements of the party's twenty-five-point programme of 1919 were quietly abandoned as Hitler assumed command.

41 St Ermin's Press, Little Brown and Co. and the Imperial War Museum, London, 2001.

42 Lampe, David, *The Last Ditch*, Cassell, London, 1968, p. 31.

43 Quoted in Alan Bullock's 'Introduction' to Schellenberg's memoirs, op.cit. p. 16.

44 Bullock, Alan ed., *The Schellenberg Memoirs*, Andre Deutsch, London, 1951.

45 Richard J. Evans' 'Foreword' to Schellenberg's Memoirs, op.cit. p. xix.

46 Canaris's behaviour during the war can be explained by the fact that he was never a Nazi and despised Hitler, eventually being executed for his part in the July plot to kill the Führer. Heydrich, as head of the rival SD, distrusted him, despite having been his disciple earlier.

47 In an article for the newspaper written in 2000.

48 Pincher, Chapman, *Their Trade is Treachery*, New English Library, London, 1981.

Chapter Five
49 Quoted in Somerville, Donald, *World War II Day by Day*, Bison Books, Canada, 1989, p. 303.

50 Quoted in Lucas, James, *Last Days of the Reich*, Guild Publishing, London, 1986, p. 246.

51 H. Neils, 1940. Quoted in Snyder, Louis L., *Encyclopaedia of the Third Reich*, op.cit. p. 372.

52 All quotations from the *Handbook* are from the St Ermin's Press edition of 2000.

53 'Hankey, Sir, brit. ND [Secret Service] Agent' is listed at 31A. It may or may not refer to this man.

54 Quoted in Kee, Robert, *The Picture Post Album*, Barrie and Jenkins, London, 1989.

55 Rauschning, Herman, *Hitler Speaks*, Chapel River Press, Canada, 1939.

Chapter Six

56 Trever-Roper, Hugh, *The Last Days of Hitler*, Macmillan, London, 1947.

57 Quoted in Cave Brown.

58 Source unknown.

59 All quotations from Ustinov, Peter, *Dear Me*, Arrow, London, 2000.

60 Quoted in Levenda, Peter, *Unholy Alliance*, Bloomsbury, London, 1995.

61 Quoted in Cooke, Andrew, *Cash for Honours: Maundy Gregory*, History Press, Gloucestershire, 2008.

ENDNOTES

Chapter Seven

62 Duff Cooper, Alfred, *Old Men Forget*, Rupert Hart-Davis, London, 1953.

Chapter Eight

63 Cadogan, Alexander, *Diaries* 1938-45, ed David Dilks, Putnam and Sons, New York, 1972.

64 In the film *Chariots of Fire* (1981, dir. Hugh Hudson), writer Colin Welland, presumably for dramatic effect, has Cecil (played by Nigel Havers) being beaten in this race by Harold Abrahams (Ben Cross).

65 The *Gestapo Handbook*, p. 86.

Chapter Nine

66 Quoted in Caedel, Martin, *The King and Country Debate 1933*, The Historical Journal 22(2), 1979.

67 Quoted in Gilbert, Martin, *Prophet of Truth: Winston Churchill*, Minerva, Trowbridge, 1990, p. 456.

68 Leigh Fermor Patrick, *A Time of Gifts*, John Murray, London, 1977, p 115-6.

69 I have only included those who are associated with universities. There are dozens more with the title 'Dr' who we can assume are academics, perhaps engaged in other work by 1940.

70 In pre-Nazi Germany, as elsewhere in the world, women, *in theory*, had access to academe but it was an uphill struggle.

71 Technically, 'Jewishness' is inherited from a mother, not a

father. The Reich had their own complex racial laws that overrode that.

72 Russell designed the ghastly Utility furniture, cheap and popular, after the war.

73 In 1936, Hitler appointed four German artists to tour all galleries and museums and remove 'degenerate, non-Aryan paintings', including the works of Klee and Kandinsky.

74 Quoted in Games, Stephen, *Pevsner: The Early Life*, Continuum, London, 2010.

75 The Third International (1919–43) was a Communist organisation pledged to establish international Communism by any means necessary.

76 Quoted in Winder, Robert, *Bloody Foreigners*, Abacus, London, 2004, p. 310.

77 Quoted in Calder, Angus, *The People's War*, Pimlico, London, 1992, p. 132.

78 In *The Jew of Linz*, Century, London, 1998, Kimberley Cornish contends that Hitler's deep-rooted anti-Semitism stemmed from his jealousy of the brilliant Wittgenstein.

79 Quoted in Rempel, Richard A., *Uncertain Path to Freedom*, Routledge, London, 2000.

80 There were minority exceptions; brave youngsters who refused to join. They were severely persecuted.

81 Warwick – the future Poet Laureate ran away after four days!

82 In his 'Foreword' to *The Nazi Kultur in Poland* (Anon), HMSO, London, 1945, p. vii.

ENDNOTES

83 Chesterton, G. K., *As I Was Saying*, Ayer Co, USA, 1936.

Chapter Ten

84 Making life very difficult for those of us tasked with researching war-time crime!

85 Only Rupert Bear in the *Express* kept going.

86 Calder, Angus, *The People's War*, op.cit. p. 505.

87 Orwell, George – quoted in Calder, Angus, *The People's War*, op.cit. p. 509

88 Quoted in Ferguson, Niall, *The Pity of War*, Basic Books, London, 1999.

89 Quoted in the *British Journalism Review*, Vol. 16 No 1, 2005.

90 Quoted in Schlesinger, Arthur, 'Men From Mars'; *Atlantic Monthly*, April 1997.

91 The current value is of 2/6d is £8 – still a bargain for a hardback book.

92 S52's date of birth is given as 1901. Either this is an error or it is a different Lytton Strachey altogether!

93 Quoted in Morresi, Renata, *Set Apart: Nancy Cunard*, 2000.

94 Taylor, D. J., *Orwell: The Life*, Vintage, London, 2003.

95 Quoted in Addison, Paul, *The Road to 1945*, Random House, London, 2011.

Chapter Eleven

96 I am grateful to Martin Connolly for drawing my attention to

this term. It features in his *The Munich Man*, Pen and Sword, Barnsley, 2017.

97 Weizmann, C., *Letters and Papers Series B*.

98 Allenby himself, as a mark of humility in that most exalted of cities, went in on foot.

99 The *Gestapo Handbook*, p. 88.

100 Quoted in a 2008 book review by Charles Kimber of *Lord Leverhulme's Ghosts*, Jules Marchal, 2008.

101 This was a jibe at the Medieval 'blood libel' belief among Christians that the Jews ate babies.

102 Goebbels, J. quoted in Snyder, Louis L., *Encyclopaedia of the Third Reich*, op.cit. p. 274.

Chapter Twelve
103 Thyssen, Fritz. quoted in Snyder, Louis L., *Encyclopaedia of the Third Reich*, op.cit.

104 Quoted in the *Gestapo Handbook*, p. 137.

Chapter Thirteen
105 The Papacy's relationship with the Reich is complicated and prone to dispute. There can be no doubt, however, that Pius XII, who succeeded in February 1939, was more accommodating to Hitler than his predecessor.

106 Jeffrey, Keith, *MI6: History of the Secret Intelligence Service*, Bloomsbury, London, 2010.

107 Mitchell, Margaret, *Honorary Degrees*, Encyclopedia Brunoniana, 1993.

ENDNOTES

108 The reference is to the massacre of 40,000 Protestants in Paris in 1572 on the eve of St Bartholomew's Day.

109 Krafft-Ebing's book (1886) was one of the first to investigate the links between sexual deviancy and murder.

Chapter Fourteen

110 Jenkins, Roy *Churchill*, Pan, London, 2001, p. 590.

111 Hankey, Sir Maurice. Quoted in Jenkins, Roy, *Churchill*, op.cit. p. 590.

112 Churchill, with his recent naval associations, wanted Admiral John Godfrey in the post. He was outmanoeuvred by Halifax at the Foreign Office.

113 The original 'C' was Captain Manfield Cumming, head of the Secret Service in 1909. In fiction, Ian Fleming turned the letter into 'M'.

114 Cave Brown, Anthony, p. 228.

115 M. R. D. Foot, *SOE in France*, HMSO, London, 1966.

116 Quoted in Hastings, Max, *The Secret War*, William Collins, London, 2015.

117 Quoted in Lownie, Andrew, *Stalin's Englishman*, Hodder and Stoughton, London, 2015.

118 Cave-Brown, Anthony, p. 198.

119 Cave-Brown, Anthony, p. 474.

120 This was almost certainly true and always had been. There was the supposition that information that was bought was

tainted and suspect. Francis Walsingham, Elizabeth I's spymaster, died heavily in debt, having funded his service largely from his own purse.

121 Sefton Delmer, Denis, *Black Boomerang*, Secker and Warburg, London, 1962.

122 A nickname also given to Sir Nicholas Winton, whom I met some years ago. Neither man welcomed the comparison (Winton, in particular, was very self-deprecating) and the jury is still out on the motives and effectiveness of the *actual* Oskar Schindler, Stephen Spielberg's brilliant film notwithstanding.

123 Hitler thought much of this was nonsense but both Heinrich Himmler and Rudolf Hess put great store by its prognostications and mystic past.

124 Sosnowski, George, interview for *Time* magazine, August 1936.

Chapter Sixteen

125 Himmler, Heinrich. Quoted in Höhne, Heinz, *The Order of the Death's Head*, Penguin, London, 1969, p. 294.

126 Not to be confused with Poland's *Black Book*, originally published in 1942 by G. Pultman's Sons, New York and currently available online. This is a list of the missing, presumed dead, who were victims of Nazi persecution from 6 October 1939 to the end of June 1941. The original ran to 615 pages with 112 photographs.

127 All quotations are from *The Nazi Kultur in Poland*, HMSO, London, 1944.

ENDNOTES

128 Quoted in Ousby, Ian, *Occupation: The Ordeal of France 1940–44*, John Murray, London, 1997.

129 Quoted in Ousby, op.cit.

130 Named after Fritz Todt, Minister for Armaments and Munitions, as he was by 1940. His workers had built Europe's first motorways (*autobahn*) and strengthened *West Wall*, the Siegfried Line.

Chapter Seventeen

131 Quoted in Cohen and Major, *History in Quotations*, Cassell, London, 2004, p. 791.

132 Quoted in Longmate, Norman, *If Britain Had Fallen*, Greenhill Books, London, 2004, p. 259.

133 Quoted in Calder, Angus, *The People's War*, op.cit. p. 130.

134 The 'habilitation' qualification entitled its recipient to teach at a university.

135 Quoted in Kershaw, Ian, *Hitler*, Penguin, London, 2010.

136 *The Rolling English Road*, 1913, was first entitled *A Song of Temperance Reform*.

137 Quoted in McDonald, Callum, *The Killing of SS Obergruppenführer Richard Heydrich*, Macmillan, London, 1989.

138 Ascherson, Neil, *The Struggles for Poland*, Macmillan, London, 1987.

ACKNOWLEDGEMENTS

'Analysing an eighty year old document that was originally written at speed on a poor typewriter in a foreign language presents problems of its own. I don't speak German and for that reason, as well as many others, I am grateful to Nicola Trow and Stefan Leidke, who do!

Thanks too, to Ciara Lloyd and her team at John Blake for taking on the project and producing such a handsome volume.

As always, my own typist, streets ahead of those available to the Reich Central Security office in 1940, holds first place in those who have helped me. Typist, sounding board, ideas woman and the love of my life, I am talking about my wife, Carol.